Native American Education
⚫❖ A Reference Handbook

CONTEMPORARY EDUCATION ISSUES

Native American Education

 A REFERENCE HANDBOOK

Lorraine Hale

A B C CLIO

Santa Barbara, California • Denver, Colorado • Oxford, England

Library of Congress Cataloging-in-Publication Data

Hale, Lorraine
    Native American education : a reference handbook / Lorraine Hale.
        p. cm. — (Contemporary education issues)
Includes bibliographical references and index.
    ISBN 1-57607-363-7 (hardcover : alk. paper)
    1. Indians of North America—Education—Handbooks, manuals, etc. 2.
Indians of North America—Education—Bibliography.   I. Title.   II.
Series.
    E97 .H138 2002
    371.829'97—dc21

                                                            2002006683

This book is also available on the World Wide Web as an e-book.
Visit www.abc-clio.com for details.

07 06 05 04 03 02   10 9 8 7 6 5 4 3 2 1

ABC-CLIO, Inc.
130 Cremona Drive, P.O. Box 1911
Santa Barbara, California 93116-1911

This book is printed on acid-free paper ∞.
Manufactured in the United States of America

✺ Contents

Series Editor's Preface, ix
Preface, xi

Chapter One: Historical Background, 1
    Advancing Colonization, 2
        Loss of Birthright, 3
        The Indian Territories, 4
        Manifest Destiny, 4
        The Civil War Period, 5
    The Growth of Community Schools, 6
        The School as Savior, 8
        Education Develops Slowly, 9
        Missionary Schools, 10
        Battles over Ideology, 12
        The Common School Movement, 12
    The Federal System of Indian Schools, 14
        The Off-Reservation Boarding School, 14
        Increasing Government Involvement in Education, 16
        Vexing Questions, 17
    Summary, 18
    References and Further Reading, 18

Chapter Two: The Twentieth Century, 21
    The Boarding-School Movement, 21
        The System's Harmful Effects, 22
        Benefits of the System, 23
    The Meriam Report, 24
    Education in the New Deal Era, 27
    World War II, 29
    Social Justice Movements, 29
    Toward Self-Determination for Native Americans, 32
    Indian Nations at Risk Task Force, 33
    Tribal Control of Education, 34
        Native Organizations, 35

Tribal Governments and Courts, 35
Native American Studies Programs, 35
Community Colleges, 36
Public Schools, 36
Summary, 36
References and Further Reading, 37

Chapter Three: Chronology, 41

Chapter Four: The Law and Native American Education, 49
European Law, 49
Early Treaties and Legislation, 53
Native Americans and Congress, 58
The Early Twentieth Century, 60
The New Deal Era, 60
Indian Reorganization Act, 60
Johnson O'Malley Act, 62
The Termination Era, 62
Post-Termination Policies, 68
The Self-Determination Era, 69
Indian Education Act, 70
American Indian Policy Review Commission, 71
Indian Self-Determination and Education Assistance Act, 71
Title XI of the Education Amendments Act, 73
Indian Self-Determination and Education Assistance Act
Amendments, 74
Tribally Controlled Schools Act, 74
Reauthorization of the Indian Education Act, 75
Summary, 75
References and Further Reading, 75

Chapter Five: Issues and Strategies, 79
Assumptions and Ideologies, 79
The Industrial Model, 80
A Paradigm Shift, 81
Assimilation versus Multiculturalism, 82
Desegregation: A Mixed Blessing, 84
Learning Styles, 84
Traditional Tribal Education, 85
Tribal Education Meets Mainstream Education, 85
Cooperative versus Competitive Learning, 86
Demonstrations of Learning, 87
Strategies for Dealing with Different Learning Styles, 89

Textbooks and Other Learning Materials, 90
Gifted and Talented Programs, 92
    Defining Giftedness, 93
    Assessing Giftedness, 93
Academic Failure and Dropout Rates, 95
    Large Schools, 96
    Uncaring Teachers, 97
    Teacher-Training Programs, 99
    Passive Teaching Methods, 100
    Inappropriate Curriculum, 101
    Inappropriate Testing, 102
    Low Expectations and Tracking, 103
    The Crossover Effect and Remedial Programs, 104
    Lack of Parent Involvement, 106
    Lack of Role Models, 106
    Reentry Strategies for Dropouts, 106
Cultural Preservation, 107
Summary, 108
References and Further Reading, 109

Chapter Six: The Basics—Language, Math, and Science, 117
Language, 117
    Development of Language Skills, 117
    Language and Writing, 118
    Key Aspects of Reading, 119
    Cognitive Academic Language Learning Approach, 120
    English as a Second Language, 121
    The Role of Language in Preserving Culture, 123
Math and Science, 124
    Science as a Second Language, 125
    Concrete Teaching Materials, 126
    Using Stories, 127
    Rational versus Holistic Science, 127
    A Bicultural Approach, 129
Summary, 131
References and Further Reading, 131

Chapter Seven: Associations, Organizations, and Tribal Entities, 139
American Indian Organizations, 139
Government Agencies, 145
Private Funding Sources, 148
Professional Organizations, 149

Tribal Colleges in the United States, 150
Tribal Contacts and State-Recognized Tribes, 154
Tribes of the United States, 156

Chapter Eight: Print and Nonprint Resources, 173
Print Resources, 173
    Articles and Reports, 173
    Books, 176
    Books for Youth, 179
    Journals, 181
    Language and Reading, 183
    Mathematics and Science, 184
Nonprint Resources, 185
    Internet Resources, 185
    Other General Web Sites, 187
    Videotapes, 188

Appendix: Selected Laws, 191
Indian Child Welfare Act, 25 U.S.C. 1901 (1978), 191
Indian Education Assistance Act (amends Indian Education Act
    through 1994), 25 U.S.C. 455 (1975), 204
Indian Self-Determination and Education Assistance
    Act, 25 U.S.C. 450 (1975), 216
Native American Educational Assistance Act (amends Indian
    Self-Determination and Education Assistance Act through
    1996), 25 U.S.C. 2001 (1988), 227
Native American Languages Act, 25 U.S.C. 2901 (1990), 269
Tribally Controlled Schools Act, 25 U.S.C. 2501 (1988), 272

Index, 289

●❖ Series Editor's Preface

The Contemporary Education Issues series is dedicated to providing readers with an up-to-date exploration of the central issues in education today. Books in the series will examine such controversial topics as home schooling, charter schools, privatization of public schools, Native American education, African American education, literacy, curriculum development, and many others. The series is national in scope and is intended to encourage research by anyone interested in the field.

Because education is undergoing radical if not revolutionary change, the series is particularly concerned with how contemporary controversies in education affect both the organization of schools and the content and delivery of curriculum. Authors will endeavor to provide a balanced understanding of the issues and their effects on teachers, students, parents, administrators, and policymakers. The aim of the Contemporary Education Issues series is to publish excellent research on today's educational concerns by some of the finest scholar/practitioners in the field while pointing to new directions. The series promises to offer important analyses of some of the most controversial issues facing society today.

Danny Weil
Series Editor

⊷ Preface

This book follows the chronological evolution of Native American education with reference to some of the significant events in mainstream American education. This comparative perspective, and an understanding of social movements affecting the development of institutions such as churches, schools, and government, shed light on the current state of native education in this country.

Before any white person came to America, the continent was divided into sections that were traditionally occupied by different Indian tribes. These tribes had their own formal and informal practices for educating their young. Scholars, intellectuals, and elders ensured that the collective wisdom identifying each tribe was preserved and handed on to the next generation. Young men and women learned the tribal customs, stories, health practices, and rites and rituals.

Every time whites claimed new territory, they were overriding a previous claim. For more than a century, settlers were continually involved in skirmishes with Native Americans. The relentless and voracious appetite of white settlers for land greatly affected the life and education of the First Nations people.

After whites had established their dominion over a particular area of the country, they worked to ensure that their community institutions and values would endure for succeeding generations. The school was seen as essential for formal education but also as the custodian of community values. Here, young people, including young Native Americans, were socialized into the European way of life. Chapters 1 and 2 cover the historical unfolding of events and trends from early colonization through the twentieth century. Chapter 3, the chronology, presents an overview of events and legislation in the first two chapters. Legislation that affected Native American education is documented in Chapter 4. Chapters 5 and 6 delineate current issues in American Indian education and offer educators some strategies for more effectively teaching Native American students. The resources in Chapters 8 and 9 are useful for those who wish to study in greater depth a number of issues raised in this book.

Regarding the use of the word "Indian" in this text, some Native Americans have indicated to me that the word is sometimes considered appropriate either for historical or traditional reasons.

Lorraine Hale

Chapter One

● Historical Background

As mentioned in the preface, Native Americans had their own well-developed system of education long before explorers and settlers came to this country. Intellectuals and scholars instructed the members of the tribes. The elders taught the young the history, geography, and customs of their people. The young learned the stories and survival and health practices. They were instructed in manual skills such as cooking, hunting, making lodges, beading, and making dresses. Storytellers passed on the wisdom of the tribe and the meaning of the sacred symbols (Trafzer 2000, 286).

The Native American model of education, with its free and more spontaneous style that involved so many tribal members, differed from the more formalized approach of the settlers. The Native American education process centered on oral tradition, and for this reason it was perceived by many colonizers as being an unreliable and lesser form of education than the traditional school format of the settlers.

Early colonists obtained the land otherwise occupied by the Native Americans either through purchase or through treaty and force. As immigrants arrived on the East Coast, they pushed the original inhabitants further and further inland. They established small communities with a school for their children. Most of the early colonizers saw little need to provide any sort of education in their form for the Native American children.

The one group that did show interest in such education was the church. The missionaries' major reason for education was the conversion of the natives—the pagans of those lands—to Christianity. The centrality of Christianity to the Europeans' way of life was a powerful impetus for the colonizers, and their conviction was reinforced by the direction of King James I as set out in the First Charter of Virginia (1606). The king urged the colony to convert those people who lived in darkness to a "true Knowledge and worship of God" (Coleman 1993, 36). These words from a monarch set the stage for the central role churches were to take in Native American education in the early days of the country.

1

It appears that throughout the seventeenth century, few of the colonists from England followed up on the king's exhortation. Even by the end of the eighteenth century only a small number of people had set about the task of educating and converting the "Indians." The English did, however, come up with the innovative concept of "praying towns." The idea underlying this approach was that the converted, or Christianized, Indians would be separated from their unconverted brethren and thus protected from falling back into their heathen ways.

After their conversion, many of the Native Americans in these towns accepted the mores and customs of the English colonists. Within these communities there appeared to be some level of appreciation of the different cultures and customs of the people who lived there. However, it is probably more realistic to assume that the Native Americans who joined these townships did so to protect themselves from the settlers and ensure the continuation of the tribe rather than because they truly accepted Christianity (Zinn 1980, 15).

ADVANCING COLONIZATION

With the ever-increasing number of settlers and their unquenchable thirst for land, Native Americans were pushed further and further westward. The California Gold Rush of 1849 added to this pressure. It soon became evident that immigrants would settle throughout the land. As the newly arrived continued to encroach on traditional hunting grounds, the number of clashes among settlers and Native Americans increased. In some settlements where the newly arrived had lived peacefully with the Indians, distrust and hostility arose and grew. Within the European community, two predominant approaches toward Native Americans became evident. Some wished to annihilate the indigenous people or, at the very least, assimilate them; others wished to help them.

To free up land for settlement, many Native American groups were forced to leave their traditional lands. Many recognized the power of the new culture that was encroaching on their way of life, and they tried to make compromises. In 1817 about 6,000 Cherokee were relocated to Arkansas; however, more than 20,000 remained in the East with the expressed hope of retaining access to their lands. Many of the Cherokee made a conscious effort to make themselves a part of the new society. They operated spinning wheels, looms, and gins, and were able to compete within the emerging cotton trade (Trafzer 2000, 150). A number of Cherokee owned African American slaves who moved west with their Native American owners. The Cherokee believed that the more they looked and acted like the new settlers, the more they would be left alone and able to maintain some level of their former life.

In the very early days of settlement there were some tribally operated schools that did meet with limited success. The Choctaw and Cherokee were two tribes able to achieve a high degree of literacy because they taught both their tribal languages and English (Skinner 1991, 3).

In addition to trying to maintain their own values, members of a number of eastern tribes appreciated the form of education that the Europeans had developed for their children. Some Native American parents had their children educated in English, math, history, and government. Many of these students attained a level of general education equal to that of the populace at large. Also, some tribal children in the East, like their European counterparts, attended schools conducted by different religious groups (e.g., Moravians, Presbyterians, Baptists, Methodists, and Congregationalists) (Trafzer 2000, 151).

Again, the main reason many tribes sent their children to school was to divert attention away from the differences between Native Americans and the European settlers. The deepest hope of the Cherokee was that through adaptation they would be able to maintain control of their ancestral lands. Such control always has been one of the core values of Native Americans.

Loss of Birthright

In 1828 Andrew Jackson was elected president of the United States, and one of his early actions was to call for the removal of all Indians from the East. Jackson gave the states permission to draw up policies that would influence and control the Native Americans. The laws and practices that ensued from his action would eventually strip the tribes of their lands. Different Native American groups tried to bring lawsuits against the states to prevent their forcible removal. In a suit brought by the Cherokee, the Supreme Court justices were sympathetic to the Native American case; however, they decided not to rule because the Cherokee were not citizens of the United States (Trafzer 2000, 153). The dismissal of this case by the Supreme Court and the consequent view of the Native Americans as noncitizens set the stage for further conflict between settlers and the indigenous population. They also provided reinforcement for those factions within the nascent society that wanted to either assimilate or eliminate Native Americans. These attitudes in turn provided the bases for many education policies directed toward the destruction of the indigenous culture. The death of the culture would be achieved through the destruction of tribal languages, customs, and beliefs.

In 1830 the Choctaw were forced to move from their land, and in 1835, the Cherokee were driven from their traditional hunting grounds and lands. In fairly quick succession the Chickasaw, Muskogee, Seminoles, and Wyandot were all made to leave their homes. After the 1830s the forcible removal of Native Americans from their traditional homelands became commonplace.

This landgrab continued throughout the nineteenth century. Native Americans were relocated onto reservations without any thought as to whether these new locations were suited to their way of life or whether such relocation impinged on other tribal groups. There were many within the European population who believed that the reservation system was advantageous to the Native American. Through this system, immigrants believed, Native Americans would be able to preserve and carry on their traditional practices.

The Indian Territories

In 1834 Congress enacted a law that was to set aside vast tracts of land for the Indian people. One of the weaknesses of this Trade and Intercourse Act was the rather vague boundaries set for the territory. The land assigned was west of the Mississippi but did not include Missouri, Louisiana, or the Arkansas Territory. The boundaries with Mexico in the Southwest and Great Britain in the Northwest were also vague. However, the land assigned to the Native Americans was roughly aligned with what is known today as the Midwest.

In the Louisiana Territory Act of 1804, Congress had approved the removal of tribes in the East to their new homelands. This treaty spelled out many protections for Native Americans. White people were not permitted to settle, hunt, introduce liquor, or trade without a license approved by the Indians. As so many treaties had been made in the past, and broken, there was skepticism among the native population that this treaty would be honored.

However, both the white settlers and Native Americans hoped that an area of settlement for the indigenous population would bring stability for all. But even as this treaty was being enacted, whites had begun to breach the upper Mississippi area. The relentless push to the Pacific had begun again.

Manifest Destiny

The right of the settlers to move westward was reinforced by lawyer and editor John O'Sullivan, who wrote in 1845, "[It is] our manifest destiny to overspread and to possess the whole of the continent which Providence has given us for the development of the great experiment in liberty" (Time Life Books 1994, 20). In an extraordinarily short space of time, the country spanned the continent. The United States annexed the Republic of Texas in 1845, the next year Oregon was added, and in 1848 the land from New Mexico to the California coast was added.

With this expansion more and more Native Americans were thrown together in a smaller space. Clashes among Native Americans and whites became intense across the plains. Tribal bands that typically would not have associated with each other joined forces to mount fierce attacks against the settlers. On the plains, where there had been a promise of a Native American country, ideals were shattered in battles and bloodshed.

Although there had been animosity between European settlers and Native Americans, many native groups welcomed the trading posts, which brought guns, liquor, and tools to the area. Whenever the traders stayed close to the outposts and did not move into the surrounding lands and interfere with the Indian way of life, all went reasonably well. However, when settlers took the land in larger parcels, the Indians fought back. The free-flowing "firewater" constituted a particularly insidious attack on the Indians' way of life (Time Life Books 1994, 23).

Diseases further weakened the Indian populace. It took time for the tribes to build immunity against diseases that were common among the white settlers. An outbreak of smallpox in 1837 devastated the Mandan, who lived along the Missouri. It continued to spread up the river and killed two-thirds of the Blackfeet population. Later the disease moved south and ravaged the Lakota; finally it reached as far as the Comanche in Texas.

The Civil War Period

By the time the Civil War broke out, Protestants and Catholics had established missionary outposts among the Omaha of the Midwest and the Nez Percé of the Northwest. During the Civil War the government gave the churches much of the responsibility for the welfare of the Indians. Ulysses S. Grant, through the Peace Policy, invited the Quakers to recommend agents and teachers for the tribes. Thus the government had merged religious and secular goals. This was not a happy marriage, and by the late 1870s there were again many conflicts between Native Americans and colonizers. In 1875 Grant invited leaders of the Sioux and Cheyenne tribes to Washington, where he threatened them with starvation if they did not stop hostilities.

The federal government, in the hope of arriving at some level of agreement with Native Americans, set up a peace commission. The members of the Peace Commission were Generals William Sherman, William S. Harney, Kenneth O. Sanborn, and Alfred Terry, together with Commissioner of Indian Affairs Taylor. The tenor and the appointees of this commission illustrate the ethnocentric attitudes of the times. Commission members believed that the difference between the Indians and the non-Indians was language. They were of the mind that if the youth had been taught English, many of the differences between the two groups would have disappeared. If all spoke the same language, all would think the same way. In any event, the peace process broke down, and conflict continued.

The changing status of Native Americans with regard to the disruption of their traditional way of life together with their experience with the federal government and treaties led to changes. Gradually the Native Americans felt that the federal government owed them a living. They looked toward the government to provide them with annuities, food, and other rations. They viewed these provisions as a form of repayment for the land that had been taken from them and the game that had been killed on their traditional hunting grounds.

A number of the treaties that had been negotiated did in fact allow for annuities to be paid to Native Americans, but only during the transitional period. The government expected that Native Americans would learn the ways of farming from the settlers and become self-sufficient. Not only would they be able support themselves, they also would fit in with the white communities and be understanding and supportive of their practices.

However, the reality facing many of the Native Americans was that much of the land allocated to them was of marginal quality for grazing. Furthermore, many Native Americans had no desire to take up the new model of farming as practiced by the settlers. The combination of poor lands and a failure to develop new farming practices led to a demoralizing dependency on governmental financial support (Reyhner and Eder 1994, 47).

THE GROWTH OF COMMUNITY SCHOOLS

The Protestants from England settled mainly on the East Coast in the first days of colonization. The belief of the early Protestant settlers, particularly the Calvinists, that reading the Bible was preparation for salvation led to the desire for children to be able to read. The responsibility for the education of children usually fell to the father of the family. However, many fathers did not carry out this obligation. Some towns and neighborhoods provided schools funded in a variety of ways. Parents were often required to pay for their children's education. In some cases children were sent to private tutors or inexpensive "dame" schools. Children of the poor either were instructed in church-affiliated schools or did not receive any formal education, but picked up the rudiments from their parents or friends.

After the formation of the republic of the United States, the founding fathers recognized the importance of an education to ensure the success of the newly established republic. Thus the legislatures took a greater interest in and responsibility for the education of the young. Thomas Jefferson, himself in the preamble of the 1779 bill for free schools in Virginia, laid out the rationale for a state-sponsored schools. He emphasized the need of the schools to ensure the education of the citizenry for the health and well-being of the republic (Kaestle, 1999,6).

When it came to the question of the education of the Native Americans, the early settlers focused on their conversion to Christianity. They perceived that this would civilize the Native Americans and save them from "savagery" (Lomawaima, 2001, 7). Native Americans who converted to Christianity were separated from the unconverted, and schools were established within the communities of Indians who had converted to Christianity. There, acculturated Indian teachers taught their young the customs and mores of the English. Other attempts to hasten the integration of Native Americans included sending some young tribal members to England or having colonists take them into their homes (Coleman, 1993, 37). There was a dual purpose to this practice: to educate and to use the labor of the Native American youth.

During the seventeenth century, the Jesuits, mostly from France, were active in the education of Native Americans in the areas of the St. Lawrence River, the Great Lakes, and the Mississippi River. Their aim was to induct the Native Americans into French culture and Christianity. The priests took children from their families and tribes and taught them French culture and customs, academic subjects, agriculture, and handicrafts.

The Franciscans of Spanish origin worked in the Southern areas of the country including such states as California, Colorado, and New Mexico. Their policy was to gather Native people into settlements around their missions. They placed greater emphasis in their schools on agriculture, blacksmithing, and weaving (Fuchs and Havighurst, 1972, 2).

In the middle decades of the eighteenth century there were numerous experiments in educating Native American youth. One of the most significant was the Moor's Charity School in Lebanon, Connecticut. An important feature of this school was that a number of its graduates became "cultural brokers" and carried the new learning back to the tribes. Thus, in these early years, the school was used as the chief agent for spreading Christianity and Western culture. There was no attempt to incorporate Native American languages, culture, or history.

During the 1800s, the United States experienced a great religious awakening and as a result of this many of the churches increased their evangelistic outreach and missionary activity. In turn this fervor supported proselytizing and the establishment of religious schools among the Indian people. In 1819, Congress allocated funds to be given to those societies and individuals who worked to "civilize" Native Americans (Fuchs and Havighurst, 1972, 5).

The School as Savior

The intermingling of religion and education in the early days of settlement is the antithesis of today's strict separation between church and state. To appreciate the prevailing attitude in these early days, one needs to understand the role of Protestantism in colonization. A brief glimpse at the later part of the eighteenth century helps put this education and religion mix into context (Tyack and Hansot 1982, 36).

On Sundays clergy used the pulpit to reinforce the message that America had a special place in God's plan. During the nineteenth century Protestant clergy looked upon America as the "Kingdom of God." This religious ideology became attached to American nationalism. One has only to read the Declaration of Independence to see that Protestant thinking and ideals were an unquestioned part of life.

Early settlers established their community schools to introduce students to a generalized form of Protestantism that they saw as supporting many of their core values and beliefs. In this burgeoning capitalist society people believed that hard work, honesty, and obedience were absolutely essential. Protestantism was perceived not only as supporting these values but also as promoting them as a basis of identifying those who were favored by God.

Just how deeply Christianity, or Pan-Protestantism, was imbedded in the ordinary way of life can be appreciated by looking at words used in a typical eulogy for an educator or community leader: "true Christian character," "earnest," "pure," "true scholar" (Tyack and Hansot 1982, 15). These were the highest words of praise, and there was no self-consciousness in using them. It was taken for granted that such encomiums were proper and fitting for an educator.

The early immigrants considered it essential that students be able to read in order to study the Bible, and in a typical school the daily routine was organized around this study. The Bible and its tenets were viewed as key for immersing students in the values and behaviors that would enable them to become part of the great American dream. Through embracing Christianity, Native Americans would partake of both prosperity in this life and rich rewards in the next.

Education Develops Slowly

In the middle of the eighteenth century America was predominantly rural. The small settlements that dotted the countryside were isolated from each other. Similarly, teachers and school personnel were isolated. All these communities followed the rhythm of the seasons. School life was organized around the cycle of agricultural growth and harvesting because children provided a cheap and valuable source of labor and thus were integral to the success of the family and settlement economies. Even though schooling was considered important, its demands gave away to the greater demands of fields and crops. This influence of the agricultural cycle gave rise to the long school break over the summer, which is still a tradition today.

As late as 1860 approximately 80 percent of Americans continued to live in what were classified as rural areas. Most of America lived in towns of less than 2,500 people. At this time most of the teachers in these schools were members of the local community. They were not highly educated, and most were poorly paid. With the isolation, and little formal education, teachers did not see themselves as belonging to a self-regulating profession. Without this perception of teachers as belonging to a profession, few influences would be uniformly adopted and consequently shape teaching throughout the country. By the same token, neither the state nor the federal government exercised extensive control or influence. In fact, the U.S. Office of Education was not founded until 1867, and at that time it had a staff of about six and a budget of approximately $13,000 (Tyak and Hansot 1982, 18). The states as a whole were somewhat slower in the development of departments of education.

Another indicator of the slow growth of formalized education in the country is the amount of money spent on education within the states. By the end of the 1890s the average size of a state department of education was two persons. One of these was the superintendent, responsible for overseeing education within the whole state. Throughout the nineteenth century there was a steady growth in the number of children who attended schools. However, there were differences in patterns of attendance as well as issues associated with different geographical areas. In the Northeast, where enrollment was generally high, the main concern was the quality of education. In the West, the main challenge was to build enough schools to house the growing numbers of children. By contrast, in the South the elite rich, who controlled education, had little interest in educating poor whites and forbade the education of the children of slaves (Tyack and Hansot 1982, 35).

With the ongoing years, a clear pattern of spending on education emerged. Even though over 70 percent of students were enrolled in rural schools, by the last decade of the nineteenth century approximately 57 percent of the money spent on educating a child went to urban schools. Part of this disparity between rural and urban spending is accounted for by the fact that it cost more in urban areas to build schools, equip them, and maintain them. Sometimes these costs were two to three times those in the country.

Missionary Schools

The missionary groups, with funding support from the federal government, controlled most of the Native American schools until 1917. The federal government also financially supported the efforts of the different religious groups. In 1802 Congress enlarged these funds through what was known as the Indian Civilization Fund Act (Prucha 1975, 19). This fund provided money to religious groups and to any other person(s) who was interested in living with Indians and teaching them the habits and arts of civilization (Prucha 1975, 33).

Another impetus to the development of schools for Native Americans was the religious revival of Evangelical Protestants. The energy generated by this movement was focused on the "heathens" of America. The American Board for Commissioners for Foreign Missions (ABCFM) was established in 1810. By the late 1820s the ABCFM had established eight schools among the Cherokee of the Southeast (Coleman 1993, 40).

The schools of the ABCFM and those established by other Protestant denominations followed essentially the same sort of curriculum. This program of studies was generally known as the 50/50 curriculum. About half the time was spent studying more traditional subjects such as the English language, arithmetic, history, and geography as well as the religion of the denomination sponsoring the school. The other half of the curriculum was dedicated to more practical skills such as farming for boys and cooking and dressmaking for girls.

The thinking behind this sort of education was that these young

Native Americans would become educated into the American way. When they returned to the tribe they would be intermediaries between the two cultures and assured of some level of prosperity. There were no elements of Indian culture included within the curriculum. There was no acknowledgment that Native Americans already had a long and successful history in farming, cooking, sewing, and other parts of the curriculum. The real aim of the schools was to take away the Native American culture so that the "barbarians" could be saved through their acceptance of Western culture, or in other words, Christianity. Through the loss of language and the Indian way of doing things, Native Americans faced the reality of losing their very identity.

The upheavals in the Midwest between whites and Native Americans (see previous section) hampered the missionaries' efforts to educate the native people. It was mainly through the leadership of part-white Indians that missionary education was able to continue. This group of Native Americans had an understanding of the missions and what they were trying to achieve and thus supported missionary education.

In addition to the conflicts between Native Americans and the settlers, there were conflicts between Catholic and Protestant missionaries. These skirmishes among the religious groups became acrimonious and contributed to undermining the relationship between churches and the government in the education of Native Americans.

Although many religious organizations desired to teach Native Americans the "superior" European lifestyle, most still wanted to save them from their heathen ways. The fundamental motive in educating Native Americans was to change them.

There were a number of missionaries, however, who appreciated the value of the native language and continued to try to preserve it. The American Board of Commissioners for Foreign Missions and the Presbyterian Board of Foreign Missions were in favor of teaching Native Americans using tribal languages. The American Board further desired to educate Native Americans to be teachers to their own people. A plan carried forward by the missionary Alfred L. Riggs. Riggs established the Santee Normal Training School to educate Native Americans as teachers. The school educated its students mostly in their Dakota language. However, there was a growing feeling among agents on the reservations that the state should be responsible for Native American education and students should be taught in English. Many officials believed that teaching in the native language kept the students Indian and using English would help them to be civilized. In 1880 the under-secretary of the interior issued regulations that all instruction must be in English (Prucha, 1973, 199).

Battles over Ideology

Whenever there was close contact between immigrants and Native Americans, there was pressure for them to give up their traditions and conform to white ways (Garcia and Ahler 1994, 13). As the nineteenth century progressed, settlers became even more diligent about ensuring the transmission of their emerging culture in this new land. As small communities were established, schools, churches, law-enforcement agencies, and political groups became responsible for shaping their further development, and struggles for power and control erupted. Who would control the community institutions? Whose values and purposes would be promoted? These were critical questions that often polarized the settlements.

Some approached Native American education with idealism and the desire to bring the indigenous people to Christianity and salvation and, as the colonizers saw it, a better way of life. Others within the European community viewed themselves as victors, and their motives had more in common with the victorious throughout history: bringing the conquered into line so that they would accept the values and assumptions of the conquerors.

Throughout the nineteenth century there were not only wars and battles between whites and Native Americans with regard to the possession of lands but also clashes of ideologies among the settlers themselves. The white community could unite to fight the common foe, the "Indian"; they also vehemently fought each other on religious or political issues.

Different factions within the communities battled over the role of education. Issues of control, responsibility, and payments, were at the center of many heated interactions. Sometimes the issues were so contentious that interactions had all the hallmarks of an out-and-out war. In fact, the differences among competing groups within one city gave rise to the title of the book *The Great School Wars* (Ravitch 1974).

It is understandable that differences became especially exacerbated in relation to education. In addition to existing conflicts about the role and control of education were differing perceptions about how and why the Native American should be educated. Whatever the motivation of the educator, intense pressure was brought to bear on the native population to conform to the ways of the settlers. Education and the school were seen as key instruments of assimilation (Reyhner and Eder 1994, 33).

The Common School Movement

At the turn of the eighteenth century and the first part of the nineteenth, people chose the type of school they would support and attend with much the same sort of freedom that they choose to support a sports team today. These choices reflected such differences as religion, social class, race, and regional needs. The local townspeople as well as governments gave money to private institutions in addition to supporting the public schools. Gradually the community came to examine the question as to who should support the many and varied schools that had emerged.

During the nineteenth century the local community, not government, took responsibility for building and maintaining the local school. The men and women of these small and often beleaguered outposts generally shared some common ideals, values, and aspirations. They wanted their community to be successful. They could hope to become part of the promised wealth and prosperity they perceived to be a part of America. For these communities, the school was an integral part of their aspirations.

Thus there was broad agreement among the power brokers within a town with regard to the nature and value of the school and its purpose within that community in particular. However, as time progressed conflicts arose as to what should actually be part of the curriculum. Local leaders often argued about the economic, political, and religious role of the school. For example, some among the new settlers saw the school as the proper vehicle to bring new methods of farming to the indigenous population. They believed that European agricultural methods were essential to Native Americans if they were to survive at all, and they could rationalize that these methods would lead to a better standard of living for indigenous groups.

As differences emerged within the community, proponents of the common school were able to ward off serious rifts by incorporating the different points into an overarching philosophy. As the nineteenth century began to draw to a close, some generalized themes about education in white America had emerged. The general populace indicated that it clearly believed education mattered. The school was to be the agent for socialization and economic opportunity within the society. Furthermore, the school became bound into a Pan-Protestant view of the American republic. Religion, politics, and economic development became inexorably bound into the fabric of the school.

The settlers saw the need to assimilate Native Americans into this ideology. If Native Americans became part of mainstream American culture, in other words, if they were assimilated, many of the troubles that were associated with their behavior in relation to whites could be overcome. Furthermore, society would not have to face such questions as whether the Native American had been treated fairly in land acquisitions, treaties, wars, and the multiple other interactions between the new settlers and the original inhabitants of the land. For many, education was viewed not only as the agent of perpetuating an ideology but as the panacea for the many unsettling questions raised through the colonization of America.

After the Civil War there was an ever-growing change in the focus of education away from conversion to assimilation. The culture and tradition of the Indians continued to be systematically ignored. In 1881 the Sun Dance was banned, and this prohibition was followed by a general policy that forbade native religious ceremonies and customs related to them.

THE FEDERAL SYSTEM OF INDIAN SCHOOLS

In 1789, a treaty was made with the Oneida Indians that contained provisions for Native American education. Some treaties provided for teachers' salaries, school construction, and general education funds. By 1838 missionary groups still controlled most of the schools for Native Americans, but the government operated six manual-training schools and eighty-seven boarding schools. There were approximately 2,900 students in the government boarding schools. In 1839, Commissioner T. Hartley Crawford formalized the development of manual-labor schools to educate Indian children in farming and homemaking (Reyhner and Eder 1994, 39). All of these government-run schools were on the reservations and were designed mainly "to devalue the traditional culture and religion of the Indian people and coercively to assimilate Indian youth into the dominant society" (Reyhner and Eder 1994, 40).

The Off-Reservation Boarding School

The federal government gradually moved away from its role of subsidizing the schools conducted by others to developing an elaborate and ambitious plan for education. The seeds of the off-reservation boarding-school system germinated when the government put down the resistance movement of the southern plains Indian tribes (Hamley 1994, 3). At the end of the war in 1875, a group of Indian prisoners from different parts of the Indian territories were sent to Florida and put into classes where they were taught English. As the Indians of the southern plains were finally quelled, the prisoners who were sent to Florida were taken to Virginia. There, some of them were admitted to the Hampton Normal and Agricultural Institute, which had opened on 1 April 1868 as a Freedmen's Bureau school (Coleman 1993, 65).

In 1879, the education of young Native Americans came to the forefront, and the first off-reservation boarding school was established in Carlisle, Pennsylvania. Some of the prisoners from the southern plains war were transferred there.

The Carlisle Industrial School was established through the efforts of Richard Henry Pratt, an advocate of the assimilation of Native Americans. Pratt had first come into contact with Native Americans who had been placed on reservations near the Red River, close to the present Oklahoma and Texas borders. Pratt believed that the Bureau of Indian Affairs was inept and untrustworthy, so he worked relentlessly to establish a school of his own.

Secretary of the Interior Carl Schurz and Secretary of the War Department McCrary gave Pratt permission to use a deserted military base for his school. In October 1879, the first students arrived at Carlisle to begin school. The students were placed in dormitories and classes began immediately. The school was structured so that students learned academic subjects for half a day and trades or manual skills for the other half. The boys learned such skills as blacksmithing, carpentry, and tinsmithing. The girls were taught sewing, cooking, laundering, and similar domestic arts. Military-style discipline was strictly enforced.

The school began with a little over 100 boys and girls. By the turn of the century there were more than 1,000 Indians enrolled in the school with representatives from more than seventy-six tribes. One of the graduates of the Carlisle School provides a perspective on the education that he received and consequently passed on.

> Teaching amounted to very little, it really did not require a well educated person to teach on the reservation. The main thing was to teach the children to write their names in English, then came learning the alphabet and how to count. I liked this work very well, and the children were doing splendidly. The first reading books we used had a great many little pictures in them. I would have the children read a line of English, and if they did not understand all they had read, I would explain it to them in Sioux. (Standing Bear 1928, 192–193)

Many of the children at the school were also part of the "outing" system. Under this system a young Native American child would spend part of his time working for a family or white firm. The thinking was that children would gain experience in the ways of the white world. They could earn money while they were learning skills that were deemed to be beneficial. Thus, even though the boarding schools did receive government funds, the students through their labors supported the school operations. However, the real goal of this experience was to separate the young child from other Indian children and the tribal way of life. By this total, solitary immersion in white life, it was hoped that the child would be saved.

The importance of the Carlisle School is that it laid the foundation for the federal system of Indian schooling, which evolved into a network of boarding schools both on and off reservations as well as day schools on the reservation. It was Pratt's influence that was mainly responsible for many students being moved from the reservation and into boarding schools. During the five years following the opening of the Carlisle School, other boarding schools opened. These included the Chemwa Indian School in Oregon and the Chiliocco Indian School in Oklahoma. Schools were also built in Genoa, Nebraska; Albuquerque, New Mexico; and Haskell, Kansas (Ryan 1931, 3).

Increasing Government Involvement in Education

In 1887, Congress passed the General Allotment, or Dawes, Act, appropriating 160 acres of free land to each Native American family and granting citizenship to the recipients. The law was intended not only to end the dependency of tribes on the federal government but to further erode Native American traditions (see also Chapter 4). Along with the Dawes Act, the federal government stepped up its efforts to educate Native Americans. By 1887 Congress was appropriating more than $1 million a year for Native American education. At this time about half the appropriations went to missionaries who were contracted to educate Indians. However, continued feuding between Protestants and Catholics, aggravated because the Catholics were much more successful in establishing schools, led the Protestants to support funding only for government-run schools. At this time, however, government-run schools still supported Bible reading and study in the regular daily curriculum.

With the appointment in 1889 of General Thomas J. Morgan, a Baptist minister, as commissioner of Indian affairs, the Republicans began a systematic effort to stop government funding of all missionary schools. Although direct funding of missionary schools had come to an end by 1989, some government support for instruction continued until 1917, when it became illegal. The different religions that maintained schools were now required to fund them from their own resources.

General Morgan set about the development of an educational plan that called for compulsory attendance and standardized curriculum, textbooks, and instruction for Native Americans. Congress passed laws permitting Morgan to enforce school attendance through withholding rations and annuities from Indian families who did not send their children to school (Reyhner and Eder 1994, 47–48). As the nineteenth century drew to a close, the BIA was clearly the entity that was taking the lead in providing schooling for Indian children. This department's budget increased from $20,000 to $3 million between 1870 and 1900 (U.S. Congress 1900, 23). At the turn of the century it was reported that government schools enrolled some 20,712 Native American students. Contract schools including some schools controlled by religious organizations along with the Hampton Institute reported enrollment of 2,903; mission schools 1,261; and state public schools 326 (Coleman, 1993, 48). Thus by the beginning of the twentieth century, the federal government was operating more Indian schools than the missionaries.

Vexing Questions

The debate that now occupied much of the educators' time and energies began to move from the content of education to the question of where education should take place. Should young Native American children be taught on the reservation or off the reservation, in day schools, public schools, or boarding schools? Was civilization to be brought onto the reservation or should students be taken to civilization? Erecting boarding schools on the reservation would bring what was perceived as a civilizing influence into the heart of "heathenism." Perhaps the school would be a moderating influence, but the more likely scenario was that the work of the school would be overwhelmed by the school's proximity to the tribe and its practices.

It was recognized by those involved in determining answers to these questions that life off the reservation could also be corrupting. There were many influences and practices in mainstream society that educators thought would be unhealthy for young Native Americans. Would these young people be strong enough to withstand the vices that would surround them off the reservation?

There was the hope among educators that as the children stayed in the boarding schools off the reservation, their natural parents would be replaced by the Christian home of the boarding schools. It was noted that children who attended the reservation day schools did not appear to give up their culture easily. In fact, they kept their regular way of life and reverted to "bad habits and loose morals," according to Commissioner of Indian Affairs William P. Dole (U.S. Congress 1863, 172).

SUMMARY

The early settlers' approach to education for Native Americans was focused on saving the heathens from their wicked and perverse ways. Many believed that through conversion, Native Americans would achieve a better livelihood. This prevailing attitude was expressed through the support that was given to the missionary schools. During the nineteenth century, educators additionally focused on literacy and civilizing the young Indian children.

Some of the Native Americans adopted forms of white education as a means of preserving their way of life. They appeared to be assimilated into the European culture, whereas they were using the system for their own purposes. Some of the tribes in the East developed a sophisticated level of European-type education for their people. However, as the tribes became dispossessed of their lands, many more clashes occurred between the Native Americans and the settlers. There were also clashes among the different missionary groups that provided a level of education to the Native American.

The need to bring some measure of peace to the countryside became an increasing issue for the government. As the government's role in controlling the clashes with Native Americans grew, so did its involvement in education. The government believed that the assimilation of the Native Americans into the white settlements would both improve the natives' lot and bring a level of peace to all. Both the missionaries with conversion and the government with assimilation wanted to change Native Americans to fit another idea and another mold.

REFERENCES AND FURTHER READING

Adams, David W. 1988. "Fundamental Considerations: The Deep Meaning of Native American Schooling, 1880–1900." *Harvard Education Review* 58 (February).

Allen, Elsie. 1972. *Pomo Basketmaking: A Supreme Art for the Weaver.* Edited by Vinson Brown. Healdsburg, CA: Naturegraph.

Armstrong, Virginia I., ed. 1971. *I Have Spoken: American History through the Voices of the Indians.* Chicago: Swallow.

Barrett, Carole, and Marcia W. Britton. 1994. *"You Didn't Dare Try To Be Indian": Oral History View of Former Indian Boarding School Students.* In *North Dakota History.* Bismarck: State Historical Society of North Dakota and the University of Mary.

Board of Indian Commissioners, U.S. Department of Interior. 1870. *Report of the Board of Indian Commissioners.* Washington, DC: Government Printing Office.

Boyer, Paul. 1989. *Tribal Colleges: Shaping the Future of Native Americans.* Princeton, NJ: Carnegie Foundation for the Advancement of Teaching.

Carter, Forrest. 1986. *The Education of Little Tree.* Albuquerque: University of New Mexico Press.

Child, Brenda. 1993. "Homesickness, Illness, and Death: Native-American Girls in Government Boarding Schools." In B. Blair and S. Cayleff, eds., *Wings of Gauze: Women of Color and the Experience of Health and Illness.* Detroit: Wayne State University Press.

Coleman, Michael F. 1993. *American Indian Children at School, 1850–1930.* Jackson: University Press of Mississippi.

———. 1999. *The Responses of American Indian Children and Irish Children to the School.* Lincoln: University of Nebraska Press.

Fuchs, Estelle, and Robert J. Havighurst. 1972. *To Live on This Earth: American Indian Education.* Garden City, NY: Doubleday.

Garcia, Ricardo L., and Janet G. Ahler. 1994. "Indian Education: Assumptions, Ideologies, Strategies." In Jon Reyhner, ed., *Teaching American Indian Students.* Norman: University of Oklahoma Press.

Grayson, G. W. 1988. *A Creek Warrior for the Confederacy: The Autobiography of Chief G. W. Grayson.* Edited by E. David Baird. Norman: University of Oklahoma Press.

Hamley, Jeffrey. 1994. *An Introduction to the Federal Indian Boarding School Movement in North Dakota History.* Bismarck: State Historical Society of North Dakota and University of Mary.

Hyer, Sally. 1990. *One House, One Voice, One Heart: Native American Education at the Santa Fe Indian School.* Santa Fe: Museum of New Mexico Press.

Kaestle, Carl E. 1999. *Pillars of the Republic: Common Schools and American Society.* New York: Hill and Wang.

Kelly, William. 1954. *Indian Affairs and the Indian Reorganization Act: The Twenty Year Record.* Tucson: University of Arizona Press.

Lomawaima, K. Tsianina. 2001. "The Unnatural History of the American Indian Education." In Karen Cayton Swisher and John W. Tippeconnic III, eds., *Next Steps: Research and Practice to Advance Indian Education.* Huntington, WV: Chapman Printing.

Molin, Paulette Fairbanks. 1988. "Training the Hand, the Head, and the Heart: Indian Education at Hampton Institute." *Minnesota History* 51.

Otis, D. S. 1973. *The Dawes Act and the Allotment of Indian Lands.* Edited by Francis Paul Prucha. Norman: University of Oklahoma Press.

Philip, Kenneth R. 1975. *John Collier's Crusade for Indian Reform, 1920–1954.* Tucson: University of Arizona Press.

Prucha, Francis P. 1994. *American Indian Treaties: The History of an Anomaly.* Berkeley: University of California Press.

——, 1973. *Americanizing the American Indians.* Cambridge, MA: Harvard University Press.

——. 1975. *Documents of United States Indian Policy.* Lincoln: University of Nebraska Press.

Ravitch, Diane. 1974. *The Great School Wars: New York City, 1805–1973.* New York: Basic Books.

Reyhner, Jon, and Jeanne Eder. 1994. "A History of Indian Education." In Jon Reyhner, ed., *Teaching American Indian Students.* Norman: University of Oklahoma Press.

Ryan, W. Carson, Jr. 1931. *Indian Schools and Education.* Circular 56759 (September 1). Washington, DC: Department of Interior, Office of Indian Affairs.

Skinner, Linda. 1991. "A Teaching through Traditions: Incorporating Native Languages and Cultures into Curricula." In *Indian Nations at Risk: Solutions for the 1990s.* Washington, DC: Department of Education.

Standing Bear, Luther. 1928. *My People the Sioux.* Edited by E. A. Brininstool. Boston: Houghton Mifflin.

Time Life Books. 1994. *The American Indians: War for the Plains.* Alexandria, VA: Time Life.

Trafzer, Clifford E. 2000. *As Long As the Grass Shall Grow and Rivers Flow: A History of Native Americans.* Orlando, FL: Harcourt.

Tyack, David, and Elizabeth Hansot. 1982. *Managers of Virtue.* New York: Basic Books.

U.S. Congress. 1863. *Annual Report of the Commissioner of Indian Affairs.* House Executive Document No. 1, 38th Cong., 1st sess., 1182, 172.

——. 1900. *Annual Report of the Commissioner of Indian Affairs,* House Executive Document No. 5, 56th Congress, 2d sess., serial, 44, 23.

Zimmerman, William. 1957. "The Role of the Bureau of Indian Affairs since 1933." *Annals of the American Academy of Political and Social Science* 102.

Zinn, Howard. 1980. *A People's History of the United States.* New York: Harper and Row.

Chapter Two

⬤⤙ The Twentieth Century

At the beginning of the twentieth century, farmers and ranchers continued to take over more and more Indian lands that were traditionally used for hunting and food gathering. These landgrabs led to almost constant conflict between Native Americans and the settlers, confirming the view that Native Americans were still a problem for the country at large. It also appeared logical to farmers that if the Native Americans were assimilated into their ways of farming, there would be less need for the hunting lands that the native farmers considered part of their territory (Ryan 1931, 18).

The focus of education was still on changing Native Americans into Europeans. This aim was upheld by the widespread belief that Native Americans would be greatly helped and their lot in life improved if they took on European ways.

THE BOARDING-SCHOOL MOVEMENT

As mentioned in Chapter 1, the boarding-school movement for Native Americans received its real impetus after the failure of the Native American resistance on the southern plains in the 1870s. By the end of the nineteenth century, the government supported about 81 boarding schools and 133 day schools (Hamley 1994, 3). With government support for the boarding schools, the missionary schools began to decrease, and more Native Americans were brought under those forces that shaped education throughout the country. In the beginning of the twentieth century the boarding school received greater attention and support from the government (Ryan 1931, 17–22). In 1917, as a result of increased squabbling among the missionary groups, particularly Catholics and Protestants, Congress refused to continue to allow the use of federal funds by the churches for the education of Native Americans. As the churches reorganized to reduce operating costs, more missionary schools closed.

The aim of the government boarding school was not only to introduce the Native Americans to new ideas but also to destroy their tribal customs and culture. This attitude is summed up by the motto of the founder of the Carlisle Indian School, Richard Henry Pratt: "Kill the Indian and save the man" (Walker-McNeil 1979, 111). Pratt believed that the transformation of the Indian child into a Euro-American was for the benefit of the child, the tribe, and American society as a whole.

The policy of separating young children from the tribe, teaching them European topics, and forcing them to work with immigrant Christian families was seen at first as an experimental phase in the Native American boarding-school movement. Although some continued to be interested in testing and developing new education methods to engage the young Native American, this experimental model became the norm of education for Indian children.

The System's Harmful Effects

As mentioned in Chapter 1, conditions in the boarding schools were harsh. Students were immediately deprived of their cultural identity with changed clothing, hairstyles, and names. The more fluid Native American approach to learning with its ease of interactions between youth and elders was replaced with rigid routines governed by the clock. Specific subjects were taught at specific times, and students used textbooks, unknown in the customary learning styles and practices of tribal education.

Jeffrey Hamley (1994, 5) enumerates some practices that were typical of boarding schools for Native Americans across the country at this time:

- Basic common school education in reading, writing, and arithmetic
- Instruction in English *and* English-only rule for school life in general
- Coeducation
- Military cadet training, stressing patriotism and citizenship
- Rudimentary industrial training, emphasizing trades for boys, domestic arts for girls, and agriculture for both
- Arduous manual labor (students worked half of each day)
- Christianization

Hamley also states that many school officials resorted to corporal punishment to force students to conform. This practice was virtually unknown among Native Americans, who held their young as sacred gifts entrusted to them. Restriction to "school jails" was also used as a method of control.

Students were crowded into unhygienic living areas. They suffered dietary deficiencies, and medical services were substandard. Contagious diseases were rampant in these living conditions and caused high morbidity rates among the students (Hamley 1994, 5). The high death rate among the children was compounded by the most frequent response of officials: When children became infected with contagious illnesses, they were sent back to their families on the reservation. This practice resulted in the spread of diseases among tribal people, who had no natural resistance to European illnesses. Typical childhood diseases resulted in high death rates not only among children but also among native adults across the country (Coleman 1993, 165).

The folklore of many tribes across the United States is replete with stories of resistance from young Native American students while at boarding schools. They endured mouth washings because they dared to use their tribal languages. They tried to run away. There are accounts of boarding-school personnel attempting to instill feelings of shame in a student about his or her traditional family. As a result of spending a number of years at boarding schools, many Native American youth developed a sense of disconnection from family and friends (Hamley 1994, 8).

One problem Native American youth who attended boarding school had to face was reentry into life on the reservation. Many students did not find it easy to fit back into the rhythms and customs of reservation life, whereas others were able to make a successful transition. Successful transitions were largely dependent on one's perspective. Many reentries were not successful from the government perspective. When some young people returned to the reservation, they began wearing their tribal dress, used their native languages, and returned to traditional customs and spiritual beliefs (Hamley 1994, 6).

Benefits of the System

For some Native American students the boarding school was not so severe and even proved helpful. It provided them with opportunities to develop skills necessary to function effectively within the emerging society. In addition to the basic training in reading, writing, math, and other areas of education, some Native American youth received advanced training that provided them with the skills necessary to take up occupations apart from agriculture. A small number of Native Americans were prepared for careers in law, medicine, art, and other professions (Hamley 1994, 7).

Over time a number of elders realized that Native Americans would not be able to succeed in this evolving society if they did not adapt to the new ways. With this in mind, in a number of instances, the elders supported young Native American youth being sent to boarding schools.

Many Native Americans managed to maintain their tribal identity and learn about the customs of other tribes with whom they lived in the boarding school. This knowledge of other tribes later aided in the formation of close, cohesive, activist Native American groups. Later, these groups were to work actively for Native American causes and issues (Hamley 1994, 7). Also contributing to communication among tribes was the common language they learned in the schools. Many of the students developed a reasonable proficiency in English (Coleman, 1993. 65).

Some other young Native Americans developed leadership skills, which gave them confidence in taking up leadership roles when they returned to the reservation. As time passed, there emerged among many Native Americans a new collective Indian identity that was expressed in the Pan-Indian movement (Hamley 1994, 7).

Thus an experience that was intended to strip the Native Americans of their culture had the opposite effect of building newer and stronger relationships among the different tribes. From bonds born in adversity grew the Pan-Indian movement, which espoused and fought for the rights of Native Americans. In 1911, it formed the Society of American Indians, which sought to advance the political rights of the indigenous people of the United States. This society fought against the Bureau of Indian Affairs because members perceived that this organization maintained a paternalistic approach instead of an advocacy role (Coleman 1993, 142).

THE MERIAM REPORT

With the Indian Citizenship Act of 1924, all Native Americans were recognized as citizens of the United States (prior to this act, Congress would enact laws making specific tribes citizens; e.g, after the member of a tribe aided the U.S. military). About this time, the secretary of the interior called together a committee to study how Native American education could be improved. During the early 1920s, the Bureau of Indian Affairs had suffered poor administration and a great deal of criticism about its policies. The assimilation policy, which was also adopted by the Indian tribal schools, was the subject of deep resentment by many native and nonnative reformers.

The education community at large had increasingly begun to appreciate the need for research into various issues affecting education. Early within the first quarter of the twentieth century George Strayer

(Tyack and Hansot, 1982, 153) was able to boast that significant progress had been made in public education for two main reasons. First, the scientific method of management had been applied to schools, and second, school leaders had been trained in universities.

In January 1926, the Board of Indian Commissioners recommended that a skilled and disinterested organization with a number of experts study the condition of Indian tribes under the control of the Bureau of Indian Affairs. In June of the same year Secretary of Labor Hubert Work appointed W. F. Willoughby the director of the Institute for Government Research. Subsequently, in 1928, the government charged the institute with conducting an investigation into Indian affairs, which resulted in the Committee of One Hundred, a new national advisory committee, investigating the Bureau of Indian Affairs (Trafzer, 2000, 343). A grant from John D. Rockefeller Jr. funded the study, and Willoughby appointed Lewis Meriam as chair (Trafzer 2000, 345).

Members of this committee included experts in health, education, Indian policy, and economics. In 1927 the committee spent seven months visiting the reservations and examining documents and records of births, deaths, illnesses, and similar data. It evaluated conditions at boarding schools, day schools, agencies, and clinics.

The following principles of progressive school reform, which had gained acceptance in public education, were used as the bases for examination of Native American education.

- Development of a clear outline of staff organization
- Reorganization of traditional uniform elementary and secondary schools into differentiated institutions, including junior high schools, that treated individuals and groups according to abilities and needs
- Creation of special classes for the "backward, delinquent, physically handicapped and the like," vocational tracks, and instruction in subjects such as health and physical education
- Professionalization of the occupations of teaching administration by upgraded standards of education, certification, tenure, specialization of function, and supervision
- Standardization of methods of "pupil accounting" and enforcement of attendance
- Introduction of "sound business administration" in budgeting, plant planning and maintenance, and finance (Tyack and Hansot 1982, 153).

The results of this study were published in 1928 in a document known as *The Problem of Indian Administration.* The report highlighted two major areas of concern. First, Indians were excluded from the management of their own affairs. Second, Indians were receiving poor-quality services, particularly in the areas of education and health care. Public officials who were supposed to be serving the needs of the Native Americans were generally performing at a substandard level.

The Meriam Report, as it came to be more commonly known, was praised for its impartial review of the Bureau of Indian Affairs and Native American education. Though the report did not really chronicle any new facts about life on the reservation or about Native American education, it brought together in one place a great deal of data so that they were more easily referenced. This compilation of data, facts, recommendations, and information provided reformers with a single document behind which they could rally.

Boarding schools were the subject of criticism within the report, which pointed not only to the inadequate facilities but also to the poor way in which the schools were operated. The writers of the report condemned the widespread practice of taking children from their homes and placing them in boarding schools off the reservations. Another focus of criticism was the curriculum. They found it to be inappropriate and stressed time and again the need for a curriculum that was relevant and adapted to the needs and backgrounds of the students. The report chided school personnel for their failure to consider or adapt to the language of the child.

The authors of the Meriam Report questioned why earlier treaty provisions, which called for the participation of parents in the directions of their schools, had not been heeded. The report was clear in its findings that a traditional public school curriculum was not the answer to either improving the educational standard of Native American youth or involving parents in the education of their children.

Another great value of the Meriam Report was that it chronicled many problems among Native Americans. These problems had their roots in poverty and the loss of land. The report pointed out the health problems that faced Indians both on and off the reservation. As mentioned earlier, many young Indians contracted diseases and illness while at the schools off the reservation and were simply sent home to die. In turn, they infected their families and others on the reservation. During his investigations, Meriam discovered that the Bureau of Indian Affairs was spending only about $.50 per Indian per year on health care (Trafzer 2000, 347).

The report condemned as assimilationist the allotment system initiated by reformers in the late nineteenth century, under which portions of reservations were divided into parcels of land and given to Indians in the hopes that they would become hard-working farmers (Trafzer, 2000, 328). The authors advised Congress to protect the remaining Native American lands and to create a loan pool for Native American enterprises. This approach could help foster the economic development of the tribes.

The report advised Congress and the Bureau of Indian Affairs to abandon assimilation (Americanization) as a primary goal of education. Schools needed to focus on a broader curriculum, better school facilities, and more qualified teachers. The report further recommended that day schools on or near the reservation (federal, public, or private) should be the schools of choice rather than overcrowded boarding schools. The report suggested that schools serve more nutritious foods and end child labor (Trafzer 2000, 345–346).

Even though this document in and of itself was not perceived as revolutionary, it provided the foundation for reform. Also, it provided the basis for government interaction with Native Americans for a considerable part of the twentieth century.

EDUCATION IN THE NEW DEAL ERA

The bureaucracy associated with schools expanded rapidly. This growth resulted in a shift of the power base away from the tribes to employees of the Department of Interior. The tribal powers of self-government and decisionmaking were whittled away and replaced by the decisions and values of the career bureaucrats.

In 1933, in an attempt to improve conditions for Native Americans, President Franklin D. Roosevelt appointed Harold Ickes as secretary of the interior and John Collier as commissioner of Indian affairs (Trafzer 2000, 350). These two had long been supporters of Native Americans and their causes. With these supporters in the executive branch of government, the new administration accelerated the rate of change to rectify problems that had been described in the Meriam Report.

The Indian Reorganization Act of 1934 (see Chapter 3) was an attempt by Congress to restore some of the power back to the tribes. Those tribes that reorganized themselves under the provisions of this act were recognized as having the powers of self-government. At about the same time, through the Johnson O'Malley Act (see Chapter 3), Congress moved to shift the responsibility of educating Native American children to the states.

John Collier was responsible for initiating other changes in Native American education. He made it clear to superintendents, administrators, and government teachers that Native American histories and traditions should be taught with the same consideration as other traditions. For years, the government had attempted to destroy Indian culture, language, and traditions, and now this policy was reversed. Collier did not go so far as to require missionary schools to accept the tribal and religious practices of the tribes. However, in 1933, Collier made somewhat of a change in his previous position when he encouraged the Hopi to conduct their Snake and Kachina dances. He also called upon the Lakotas to reinstate their Sun Dance, the Palouses to offer their First Food Feasts, and natives in general to conduct other traditional ceremonies (Trafzer 2000, 351). Additionally, Collier was active in promoting Native American arts and crafts and theater.

John Collier was responsible for such innovative programs as bilingual education, adult basic education, the promotion of higher education for students, and student loans. He made provision for the inservice teacher training for native teachers in the federal school system. In addition, he began programs in native culture and life. During this time, the number of Native American boarding schools was reduced and new day schools added.

Collier's personality undermined many of his efforts to improve conditions for Native Americans. He was an impatient person and wanted to redress, immediately, many of the wrongs that had been perpetrated against the Indians. Native Americans, in contrast, reached their decisions through a slower process of consensus—rather than majority rule. Collier pushed through many of his changes without taking into account the input of Native American tribal leaders. Ultimately, it was Collier's impatience that cost him the support he needed from the tribes. At various meetings across the country, Native American leaders indicated that they would not commit to new legislation until they knew more about it and had time to inform their people (Reyhner and Eder 1994, 51).

Collier exhibited the same characteristics as many superintendents and administrators in the school system. He believed that he knew what the issues were and how to deal with them. Though he did consult, he most often ignored others' recommendations and followed his own thoughts and solutions. The federal government itself moved into a similar mode of operation. As it became more involved in Native American education, the government, too, relied on committees of experts to identify the issues and recommend the solutions. Often Native Americans were not on these committees, and the government failed to listen to or consult the American Indian people themselves, the ones for whom it was providing solutions.

WORLD WAR II

The challenges of World War II caused many Americans to question whether the country was really the utopia they thought it to be, but the war had a much greater effect on Native Americans than even the populace at large. Its effects were more far reaching than the other wars, skirmishes, and events that had taken place during the past four centuries (Trafzer 2000, 371).

More than 24,000 Native Americans enlisted and served in the armed forces. War provided them with the opportunity to join another group of braves fighting for a cause. This feeling resonated with many of the deep traditions of tribal society. Additionally, experiences in the services exposed the Native Americans to a different way of life and other ways of interacting with the immigrants in their country. During the war itself and immediately after, many Native Americans left the reservations to work in the cities. As they took their place in mainstream society, they got jobs and had regular paychecks. This meant that they became part of the cash economy, and this way of conducting business soon spread onto the reservation. As the use of cash increased, the trading in goods on the reservation came to an end (Reyhner and Eder 1994, 52).

SOCIAL JUSTICE MOVEMENTS

During the 1960s momentum for the general availability of social services for students in and through schools increased. As local funding for school operations decreased, funding from states and the federal government, together with specific guidelines for its use, was increased. Much of the money from state and federal coffers was directed toward special programs for specific segments of the school population. Some of these programs were focused on exceptional students, as well as on providing compensatory aid for disadvantaged youth (Tyack and Hansot 1982, 226).

The social justice movements initiated in the 1960s not only caused great upheaval within the United States but also affected all education, including that of Native Americans. Rosa Parks in Montgomery (1955) and Martin Luther King Jr. at the Lincoln Memorial (1963) were part of a crusade to bring about social justice to all people within the

United States. Their actions had a ripple effect on the education system not only for African Americans but also for all minority groups. The U.S. Supreme Court in 1954 with its decision on the desegregation of schools ushered in an era of re-creation of the public school system. Reformers targeted the schools as the instruments for change just as their predecessors had done in the middle of the nineteenth century.

The emphasis in this reform was not to build a new system of education for the United States but rather to use the schools for the betterment of those at the bottom of the social ladder. Schools were to be agents in the war against poverty. They were to speed up desegregation, break down economic divides, and provide all peoples with the opportunity to be part of the American dream.

Schools became the battlefield where social justice skirmishes were fought. As all children had to go to school, it became the place where many federally funded programs were initiated and carried out. These school programs helped the poor and gave new entitlements to handicapped students.

With increased funding for social programs in schools, the courts began to scrutinize more closely school governance and financing and became more actively involved in setting guidelines for schools. Court decisions at both the state and federal levels set limits on religious instruction and ceremonies, set guidelines for assigning students to special classes, ordered desegregation, revised school financing, and proscribed racial and sexual inequities. Thus, in their way, the courts also exerted pressure on schools to carry out social and change agendas.

With so much time, energy, and money being poured into the schools, many competing forces were unleashed within the school itself. It was not so much that schools were viewed as particularly dysfunctional or oppressive; rather they were viewed as the places of opportunity to access different levels of society (Tyack and Hansot 1982, 224). Equal access and status for differing groups were seen as the first and essential requirements of schools. Different groups made different demands; for example, many protest leaders pressured schools to teach the values and languages of differing cultural groups. With such issues now coming to the fore in the general society, the spotlight was on the state of education of Native Americans.

Superintendents during the1950s and 1960s, who had been educated to work from a base of power and control the agenda, found for the most part that they were not well prepared to deal with the social ferment. Many tried to control the issues by redefining them and attempted to regain the initiative in terms of what should and could be expected of schools (Tyack and Hansot 1982, 232). They believed that the schools had not created the social problems and in many cases had done much to alleviate them. Superintendents did not deal well with the direct confrontations of protestors.

Some groups sought a voice by following the strategies of the civil rights movement as outlined by black activists. Hispanics, feminists, and Native Americans made new and more demands on the public schools. Each group confronted the structural inequalities that it saw as hindering its progress. Many and varied issues claimed media attention for short periods. Every law passed and every court decision made was a lever for another group to obtain change.

In this environment of upheaval and questioning society's institutions, major changes occurred in the organization of schools. The public school system altered the way in which decisions were made for individual schools and school districts. Another significant development during this period was the emergence of a strong teachers' union. Teachers joined the union in ever greater numbers and used their collective bargaining power not only to improve wage and working conditions but also to exert influence over education programs for different groups of students. Many turned toward Native American issues and their difficulties within the system (Tyack and Hansot 1982, 241).

The civil rights movement, the push for equality among different groups, and the work of the teachers led to many programs and changes not only within the schools but also in textbooks for all groups, including Native Americans. Consciousness of and respect for the many cultures and the diversity within the classrooms in turn led to a growing concern that schools would promote ethnic divisions and conflict rather than unity and harmony (Nash 1995, 141). As a result, schools were charged to promote national identity as well as enhance ethnic diversity. An increasing numbers of scholars from different ethnic groups conducted research on the schools, their histories, and their role in the community. These scholars questioned the extant historical views of the emergence of the school system within the United States (Nash 1995, 141).

It became obvious that many of the observations of the past came out of the worldview of the dominant group. Furthermore, social justice issues in previous times appeared to have been raised by individuals and not groups. By the end of the twentieth century, social justice themes were being raised by groups within the society, and this change affected whether these views were accepted and how they were implemented. Gradually, ethnic differences were given the same reverence that had been reserved for the national identity (Ueda 1995, 128). Society at large began to appreciate more the mosaic that different cultures provided, and with that appreciation, respect for differences grew. Schools promoted cultural groups rather than trying to assimilate them.

TOWARD SELF-DETERMINATION FOR NATIVE AMERICANS

With the acceleration of social movements in society at large, the winds of change swept through the tribes. Within the tribes there were those who wanted radical change and wanted it immediately. Others were more willing to work within the system and were content with a slower rate of change.

During the 1950s and 1960s a core of leaders emerged from among many different tribes. A number of the new leaders were willing to engage the federal government in debate about tribal needs and issues relevant to advancement. These leaders made it clear that they wanted self-determination. Nixon set the stage for a different approach by the federal government when he sent the following message to Congress in 1970:

> It is long past time that the Indian policies of the Federal Government began to recognize and build upon the capacities and sights of the Indian people. Both as a matter of justice and as a matter of enlightened social policy, we must begin to act on the basis of what the Indian themselves have long been telling us. The time has come to break decisively with the past and to create the conditions for a new era in which the Indian future is determined by Indian acts and Indian decisions. (Reyhner and Eder 1994, 54)

Native American educators became more active, and toward the end of the 1960s formed the National Indian Education Association (NIEA). Many Indian leaders lobbied and worked with Congress; some of the more militant young Native Americans followed the example of the Black Panthers and formed the American Indian Movement (AIM). This group damaged the BIA headquarters in Washington and in 1973 took over the village of Wounded Knee in South Dakota. There, AIM members engaged in a gun battle with the Federal Bureau of Investigation that left both Native Americans and federal agents dead and wounded.

During this time of turmoil, two major studies were being conducted on American Indian education. Estell Fuchs and Robert J. Havighurst (1972) of the University of Chicago conducted one of the studies.

The results were summarized in the publication *To Live on this Earth.* The other was a Senate inquiry, summarized in the report *Indian Education: A National Tragedy, a National Challenge* (U.S. Senate Special Subcommittee on Indian Education 1969) (Reyhner and Eder 1994, 55).

A special subcommittee on Labor and Public Welfare headed by Senator Robert Kennedy held hearings for eighteen months.This Senate report, which encouraged the establishment of community-run schools in which Native American parents were fully involved, was later known as the Kennedy Report because leadership of the effort passed from Robert Kennedy to Senator Edward Kennedy. One result of this report was the passage, in 1972, of the Indian Education Act. The act provided funding for tribal involvement in curricula development (also see Chapter 3).

Even though the Indian Education Act of 1972 (see also Chapter 4) resulted in an increase in the number of Native American schools that were tribally run, tribal leaders did not always find education institutions responsive to their demands. Furthermore, the schools did not provide curricula sensitive to Native American culture and insights (Reyhner and Eder 1994, 192, 56). These realities were a source of ongoing irritation and discontent to tribal leaders.

The Indian Self-Determination and Education Assistance Act of 1975 (see Chapter 4) provided added impetus to the involvement of Native Americans both in their own government and in education. This act led to the establishment of Native American studies programs in colleges and universities.

An initiative of the American Association for Colleges for Teacher Education (AACTE) in collaboration with the Teacher Corps, U.S. Department of Education, published in 1978 the document: *The Schooling of Native Americans.* Though the document was considered a comprehensive blueprint for action in Native American education, it does not appear to have had the impact that it deserves (Skinner 1990,10).

INDIAN NATIONS AT RISK TASK FORCE

In March 1990, the Department of Education commissioned a task force entitled Indian Nations at Risk with Lauro F. Cavazos, the secretary of education, at its head. The purpose of the task force was to make "practical recommendations for action to be taken by boards of education, public officials, state and local government, the federal government, affected tribes, parents, students, and others having a vital interest in the education of American Indians/Alaska Natives" (Charleston and King 1991, 1).

The task force worked in conjunction with the National Advisory Council on Indian Education (NACIE). Through site visits, a conference, and regional hearings, investigators gathered information about issues concerned with Native American education. Visitors examined specific programs at each site. They reviewed those programs that dealt with dropout prevention, bilingual teacher training, native language and culture. Also of interest was education reform to increase the academic achievement of native students in rural sites.

The study identified a number of significant problems, such as chronic underfunding of all native education programs. This finding was ironic given that funding for education programs was often a part of treaty obligations. However, the government had made deep cuts in essential services for Native Americans in efforts to balance the budget.

The writers of the report identified a critical need to educate "American Indian and Alaska Native teachers, administrators, counselors, and specialists" for all levels in the education system. Even though the government had mandated earlier that parents should be involved in education, the framers of the report found that this goal had not been achieved. Schools were also found wanting in regard to integrating native language and culture into the general education process.

TRIBAL CONTROL OF EDUCATION

Native parents have always been highly committed to the education of their children. Among parents' concerns has been and continues to be the adequacy of education for their children in terms of content and values. Over time, though, the tribal role in education has been limited by inadequate funding of schools and continuing conflicts with federal agencies over local control and decisionmaking authority.

Through the passage of laws, the government promoted greater participation in and control of Native American education by the tribes themselves. Professional organizations such as the National Council for the Accreditation of Teacher Education (NCATE) also contributed to the raising of consciousness through the adoption of requirements that teacher-education institutes give evidence of planning for and instruction in multicultural education. In areas with a Native American population, students were required to take at least one course in Native American education.

Native Organizations

Concerned native people have formed organizations to help improve educational opportunities for their children. These organizations have also aided native community members to negotiate the political steps necessary for the parents to take control of the local schools. Examples of these organizations are the National Indian Education Association, already mentioned, and the Coalition of Indian Controlled School Boards formed in 1971. The coalition serves some ninety communities, parent groups, and school districts.

Tribal Governments and Courts

During the 1960s, the U.S. public became more tolerant of different cultural groups. A number of the tribes and communities took advantage of the changing attitudes by contracting with the Bureau of Indian Affairs to set up school boards. However, tribal government and courts themselves did not always perform well. The U.S. Civil Rights Commission issued a report critical of tribal courts (*Congressional Record* 134, Nov.10, 1988, Secs. 17392, 17393). The Senate Select Committee on Indian Affairs also issued a report critical of tribal government operation in 1989 (U.S. Senate 1989, 13). The 1990 conviction of a Navajo tribal chairman, Peter MacDonald, on corruption charges has been judged by some as casting the same shadow on tribal governments that was cast on local county government by the Oklahoma county commissioners scandal.

Recent indications are that some tribes are recognizing their problems and have moved to rectify them. Native governments are working to revitalize themselves in order to better serve the needs of their people. Education continues to be one of the top priorities of the tribes. They want improved education opportunities to be available to all of their youth.

Native American Studies Programs

The social upheavals of the 1960s and 1970s led people toward awareness of the differences among cultural groups and the need for supporting these differences. As mentioned, as a result of the Indian Self-Determination and Education Assistance Act of 1975, departments of Native American studies opened in colleges and universities throughout the country. With the establishment of these centers, more focus was directed toward the study of Native American cultures, rituals, languages, and the development of appropriate curriculum materials. New studies and materials were used in training teachers, especially in those areas of the curriculum that served Native American children. By the close of the twentieth century, Native American studies within colleges and universities existed as a discipline in its own right.

Community Colleges

Generally speaking, reservations are far from urban areas, and thus Native Americans have limited opportunities to attend colleges and universities. To address the problem, in 1972 a number of tribes formed the American Indian Higher Education Consortium. The consortium was able to achieve its financial goals by lobbying Congress for accreditation of tribally run colleges.

By the end of 1989 the tribes had established twenty-four colleges in ten states throughout the country. Two were four-year institutions. Sinte Gleska University in South Dakota later expanded its program to offer a masters degree in education. Native American students have had a greater level of success in these colleges, which are located on the reservations.

Public Schools

By 1990, tribes operated fifty-eight elementary and secondary day schools, some on or near reservations, twelve boarding schools at further distances from reservations, and six dormitories that provided residential accommodations for Native American children attending off-reservation public schools.

Some tribes have developed guidelines for regulating public schooling on the reservations. The Rosebud Sioux, for example, address curriculum and education standards and require instruction in Rosebud Lakota language and history as well as modern federal-tribal-state relations. Their guidelines stipulate programs to deal with alcohol and substance-abuse prevention; increased parental and community involvement; the hiring of more native teachers and administrators; and goals unique to tribes, such as the preservation of tribal culture.

SUMMARY

At the beginning of the twentieth century, few in the mainstream believed in the value of the Native American way of life. The wars in which the United States was engaged throughout the century as well as the emergence of the social sciences and new social movements promoted questioning of the way in which the mainstream culture had interacted with American Indians. The civil rights movements impacted both the education and the status of Native Americans within the country. By the close of the century, radical changes had occurred in approaches to Native American education. Native Americans were somewhat more appreciated as a group of people with different cultures, mores, and traditions. Rather than being a problem that needed to be overcome, they were viewed as people who needed support and restitution for the wrongs that had been done them.

At the beginning of the twenty-first century with the availability of many written and electronic research reports and resources about Native American education, there is a possibility that improvements will be made more quickly. These improvements will be dependent on an increase in funding as well as the ability of Americans to rise above the racism that is embedded in many of society's attitudes and structures.

REFERENCES AND FURTHER READING

Adams, David W. 1988. "Fundamental Considerations: The Deep Meaning of Native American Schooling, 1880–1900." *Harvard Education Review* 58 (February).

Allen, Elsie. 1972. *Pomo Basketmaking: A Supreme Art for the Weaver,* ed. Vinson Brown, Healdsburg, CA: Naturegraph.

Armstrong, Virginia I., ed. 1971. *I Have Spoken: American History Through the Voices of the Indians.* Chicago: Swallow.

Barrett, Carole, and Britton, Marcia, W. 1994. "You Didn't Dare Try to Be Indian," Oral History View of Former Indian Boarding School Students." In *North Dakota History.* Bismarck: State Historical Society of North Dakota and the University of Mary.

Board of Indian Commissioners, U.S. Department of Interior. 1870. *Report of the Board of Indian Commissioners.* Washington, DC: Government Printing Office.

Boyer, Paul. 1989. *Tribal Colleges: Shaping the Future of Native American.* Princeton, NJ: Carnegie Foundation for the Advancement of Teaching.

Carlson, Leonard, A. 1981. *Indians, Bureaucrats and Land: The Dawes Act and Decline of Indian Farming.* Westport, CT: Greenwood Press.

Carter, Forrest. 1986. *The Education of Little Tree.* Albuquerque: University of New Mexico Press.

Child, Brenda. 1993. *Homesickness, Illness, and Death: Native-American Girls in Government Boarding Schools.* In Blair, B. and Cayleff, S. (eds) *Wings of Gauze: Women of Color and the Experience of Health and Illness.* Detroit: Wayne State University Press.

Charleston, G. Mike, and Gaye King. 1991. "Indian Nations at Risk Task Force: Listen to the People." In *Indian Nations at Risk: Solutions for the 1990s.* Washington, DC Department of Education.

Coleman, Michael F. 1993. *American Indian Children at School, 1850–1930.* Jackson: University Press of Mississippi.

———. 1999. *The Responses of American Indian Children and Irish Children to the School.* Lincoln: University of Nebraska Press.

Collier, John, and Ira Moskowitz. 1947. *Indians of the Americas.* New York: W. W. Norton.

———. 1963. *From Every Zenith.* Denver: Sage Books.

———. 1972. *American Indian Ceremonial Dances.* New York: Bounty Books.

Department of Education. 1991. "Preamble." In *Indian Nations at Risk: Solutions for the 1990s.* Washington, DC: Department of Education.

Forbes, Jack D. 1981. *Native Americans and Nixon: Presidential Politics and Minority Self- Determination, 1969–1972.* Los Angeles: American Indian Studies Center, University of California.

Fuchs, Estell, and Havighurst, Robert J. 1972. *To Live on This Earth: American Indian Education.* Garden City, NY: Anchor.

Grayson, G. W. 1988. *A Creek Warrior for the Confederacy: The Autobiography of Chief G. W. Grayson,* ed. E. David Baird. Norman: University of Oklahoma Press.

Hamley, Jeffrey. 1994. *An Introduction to the Federal Indian Boarding School Movement.* Bismarck: State Historical Society of North Dakota and University of Mary.

Hyer, Sally. 1990. *One House, One Voice, One Heart: Native American Education at the Santa Fe Indian School.* Santa Fe: Museum of New Mexico Press.

Kelly, William. 1954. *Indian Affairs and the Indian Reorganization Act: The Twenty Year Record.* Tucson: University of Arizona Press.

Meriam, Lewis. 1928. *The Problem of Indian Administration.* Baltimore: Johns Hopkins University Press.

Molin, Paulette Fairbanks. 1988. "Training the Hand, the Head, and the Heart: Indian Education at Hampton Institute." *Minnesota History* 51.

Nash, Garry. 1995. "American History Reconsidered: Asking New Questions about the Past." In Diane Ravitch and Maris Vinovskis, eds., *Learning from the Past.* Baltimore and London: Johns Hopkins University Press.

Orfield, Gary. 1965. *A Study of the Termination Policy.* Denver: National Congress of American Indians.

Otis, D. S. 1973. *The Dawes Act and the Allotment of Indian Lands.* Francis Paul Prucha, ed. Norman: University of Oklahoma Press.

Philip, Kenneth R. 1975. *John Collier's Crusade for Indian Reform, 1920–1954.* Tucson: University of Arizona Press.

Prucha, Francis P. 1985. *American Indian Treaties: The History of an Anomaly.* Berkeley: University of California Press.

Reyhner, Jon, and Eder, Jeanne. 1994. "A History of Indian Education." In Jon Reyhner, ed., *Teaching American Indian Students.* Norman: University of Oklahoma Press.

Ryan W. Carson, Jr. 1931. *Indian Schools and Education.* Circular 56759. Washington, DC: U.S. Department of the Interior, Office of Indian Affairs, September 1.

Skinner, Linda. 1991. "Teaching Through Traditions: Incorporating Native Languages and Cultures into Curricula." In *Indian Nations at Risk: Solutions for the 1990s.* Washington, DC: Department of Education.

Stein, Gary. 1972. "The Indian Citizenship Act of 1924." *New Mexico Historical Review* 47.

Trafzer, Clifford, E. 2000. *As Long As the Grass Shall Grow and Rivers Flow: A History of Native Americans.* Orlando, FL: Harcourt.

Tyack, David, and Elizabeth Hansot. 1982. *Managers of Virtue.* New York: Basic Books.

Ueda, Reed. 1995. "Ethnic Diversity and National Identity in Public School Texts." In Diane Ravitch and Maris Vinovskis, eds., *Learning from the Past.* Baltimore: Johns Hopkins University Press.

U.S. Congress. 1863. *Annual Report of the Commissioner of Indian Affairs,* House Executive Document, No. 1, 38 Congress, 1 sess., serial 1182, p. 172.

U.S. Congress. 1900. *Annual Report of the Commissioner of Indian Affairs,* House Document No. 5, 56 Congress, 2 session, serial 44, p. 23.

U.S. Senate Special Subcommittee on Indian Education. 1969. *Indian Education: A National Tragedy, a National Challenge.* Senate Report No. 91–501.Washington, DC: Government Printing Office.

Walker-McNeil, Pearl L. 1979. "The Carlisle Indian School: A Study of Acculturation." Ph.D. diss., American University. (Original source cited by author: Wilson, Flora Warren. 1941. *Indian Agents of the Old Frontier.* New York: D. Appleton-Century.)

Zimmerman, William. 1957. "The Role of the Bureau of Indian Affairs since 1933." *Annals of the American Academy of Political and Social Science* 102.

Chapter Three

●← Chronology

1492   The Spanish conquistadors seek to exploit Native Americans by using them for forced labor. They also attempt to convert natives of the new land to Catholicism.

The Jesuits, primarily from Spain, establish most of the missionary schools during the early days of European settlement of North and South America. They teach the natives in Spanish and work hard to convert them to Catholicism.

1568   A school for Indian youth is established in Havana, Florida, by the Jesuits. This school marks an era when Catholic and Protestant religious groups dominate the education of Native American youth. For the next 300 years these religious groups remain most prominent in non-Indian attempts to educate Indian children.

1607   The British begin settlement of North America with the establishment of Jamestown, Virginia. The British are interested not only in colonizing the new lands but in educating American Indians. Native Americans are not as interested in availing themselves of the opportunities provided by the English colonists.

1617   King James asks the Anglican clergy to collect money for building churches and educating the native youth of Virginia.

1631   Reverend John Eliot establishes a school in Roxbury, Massachusetts, where he instructs some of the Pequot Indians captured in a war with the Europeans. His instruction focuses on the principles of industry.

1636   Harvard is established. The charter includes education of Native Americans with the aim of "civilizing" them and converting them to Christianity.

1693   The College of William and Mary is founded and takes as part of its mission educating Native Americans to become educators for their own people. Generally speaking, Native Americans do not want to send their children to European schools. Some, however, believe that if their people are to survive under colonization, they needed to take advantage of the education offered by the colonials. However, the experience of the Native American students is that their teachers do not appreciate the complexity and depth of Indian cultures.

1756   Dartmouth College also determines to educate Native Americans so that they will in turn become missionaries to and educators of indigenous people of the land. Some Native Americans are successfully educated there but not to the extent that the founder had envisaged.

           Many missionaries advocate taking native children away from their parents so that they can be immersed in European culture. Thus, boarding schools for Native American children are initiated. For nearly 300 years, many European educators advocate the use of boarding schools for Native American youth. Some Native American parents disagree with this practice and refuse to have their children taken away from them.

1775   The Continental Congress, to demonstrate its power, declares that it has jurisdiction over Indian tribes. The Congress creates three departments of Indian Affairs and appropriates $500 to educate Indians at Dartmouth.

1778   The treaty-making era with Indian tribes begins. Almost 400 treaties are made between the U.S. government and Indian tribes between 1778 and 1871. Of those 400 treaties, 120 contain educational provisions, including provisions for teachers' salaries, school construction, and supplies.

1789   A treaty made with the Oneida Indians is the first to contain educational provisions. Congress establishes the War Department, whose secretary is responsible for all matters pertaining to Indians.

1802   Congress authorizes the allocation of up to $15,000 per year for a "civilization" program for the "aborigines." At this time most of the money is used by missionaries with the Protestant Board of Foreign Missions receiving the largest amount.

1820   A plan is developed to move the tribes from the East to the Midwest. The Cherokee tribe is slated to be moved west of the Mississippi. This movement of eastern tribes is intended to provide more land for European settlers; it leads to many skirmishes and wars between Native Americans and Europeans.

1830s   The Cherokee develop an educational system based on a language developed by Sequoya, a member of the tribe. The Cherokee teach their students in their native language as well as in English.

1832   The federal government creates the position of commissioner of Indian affairs within the War Department, marking its greater role in the education of Native American students. By 1838 the U.S. government operates six manual-labor training schools with approximately 800 students. The government also runs eighty-seven boarding schools with about 2,900 students.

1834   Congress provides for the organization of the department of Indian Affairs.

1839   Manual-labor training schools are formalized by Commissioner T. Hartley Crawford. These schools aim to train Indian children to be efficient farmers and homemakers.

1835   Congress establishes the Home Department of the Interior and the Bureau of Indian Affairs passes from military to civil control.

1851   This year marks the beginning of the period when the federal government removes Indians to reservations. This period continues until the end of the 1930s. Forced settlement on reservations causes an almost total dependence on the government for food, shelter, and clothing. (This is especially true for the plains tribes, which were formerly dependent on buffalo, rapidly decimated in the third quarter of the nineteenth century.) Reservation schools, modeled after boarding schools, are designed to devalue the traditional culture and religion of Indian people and coercively assimilate Indian youth into the dominant society.

1869 After the conclusion of the Civil War, President Ulysses S. Grant appoints a commission on Indian affairs. This commission's purpose is to supervise the selection of Indian agents, schoolteachers, and farming instructors and to oversee the purchase of supplies. The Board of Indian Commissioners functions until 1933. (Commissioners of Indian affairs continue to operate under the Bureau of Indian Affairs.)

1870 Congress appropriates $100,000 to support industrial and other schools among the Indian tribes. Education for Indians comes under direct control of the Bureau of Indian Affairs. Day and boarding schools emphasize basic arithmetic and speaking, reading, and writing English as well as vocational training.

1873 The Civilization Fund Act is repealed and the federal government becomes more involved in the operation of Indian schools maintaining the aim of transforming Native American children, with their so-called ignorance and attachment to superstition, into "productive" European-type farmers.

1879 The first government-run boarding school that is not on a reservation opens at Carlisle, Pennsylvania. Captain Richard Henry Pratt is the first director of the school. The school is determined to "take the Indian out of the student."

1880 Under the direction of Secretary of Interior Carl Schurz, the Bureau of Indian Affairs issues regulations that all instruction for Native American children be given in English. This directive must be carried out in both mission and government schools under the threat of loss of government funding.

1887 Congress passes the General Allotment (Dawes) Act. One purpose of the act is to help Native Americans move away from their growing dependency on the government. The act grants 160 acres to each head of an Indian family and 80 acres to each single person over the age of eighteen. The Indians are given four years to decide which land they want; if they fail to decide, the government will decide for them. Indians who accept land are granted citizenship. Unclaimed land is to be sold and the proceeds used for the education and "civilization" of Native Americans. Along with this act, the government steps up its efforts to educate Indians by increasing spending on their education to approximately $1 million per year.

1900   The federal government stops directly funding missionary schools because Catholic and Protestant missionaries have engaged in many acrimonious feuds over the education of Native American students.

1924   Congress passes the Indian Citizenship Act, which makes all Indians citizens of the United States. The secretary of interior, in an attempt to improve education for Native Americans, forms the Committee of One Hundred Citizens. This group examines and discusses current practices and makes recommendations for improvements in Indian education. The committee recommends that school facilities be upgraded, personnel be better trained, Native American students be encouraged to attend public schools, and the government provide scholarships for high school and college.

1927   The Board of Indian Commissioners directs that there be a study of Native American education throughout the country, under the leadership of Lewis Meriam. The subsequent report, *The Problem of Indian Administration,* is known as the Meriam Report and is published in 1928. The report condemns the allotment policy and the poor quality of services provided by the Bureau of Indian Affairs and recommends that Indian property be protected and Indians be allowed more freedom to manage their own affairs. The report argues that since the conditions of boarding schools are shocking, elementary-age children should not be sent to boarding schools at all, and he urges an increase in the number of day schools.

1934   Congress passes the Indian Reorganization (Wheeler-Howard) Act. This act ends the practice of allotment of Indian lands. The act also provides religious freedom for Native Americans, a measure of tribal self-government, and the preference of hiring Native Americans as Bureau of Indian Affairs employees.

Congress passes the Johnson-O'Malley Act. Through this act the secretary of interior is given the authority to enter into contracts with states or territories to pay these entities for providing services to Indians. As a result, the federal government can pay the states for educating Indians in public schools. Before the act, the money went into the general operating fund of the school districts and thus could be used to support the education of non-Indian students. As of the year 2002, the act still provides money to public schools educating Indian children; however, the money is supplemental to other programs. An additional requirement is that these programs are approved by an Indian parent advisory committee (PAC).

1953   Congress passes six termination bills, causing the states to assume responsibility for the education of all Indian children in public schools. The first tribe to take advantage of the bill and have their reservation status terminated is the Menominee tribe, in 1954. The termination policy is quickly judged a failure by Native Americans.

1960s   During the 1960s, two major studies of Indian education are undertaken. *The National Study of American Indian Education* is carried out from 1967 to 1971 under the direction of Robert Havighurst of the University of Chicago. The results of the study are summarized in the document *To Live on This Earth* (Fuchs and Havighurst 1972).

The second study is conducted by the Special Senate Subcommittee on Indian Education. The testimony from hearings held by this committee fill seven volumes, and a summary report titled *Indian Education: A National Tragedy, a National Challenge* is published by the U.S. Senate in 1969. This report is also known as the Kennedy Report.

1970s   During this decade more tribally controlled schools and colleges are established. Also, many mainstream colleges and universities across the country develop departments of Native American studies.

1972   The Kennedy Report results in the passage of the Indian Education Act. This act provides funding for special programs for Indian children in reservation schools and, for the first time, programs for urban Indian students. The act also promotes the establishment of community-run schools, encouraging the use of culturally relevant and bilingual curriculum materials.

1975   The Indian Education Assistance Act requires that committees of Indian parents be involved in planning these special programs. Congress also passes the Indian Self-Determination and Education Assistance Act. The act encourages the transition of authority regarding Indian programs from the federal government to the Indian people. Native Americans are to take over planning, implementing, and administering their own educational programs.

1978   Congress passes the Indian Child Welfare Act, which restricts non-Native social agencies from placing Native children in non-Native homes. The act recognizes the role of tribal courts over child custody issues.

Title XI of the Education Amendments Act of 1978 promotes Native American self-determination. According to the amendment, the Bureau of Indian Affairs is to take a more active role in ensuring that Native Americans take control of all matters regarding the education of Native American children. Furthermore, the amendment directs the Bureau of Indian Affairs to fund Native American schools according to a formula that ensures an equitable distribution of funds.

1988   Congress amends the Indian Self-Determination and Education Assistance Act, introducing new language into the law by declaring the U.S. government's commitment to supporting and assisting Indian tribes in the development of strong and stable governments. These governments will be responsible for the administration of quality programs and the development of the economies of their communities.

1990   Under the auspices of the Department of Education, Lauro F. Cavazos establishes the Indian Nations at Risk Task Force, composed of fourteen individuals, to study solutions to the problems facing Native American education. The task force is directed to summarize and make recommendations for actions to be taken by the federal government, state and local governments, and public officials of local governments. The results of many interviews conducted by the task force are published in 1991 as *Indian Nations at Risk: Task Force Commissioned Paper.*

Congress passes the Native American Language Act, recognizing the role of learning language in preserving culture.

Chapter Four

✒ The Law and Native American Education

Throughout the history of interactions between Europeans and Native Americans in the United States, many laws and treaties have been passed to both regulate those interactions and define their parameters. This chapter focuses on some of the treaties and laws that highlight the prevailing attitudes toward Native Americans or are concerned with the education of Native Americans. Sometimes, treaties were made with specific tribes, and later those conditions were extended to other tribes, particularly surrounding groups. At other times the actions of a particular state influenced what was done at the federal level. In some periods politicians took the lead in forging Native American legislation; at other times the Supreme Court led the way.

EUROPEAN LAW

The early European explorers and settlers who came to the land that was to become the United States of America were from countries where there was already a system of law. In some instances the system was still in the process of development, and generally speaking, even though law was not uniform across the different countries, there were common elements.

Before the settlement of America many Europeans had grappled with the question of parameters for their continuing relationships with those inhabitants of the land masses outside Europe and Asia. A number of countries had established procedures for these interactions.

The king of Spain took an ongoing and particular interest with regard to the rights of "Indians" in the newly discovered lands. Some of his advisers were of the opinion that the Indians had no rights because they were not Christians. The king, however, was swayed by the opinions of Franciscus de Victoria, a theologian and jurist. In 1532, he advised that there could be no change in the ownership of the lands of the Americas. It was also his opinion that " the aborigines in question were true owners before the Spaniards came among them, both from the public and private point of view" (Cohen 1948, 46). Furthermore, there could be no change in the independent status of tribes within the Americas unless the inhabitants gave their consent.

Victoria further advised the king that the Doctrine of Discovery, which stated that there could be no change in land ownership unless the Indians gave consent, a view popular in many European countries at the time, could be applied only to those lands that were uninhabited before the arrival of the explorers. Victoria's advice provided the backdrop for the many treaties that were negotiated between Europe and the native nations of the Americas (Cohen 1948, 46).

From the early days of treaty negotiations, different groups held widely divergent opinions. Some supported Victoria and the rights of the indigenous, and some opposed native rights because the natives were not Christians. From these different bases developed what has become known in the United States as federal Indian law.

According to L. K. Cohen (1960, 240–247), the effectiveness and justice of the interactions between the federal government and Native Americans can be measured in relation to how well the government has recognized and protected the following four principles enunciated by Victoria:

- The recognition by government of the political equality of the races
- Government support of established tribal self-government
- Tribal government control of native affairs
- Government protection of native rights (Cohen 1960, 240–247)

According to Victoria's principles, the Doctrine of Discovery did not apply to the newly discovered Americas because the lands were inhabited before the Europeans arrived. Therefore, it was incumbent on new settlers to develop a set of principles to regulate the competition that developed among them in regard to settlement of the land (Cohen 1948, 46).

The new arrivals declared that the Principle of Discovery should now be followed. The first right to take over the ownership or title rights from the native inhabitants, if they wished to sell, should go to the discovering nation. This approach settled the question as to who had the first right among the European powers to obtain land titles from the natives. It did little, however, to settle the question of rights between the natives and Europeans (*Worcester v George*, 31 US 515, 543–544 [1832]).

Most of the competition for land in the United States was among Britain, Spain, and France. Just as these nations vied to carve up other parts of the world to their advantage, so they competed for control in the territories of North America. Part of the powers' modus operandi was to engage native groups as allies, often using trade as the incentive. In North America at this time, the natives provided primary products such as furs, fish, tobacco, and other agricultural products in exchange for guns, firewater, and other manufactured goods. From time to time, trading conflicts arose between the colonial and tribal governments. To resolve these conflicts, the British Crown issued its Royal Proclamation of 1763. This proclamation also included provisions for the trade in land. The other important parts of the proclamation dealt with the establishment of the boundaries of Indian and confirmation of its policy for acquiring native land by purchase (Kickingbird and Charleston 1991, 3).

Honoring Victoria's principle of the political equality of indigenous people, the British Crown established the practice of dealing directly with the official native governments. Its continued interactions upheld this custom and, in so doing, strengthened the authority of tribal governments. Many statutes in force today implement Victoria's principles of equity. Now, however, the primary responsibility regarding Native American matters is assigned to the Bureau of Indian Affairs, U.S. Department of Interior (Kickingbird and Charleston 1991, 3).

In the early days of settlement, the main colonial powers generally recognized the sovereignty of native nations and entered into numerous treaties with native governments. America's Revolutionary War brought with it not only newfound freedoms but also many issues for the new government to face. After the end of the war the newly formed government operated under the Articles of Confederation. An issue that came to the fore quickly was that of the ownership of land.

The laws that had guided the colonial powers were not part of the routine of the new federal government. In fact, after the success of the Revolutionary War, many within the country's government suggested that the land that belonged to those tribes who had sided with the British should be treated as land subjected to the Doctrine of Conquest. Secretary of War Henry Knox did not favor that position and pointed out the pitfalls of taking this stance.

Knox held that the tribes were fed up with war and conquest and that the British had already established the practice of purchasing land from the Indians. Furthermore, if the government were to pursue the path of conquest, the country would be in continuous war with Native Americans. At this time, the Treasury was depleted from the recent war and the government could not afford more warfare. As far as Knox could judge, the least expensive course of action was to purchase the land from the Native Americans through treaties (Mohr 1933, 132, 219).

Congress debated the issue of landownership and decided to try another method, appropriating funds from the settlers so that land could be acquired by the U.S. government. Upon the purchase of the land, the rights of Native Americans to the land were abrogated. Although many at the time believed that most Native American lands were acquired by purchase and although some land was purchased, most Native American lands were taken by treaty or by force (U.S. Indian Claims Commission 1979, 1).

The new federal government had difficulty because there were no clear-cut rules in the Articles of Confederation about the powers of the central government in relation to the states. While developing the Constitution of the United States, the thirteen original states of the federation had to deal with the issue of the distribution of power between the federal and state governments. The states, although they wanted to keep as many powers as possible, realized that it was expedient to delegate some to the federal government. Among these delegated powers was the responsibility for Native American affairs. (Kickingbird and Kickingbird 1979, 23–24). This relationship between the U.S. government and the native tribal governments evolved over time into one of guardian and ward. The guardian-ward-type interaction was further reinforced by the Commerce Clause and the Treaty-Making Clause of the Constitution together with decisions from the Supreme Court (Cohen 1972, 170).

The laws that controlled the government's interactions with the tribes led to the theory that when tribes accepted the protection of the federal government through treaty, they relinquished their *external sovereignty*. A number of tribes did choose to place themselves under the protection of the federal government and also agreed they would not enter into any form of treaty with any other country. In return, the federal government committed itself to fulfill all the treaty terms and protect the property and rights of the native governments. The net effect of the laws was that the tribes who chose protection gave large tracts of land to the federal government.

These laws of themselves did not alter the internal workings within the tribal communities. Thus, the *internal sovereignty* of the tribes as self-governing, independent native nations was maintained. Each of the tribal governments kept its right to make treaties with the federal government, and over time, some tribes negotiated multiple treaties.

Perhaps one of the most revealing documents in relation to the way the government interacted with the Native Americans is the Doctrine of the Law of Nations. The U.S. Supreme Court decisions involving the Cherokee cases (*Cherokee Nation v Georgia,* 30 US 1 [1831] and *Worcester v Georgia,* 31 US 515 [1832]) provided the guiding principles for the way in which the Doctrine of the Law of Nations was applied.

These cases resulted from the actions of the state of Georgia when it attempted to assert jurisdiction over the territory of the Cherokee and the tribe took Georgia to court. The Court determined as follows:

- Indian country did not come under the state's jurisdiction.
- Each native government was a distinct political and independent entity.
- The United States had a relationship with the government of different Native American tribes analogous to the relationship of a guardian to a ward (Kickingbird and Kickingbird 1991).

In decisions that it handed down later, the Supreme Court indicated that native governments also had the power to wage war with other colonial powers (and, in a later case, the United States). By upholding the right of a tribe to declare war, the Court was in fact ratifying the *sovereignty* of each of the tribal governments. In the cases *Montoya v U.S.* (180 US 269 [1901]) and *Marks v U.S.* (161 US 297 [1896]), the sovereign power of a tribal government was well outlined and defined. For many within the United States the acknowledgment of the sovereignty of the native governments was a source of annoyance and contention. They complained that it was not proper to view the native governments as independent nations. With the growing criticism the Court pointed out that the words "treaty" and "nation" were part of the diplomatic and legislative language of the country. The Court also stated that the meanings, as generally understood, had to be applied to the Native American nation as they would be to any other nation (*Worcester v Georgia,* 31 US 515, 559 [1832]).

EARLY TREATIES AND LEGISLATION

As was mentioned, many Native American governments entered into numerous treaties with the federal government. Usually the treaties dealt with military, political, or economic matters. However, within the terms of a particular treaty a wide variety of subjects was often addressed. In treaty negotiations, many times the issue of the self-governance of the tribe intruded itself into the discussions. Upon signing a treaty, the federal government reaffirmed many aspects of the agreement through federal legislation. This practice of supporting agreements with Native Americans through legislation has continued to the present day.

As was discussed in Chapter 1, churches as well as interested and concerned individuals provided the initial impetus to educate Native Americans. A number of wealthy patrons gave money to prestigious universities, for example, Dartmouth, to support Native American education. In 1691, the Honorable Robert Boyd made a bequest to the College of William and Mary. This money was to be used specifically for the development of the Christian faith among native boys from the West. It covered tuition for instruction in reading, writing, arithmetic, and the catechism as well as living expenses (Kickingbird and Kickingbird 1979, 14–15). In fact, only a few Native American boys were ever admitted to the college.

At the signing of the Treaty of Lancaster between the government of Virginia and the six nations of the Iroquois Confederacy, the Virginia commissioners offered to educate six young Seneca men in the College of William and Mary. The European delegation perceived this offer as generous, but the Native Americans saw it otherwise. They understood that white people valued their colleges. However, they were sure that these men would understand that different native nations held varying views of the world. Therefore, it was reasonable that the Native Americans could not take advantage of this offer (Kickingbird and Charleston 1991, 5).

A significant piece of legislation, and one of the earliest, from the Continental Congress resulted from a Mohegan chief's request for instructors so that the Native Americans could learn milling and the new settlers' ways of tilling the soil. On 12 July 1775 the Congress appropriated $500 to be used for the education of Indian youth at Dartmouth, New Hampshire.

At a later date the Seneca chief Cornplanter requested that President George Washington provide instruction for the Seneca people in such practical areas as plowing, milling, and smithing as well as in reading, writing, and arithmetic. Washington was pleased by the request. Through his secretary of war, he informed Cornplanter that during a treaty negotiation or at some other similar and convenient time, formal arrangements would be made. As it happened, Cornplanter's request was never fulfilled. What did result was the idea that educational provisions could be included within the context of a treaty.

The first federal government treaty with a native tribe was signed in September 1778 between the Delaware Indians and the Continental

Congress. It laid out the guidelines for conducting legal interactions between native governments and the federal government. The provisions of this treaty were followed for almost a century (American Indian Policy Review Committee [AIPRC] 1976, 29). Essentially, it was a treaty of alliance between the United States and the Delaware (Kappler 1929, 3). The treaty was of particular significance because of the emphasis on the language of equality. Article 6 is of interest from the perspective that Congress wanted to distance itself from rumors that the government wished to exterminate Native Americans.

> Whereas, the enemies of the United States have endeavored, by every artifice in their power, to possess the Indians in general with an opinion, that it is the design of the states aforesaid to extirpate the Indians, and take possession of their country; to obviate the Indians, and take possession of their country; to obviate such false suggestion, the United States do engage to guaranty to the aforesaid nation of Delawares, and their heirs, all their territorial rights, in the fullest and most ample manner, as it hath been bounded by former treaties, as long as the said Delaware nation shall abide by, and hold fast, the Chain of friendship now entered into. (Kapler 1904)

Congress also speaks in this treaty about its relationship with the "Indians," acknowledging the stature and status of native governments. In Article 4 the treaty makes allowance for the Delaware and other tribes allied with the federal government to form a state and send a delegate to Congress. Native Americans chose not to follow up on this opportunity because it was obvious to them that they were being treated as a conquered people. Dissatisfaction spread among native peoples.

It was not until another thirteen treaties had been signed that the first educational provisions were included. The Treaty of 2 December 1794 was signed by the federal government and the Oneida, Tuscarora, and Stockbridge tribes. It included provisions for instructing the young men of the three nations in the skills of millers and sawyers. In addition, the government would provide teams and utensils for the continuance of millwork (*Stats. at Large USA*, vol. 7, 47). During the next eighty years, there were ninety-five more treaties containing education-related services for different native tribes (Kickingbird and Charleston 1991, 6).

An important part of these treaties is the provision for a particular person or group to educate tribal people. An example is in the Treaty of 1803 with the Kaskaskia. In this case, the United Sates agreed to pay $100 annually to support a Catholic priest "to perform for the said tribe the duties of his office and also to instruct as many of their children as possible in the rudiments of literature" (*Stats. at Large USA,* vol. 7, 78). In another treaty with the Delaware signed on 18 August 1804, a "civilization" program was included and was to be funded through the allocation of $300 for ten years. As part of the civilization process, Native Americans were to be taught fencemaking, cultivation, and "such domestic arts as are adapted to their situation" (*Stats. at Large USA,* vol. 7, 81). These treaties and other similar ones illustrate the prevailing attitudes of the times, namely that the Native American needed to be converted to Christianity and taught European agricultural methods.

Although most treaties dealt with the ceding of land from the native tribe to the federal government, officials soon realized that it was important to include provisions for education. The more the natives became like the European settlers, the easier it would be to negotiate with them. Also, if the natives adopted the new settlers' ways of agriculture and put the land under cultivation, they would have less need of large tracts of land for hunting.

The government found it expedient to work with both the Catholic and the Protestant churches because it believed that their goals to "Christianize the heathens" would lead to more peaceful settlement of the land and thus further its goals (Kickingbird and Charleston 1991, 8). As Kickingbird and Charleston observe, the only separation issue involved in the relationship of church and state appeared to be a common concern to separate natives from their land.

Congress was also supportive of converting the Native American to the European way of life, as members believed this would bring peace between the natives and the settlers. In the hope of achieving this goal, on 3 March 1819, Congress passed an act establishing the Civilization Fund (15 U.S.C. 87). Through this legislation Congress appropriated an annual sum of $10,000 to provide "against the further decline and final extinction of the Indian tribes adjoining the frontier settlements of the United States, and for introducing among them the habits and arts of civilization." This act formed the cornerstone for Indian education until it was repealed in 1873.

Through the Civilization Fund Act, the United States assumed general responsibility for the "civilization" of natives without reference to treaties or treaty-related responsibilities previously assumed. However, the main intent of the act was to assimilate natives into mainstream society (AIPRC 1976, 34).

The federal government clearly embraced the popular idea that Native Americans needed to be changed. This change would be achieved through "education" and "civilization." The government reflected the prejudices of the time and did not appreciate the level of civilization of the different Native American tribes. In order to promote this agenda, in 1832 Congress established the position of commissioner of Indian affairs. The commissioner was housed within the Department of War, and Native American education was part of his responsibilities. The attitude of the early commissioners is perhaps well summed up by Commissioner T. Hartley Crawford. In his report of 1838, he stated that the way to bring Indians out of the "mire of folly and vice" into which they had fallen was through education (Kickingbird and Charleston 1991, 7).

Commissioner William Medill, in his annual report of 1847, also emphasized the great need for the Native American to be educated. It was Medill's contention that if the tribes were allowed to continue their simple way of living through hunting, they would not appreciate the role and values of reading and writing. Medill believed that teaching Native Americans the use of farm implements would awaken their interest in further education and thus lead to a more peaceful and productive interaction with the new settlers.

Even though there were monetary provisions for education within many treaties, throughout most of the nineteenth century the tribes themselves still had to contribute substantial sums of money toward building schools and hiring teachers. The commissioner of the Indian Office in 1849 confirmed that Native Americans bore the bulk of the cost of operating and maintaining their schools the (Kickingbird and Charleston 1991, 9).

The following incident sums many of up the prevailing attitudes toward Native Americans in the later part of the nineteenth century. In 1879, Chief Standing Bear's small son died, and the chief decided to bury his son's remains in the land of his birth. Standing Bear and his followers began the journey to Nebraska to bury the boy. The chief traveled in a wagon with his son's body. The slow and solemn party of Indians frightened the European settlers, and they circulated rumors that Standing Bear was leading a war party against them. In Nebraska, the Omaha Indians joined Standing Bear and his people to bury the boy.

In the meantime, General George Crook was ordered to arrest Standing Bear. The general and his soldiers tracked down Standing Bear, and he and his party were confined to a jail in Omaha while they awaited deportation to Indian territory. After the settlers in Omaha learned the nature of Standing Bear's journey, they were upset that the chief had been jailed. The press and many settlers joined to demand that the Poncas and Standing Bear be freed. The incident became quite a cause throughout the area. The immigrant settlers went so far as to hire legal counsel for Standing Bear, who sought a writ of habeas corpus in a federal district court.

By the time the federal court convened to hear the case, the room was filled with Standing Bear's supporters. The government attorneys argued that under the Constitution, Standing Bear was not a person and thus could not legally petition for a writ of habeas corpus. Chief Standing Bear's purpose moved the judge so strongly, however, that he declared Standing Bear a person within the meaning of U.S. law and found in his favor. He indicated that Standing Bear had a right to personal freedom and civil rights (Standing Bear 1928).

NATIVE AMERICANS AND CONGRESS

As mentioned earlier, the Constitution established the authority of Congress over relations with native nations. The states delegated to Congress the authority to regulate trade and enter into treaties with native governments. "Unquestionably a treaty may be modified or abrogated by an Act of Congress but the power to make and unmake is essentially political and not judicial" (*Old Settlers v U.S.* 148 US 427 [1893]; Kappler 1929, 1153). Congress also had the authority to enter into a treaty that superseded a prior act of Congress or enact law to override a prior treaty (*Patterson v Jenks*, 2 Pet. 216 [1829]; Kappler 1929, 1153).

Even though Congress had authority from the states and local governments to deal with the native tribes, the tribes themselves had limited this power through treaty. In other words, Congress had authority and power with regard to tribes only in accordance with the conditions of treaties. For Native Americans, the native government was superior to the authority of state and local governments, since such authority was delegated by the states to Congress in the Constitution. Either Congress or the native government that had signed the treaty had the power to renegotiate or abrogate the terms of the treaty. Furthermore, at no time did the authority of Congress extend to the internal governance of the tribe.

When the federal government saw that the churches were not achieving its desired goals for education, it gradually assumed a more active role in the education of Native Americans. During the last three decades of the nineteenth century, the federal government's role accelerated so that it became the major agent in native education. The Board of Indian Commissioners, established in 1869, recommended to the federal government that more schools for Native Americans be established and that the government employ teachers to instruct all tribes in English. Congress passed the act of 15 July 1869 so that more funds could be provided for these increased activities. This act provided for the appropriation of $100,000 to support "industrial and other schools among the Indian tribes not otherwise provided for" (41 U.S. 296 [1869]).

Another Act of Congress on 17 May 1882 established the position of superintendent for Indian education. After approximately another five years, a full department of education for native affairs was established. The Indian Department of Education's general policy was that Native American students should be taught reading and writing in the English language, fundamental arithmetic, geography, and U.S. history. Additionally, they should be instructed in farming, raising livestock, and performing domestic chores.

Meanwhile, the number of native students had increased, but there was little new construction of schools. The schools that were available for the native students were dilapidated, overcrowded, and generally inadequate. The act of 31 July 1882 was passed to ameliorate these conditions (22 US 181 [1882]). This act gave the secretary of war the authority to set aside unused military installations, forts, and stockades for native education. Additionally, he was to assign one or two army officers to oversee native education.

The Bureau of Indian Affairs (BIA) operated as though it were all powerful. More often than not, it ignored tribal governments and took over control of all aspects of Native Americans' lives, property, schools, and governments. A federal judge was to characterize the bureau's conduct, which was without any statutory authorization, as "bureaucratic imperialism" (Kickingbird and Charleston 1991, 10). In the *Harjo v Kleppe* decision (420 F. Supp. 110, [1976]), the U.S. Supreme Court stopped the Bureau of Indian Affairs from interfering in the Creek government. The Court took this position largely because the treaty of 1867 between the Creek and the United States guaranteed Creek self -government.

Another significant act of the late nineteenth century was passed on 3 March 1871 (25 U.S.C. 71). This act ended the era of treaty making between the native tribes and the federal government. It did, however, uphold the terms and conditions of the treaties that had been previously ratified. Now the movement shifted toward making agreements with the native governments.

In 1887, Congress passed the General Allotment Act, which became known as the Dawes Act. The intent of this legislation was to end the growing dependency of the tribes and destroy traditional Indian tribal life. The Dawes Act provided that each head of a Native American family would receive free title to 160 acres of land. A single person older than eighteen received 80 acres, and an orphan younger than eighteen also received 80 acres. This fee title was held in trust by the government for twenty-five years. All recipients would be given citizenship, and land left over after allotment was to be sold to the U.S. government with the profits to be used for Native American "education and civilization" (Otis 1873, 36).

THE EARLY TWENTIETH CENTURY

During the early twentieth century, there were some landmark pieces of legislation. These laws were instrumental in changing the course not only of federal but also of state interactions with Native Americans. The Snyder Act, in 1921, directed that the Bureau of Indian Affairs provide services to all Native Americans. This provision was to be carried out regardless of other provisions in specific treaties or the Indian Citizenship Act of 1924, which recognized all Native Americans as U.S. citizens.

By the end of the first quarter of the twentieth century, the number of Native American children attending public schools had increased greatly. In order to keep up with the growing numbers of students, Congress made appropriations to subsidize public schools that educated native students. As the money was expended quickly, many students had to turn to federal boarding and day schools for education. During these years of rapid expansion when native youngsters were educated in different sorts of schools, educators realized that native students were most successful when they went to schools (public or federal) near their homes (Kickingbird and Kickingbird 1979, 19).

THE NEW DEAL ERA

The bureaucracy associated with schools had expanded rapidly, and this growth had resulted in a shift of the power base away from the tribes to employees of the Department of Interior. The tribal powers of self-government and decisionmaking had been whittled away and replaced by the decisions and values of the career bureaucrats.

Indian Reorganization Act

There was a need to correct the many previously enacted laws that had eroded tribal government powers. The Indian Reorganization Act of 1934 (IRA), among the most influential acts passed, was an attempt by Congress to restore some of this power. The act, also known as the Wheeler-Howard Act, did not "give" a government to each tribe but recognized the current government of the tribe; tribes had been governing themselves for many generations. Thus the U.S. government acted to reaffirm practices that had been in operation for a very long time. Most tribal governments operating today have been in some way influenced and shaped by this act.

Senator Charles E. Wheeler, one of the cosponsors of the law, presented the final report (Senate Report No. 1080, 73d Cong., 2d sess. 1934, in which he summed up the objectives of the legislation:

1. To stop the alienation, through action by the Government of the Indian, of such lands, belong to ward Indians, as are needed for the present and future support of these Indians.
2. To provide for the acquisition, through the purchase, of land for Indian, now landless, who are anxious and fitted to make a living on such land.
3. To stabilize the tribal organization of Indian tribes by besting such tribal organizations with real, though limited authority, and by prescribing conditions which must be met by such tribal organizations.
4. To permit Indian tribes to equip themselves with the devices of modern business organization, through forming themselves into business corporations.
5. To establish a system of financial credit for Indians.
6. To supply Indians with means for collegiate and technical training in the best schools.
7. To open the way for qualified Indians to hold positions in the Federal Indian Service (Seaton 1958, 129)

Another important feature of the Indian Reorganization Act was provisions for Native American students to take out education loans. They were able, through this funding, to pursue their education at vocational and trade schools and in high school and college.

The leadership of Commissioner of Indian Affairs John Collier (1933–1945) and the passage of the IRA were two significant factors that affected Native American education greatly in the next years. John Collier was responsible for such innovative programs as bilingual education, adult basic education, the promotion of higher education for students, and student loans. He made provision for in-service teacher training for native teachers in the federal school system. In addition, he began programs in native culture (see also Chapter 2). During this time, the number of Native American boarding schools was reduced and new day schools added.

The IRA provided native people and tribes with an opportunity for orientation to and experience in the political system and government structure of mainstream America. This new structure of government was considered carefully by most tribes. The more traditional of them rejected the reorganization (Lynch and Charleston 1990, 5).

Johnson O'Malley Act

During the first part of the twentieth century, the main views on Native American education did not change very much. The central governments of France, Spain, Britain, and the United States had outlined the parameters and the goals as well as set the standards of native education. However, early reports from various studies began to question whether federal boarding schools were meeting the needs of Native American children. Later recommendations led to the passage of the Johnson O'Malley Act of 1934 (25 US 452). The Johnson O'Malley Act provided financial incentives and authority for state school systems to assimilate native children into mainstream public schools. The act shifted the locus of control of Native American education from the federal administration to that of the states. The act additionally required that supplemental programs be funded for native children and that these programs be approved by an Indian parent advisory committee (PAC).

The states wanted the federal dollars for the education of Native American students, but they had other issues. They did not want to lose control over the funding because of a greater role in education having been assigned to native parents and communities. The states also feared that if the Native Americans controlled the funding, they would in turn have greater political power. There was no real change from the basic assumption that non-Native officials should be in charge of Native American education. The Federally Impacted Areas Act in the 1950s and Title I of the Elementary and Secondary Education Act of the 1960s ensured that nonnatives would control native education even to the present day.

THE TERMINATION ERA

After World War II, Native American experiences of receiving a regular salary and having control of personal finances versus living on the reservation led to a call, supported by the population at large, to free the Native American from the reservation system.

Conservative members of Congress, unhappy with the positive reforms enacted during the New Deal, worked to have them rescinded even before Roosevelt left office. The members wanted to redefine Indian policy and terminate federal relations with some tribes. Their sentiments reflected the national mood of intolerance toward cultural diversity together with a desire to trim the federal bureaucracy created by the Roosevelt administration. They saw withdrawing services to Native Americans as one way to cut federal spending.

Some in Congress determined that it was in the best interest of Native Americans to phase out tribal governments and any guardian responsibilities of the federal government. Thus Congress would remove its protection from native lands and encourage business leaders to help Native Americans develop their own resources. These same congressmen maintained that Indians would assimilate faster into the population if they owned their lands outright and were allowed to trade freely. This approach would also open the way for states to tax Indian lands so that Native Americans could help pay for public services (Trafzer 2000, 389).

The Indian Claims Commission Act of 1946, which was part of the termination movement, turned out to be beneficial for the Native Americans. Under the provisions of this act, Native Americans were allowed to file claims against the federal government for lands that had been illegally seized. Even though Native Americans could receive monetary compensation, no amount of money could make up for the upheaval and disruption to their way of life. Through the seizure of sacred lands and traditional hunting areas, the deeply held and sacred values of the tribes were disrupted and their usual means of support destroyed. However, compensation did provide Native Americans with funds that enabled them to get their economies moving, at least to some degree.

With conservatism growing strongly within the government and society, John Collier's successors, Commissioners of Indian Affairs William Brophy and John Nichols, were not able to withstand the pressure to roll back change. Conservative congressmen and Dillon S. Myer, chosen by President Harry S Truman in 1950 to head the Bureau of Indian Affairs, favored termination. They were able to push through their agenda.

During World War II, Myer had been the director of the War Relocation Authority, which had forcibly removed Japanese Americans from their homes into internment camps. Myer had also been responsible for managing the rural relocation of thousands of people. Throughout the war, Myer maintained the position that Japanese Americans and cultural groups should be assimilated into the dominant society, thereby reducing racial conflicts.

It is not surprising that when Myer became commissioner, he would act to have Native Americans assimilated into U.S. society. Toward this end, he launched a major counterrevolution against John Collier's policies. Myer believed that a Native American culture was nonexistent and that it was wrong for the government to encourage native languages, arts, literature, and governments. Myer had little interest in cultural preservation programs and little concern for cultural pluralism and ordered an end to these programs.

Myer played down the role of Indian Day Schools, especially those that were on or near the reservations. He perceived that these schools made too many accommodations to the culture and the customs of the Native American tribes. Myer wanted boarding schools to be enlarged so that more children could be taken from the reservations and their parents. He wanted students to be taught the regular class subjects so that their assimilation would be hastened.

After the election of Dwight D. Eisenhower as president in 1952, Myer realized he would have no place in the new administration. He then offered his services to Glenn Emmons, the new commissioner for Indian affairs. In this capacity he helped draft a document for Congress endorsing termination. Through Myer's work and influence, the Bureau of Indian Affairs had already advocated termination as the "new" national Indian policy by the time that Emmons took over the position of commissioner of Indian affairs in 1953. It is of interest that neither Myer nor Emmons considered it necessary or appropriate to seek Native American advice in formulating the new policy.

It was the view of some, for example, Donald Fixico of the Creek (Trafzer 2000, 389), that termination was a policy designed by politicians to achieve the withdrawal of federal services and funds that had been promised in treaties, laws, and agreements. Fixico also maintained that the attempt by Congress to desegregate Indian communities was also intended as the final destruction of native tribal cultures (Fixico 1991).

The administrators implemented the policy quickly before Native Americans had time to respond to the new threat. It would appear that Emmons had his own agenda in supporting termination. He was a former banker from New Mexico, a state with a large Native American population. Many business interests within the state were eager to re-open reservation lands. Emmons and Senator Arthur V. Watkins of Utah, chair of the Senate Committee on Indian Affairs, championed termination as a way of abolishing the tax-exempt status of tribes. Conservative congressmen chaired the committees on Indian affairs in both houses. They spent time and energy to move a resolution quickly through Congress. On 1 August 1953, Congress unanimously passed House Concurrent Resolution 108.

The thrust of the resolution was that Indians would be "subject to the same laws and entitled to the same privileges and responsibilities" as other Americans. The resolution abolished the status of native peoples as wards and listed tribes in various states that were prepared to have federal services ended. Although House Concurrent Resolution 108 was not in itself law, it had the full support of Emmons and the Bureau of Indian Affairs and marked the beginning of an official congressional termination policy.

The Federally Impacted Areas Aid Act (20 U.S. C. 236), passed by Congress in 1951, was the second act—the first being the Johnson O'Malley Act of 1934—designed to to aid Native American education in public schools. The Impacted Aid Act assisted school districts that had a reduced tax base because of federally owned land, that is, it provided monies to schools responsible for educating children from armed service bases so that the local schools would not have to sustain an unfair burden. It also provided monies for the education of Native Americans. With this increased funding, local schools now saw the Native American student as fiscally desirable.

In spite of the Johnson O'Malley Act of 1934 and the Impacted Aid Act (20 US 236), it was evident that the federal government would continue to play a primary role in the funding of native education. The federal-Indian trust relationship, the statutes passed by Congress to maintain that relationship, and the federal funding required to execute the responsibilities in native education ensured that the federal government would continue to be involved. For their part, the native communities were concerned with the degree of control that the federal government exerted through the maintenance of its responsibilities (AIPRC 1976, 167–170).

In the early days of the Impacted Aid Act and its amendments, the states officially were required to make a choice between the Johnson O'Malley or Impact Aid. The Johson O'Malley Act of 16 April 1934, as amended (Pub.L.73–471; 48 Stat. 596; 25 U.S.C. 452) provided supplemental funds to support education programs for Indian students attending public school, for programs and for the culturally related and supplementary academic needs of Indian children attending public schools. The Impacted Aid Act was amended in 1958 to allow state school systems to collect both through Impact Aid for the basic support of schools and the Johnson O'Malley Act for the support of the special education needs of Indian students.

Debate in the federal government resulted in the passage of six termination bills in 1953. In the course of only two weeks, both houses of Congress passed Public Law 280. The president signed the law, but he noted that Congress had not included a provision asking for native consent to the law. The law placed Indian lands in Minnesota, Wisconsin,

California, Nebraska, and Oregon under criminal and civil jurisdiction of the states. The law also invited other states to assume jurisdiction over Indian lands (Trafzer 2000, 390–392). As a result, states were to assume responsibility for the education of Native American children.

In 1954, Congress passed the Klamath Termination Act. As a result, in 1958 approximately 77 percent of the Klamaths voted to terminate and receive a one time per capita payment of $43,000. The 23 percent who voted to retain their Klamath status in 1973 voted to withdraw from the tribe and receive a payment of $173,000. Even though Klamaths had terminated their sovereign relationship with the federal government, they still identified as Indians. The termination did not work out. The Klamath tribe found that it did not have the infrastructure to function successfully in the changed economic conditions. In 1975 the Klamaths readopted their tribal status, and in 1978 Congress recognized the Klamaths and restored their status (Trafzer, 2000, 393–395).

In 1961, the Menominee tribe of Wisconsin was selected by the federal government for release from its governmental ties under the Termination Act. This termination was a disaster for the tribe. As a result of misunderstanding the terms of the act, members of the tribe failed to invest the money they received or plan for a future without regular subsidy from the government. The tribe quickly used its cash reserves and was left without resources to satisfy basic needs and continue education services. When the Menominee did not receive money regularly, as was the custom, poverty and then diseases ravaged the tribe. As conditions worsened, the tribe sold much of its prime lands along the rivers and surrounding areas and left itself without resources (Trafzer 2000, 394).

In all there were about 70 tribes that were part of the termination era policies. The Menominee of Wisconsin had previously experienced quite a high level of economic development. Termination brought economic and health disaster to the tribe. They experienced the effects of tuberculosis as well as a rapidly increasing infant mortality. When the Menominee's experienced threats to their power and self determination they formed the group Determination of Rights and Unity for Menominee Shareholders (DRUMS) to reverse the effects of termination. President Nixon signed the Menominee Restoration Act 22 December 1973, (87 Stat730, 25 U.S.C. 903 et seq.) restoring most of the reservation to the tribe and recognized them as tribe. Thus began the end of termination.

Another outcome the Termination Act was the relocation of many other tribes to urban areas. This relocation also proved disastrous, as many Native Americans had great difficulty adjusting to their new surroundings. When they did not adjust to life in the city, they returned to their lands only to find that they were greatly reduced in size. Tribes had been forced to sell large tracts of land, as they needed money for survival. It did not take too long for the government and the tribes to recognize that the termination program, as it was passed and implemented, was a failure (Reyhner and Eder 1994, 52).

The policies of the termination era were in conflict with the existing body of federal Indian law. This body of law, which had set the groundwork for interactions between the federal government and the Native Americans, had been consolidated in 1948 by Felix S. Cohen in the *Handbook of Federal Indian Law.* Beginning with the 83rd Congress passing House Concurrent Resolution 108, declaring that U.S. policy for Indian tribes was termination, legislation from the late 1940s to the early 1970s represented the confluence of a number of factors: the decentralization policy of the federal government, a desire to open up Indian lands, a desire for Native Americans to be assimilated, and a wish to cut back on social programs. In order not to emphasize the discrepancies between new legislation and previous laws, the BIA simply revised Cohen's 1948 book, deleting or changing sections that were in contradiction with new legislation. The bureau included new opinions to support new policies. The final move was to issue a new edition of Cohen's book in 1972 without mention of any previous editions. This version was and continues to be a highly regarded legal reference (Kickingbird and Charleston 1991, 16).

Congress became aware of and understood that Native American parents had minimal political clout with regard to school policies and boards. It also appreciated that the parents wanted to be involved in their children's education. The parents of native children were encouraged to become involved in the operation of schools serving their children on the reservations. Some of this influence could be exercised through the election of the tribal officials on the reservation. Outside of Indian country, the parents of native children had much less influence on education programs serving their children. The parents formed such a small minority that they had little influence in the election of school board members. Thus Congress amended the Federally Impacted Areas Act with the Education Amendment of 1978, which required the involvement of native parents and tribes in planning, developing, and operating programs funded in the act. Even though parents are supposed to be involved in those practices that affect their children the reality has been otherwise. The very requirements that parents have to follow are so complex that they more or less preclude the successful filing of a grievance. As of 1990 there had been no official grievances filed with the Office of Impact Aid (Kickingbird & Charleston, 1991, 17).

It is probably fair to say that during the termination era, reservation schools, whether they were public, bureau, or mission schools, were similar to one another. Typically, they were surrounded by a fence. Parents were not encouraged to come to the schools, and teachers did not go to the students' homes. When one considers that Native American parents held their children as sacred gifts, separating the schools from the rest of the community was particularly offensive and disrespectful. Classes were taught in English, which in reality was a second language for the Native American child. By the time the child became comfortable with English, he or she had fallen well behind in basic skills (Reyhner and Eder 1994, 53). As a result of this disadvantage, Native American students were not able to keep up with the progress of European children.

POST-TERMINATION POLICIES

The Economic Opportunity Act of 1965 gave Native Americans the first real chance to develop and implement their own work programs outside the framework of the BIA and the states. From these endeavors grew such projects as Head Start for preschool children, Upward Bound and Job Corps for teenagers. The programs also provided the occasions to train tribal people for management and administrative positions. This concept of community involvement in education had been put forward sporadically for almost a century. The mechanism and funding to develop these ideas were now provided through the Economic Opportunity Act. The ability to take part in their schools and be involved in the education of their children provided many Native Americans with the impetus for learning. This in turn aided in the development of community-controlled schools.

The idea of bringing education and other support programs to the native communities was supported by Presidents John Kennedy and Lyndon Johnson. Neither of these presidents apparently grasped that without significant reorganization of the bureaucracy, native initiatives, which had been stymied for well over a century, would continue to be thwarted. There was no real opportunity for the tribes to accomplish many of their educational goals. Even though the Economic Opportunity Act provided money, there was often not enough to begin a worthy project. Further funding was needed from other sources, such as the BIA or the Department of Health, Education and Welfare (HEW) to expand and continue initial efforts.

Congress passed the Elementary and Secondary Education Act

(ESEA) in 1965. This act provided supplementary funds for innovative educational programs for disadvantaged youngsters, including Native Americans. Under Title I, monies went to school systems where native children were enrolled and to the BIA for use in the federal school system. The program had great potential, but due in part to the inefficiency of the BIA's delivery systems and poor monitoring on the parts of both the BIA and the U.S. Department of Education, some of the money was misused. The problems with money use were detailed in the NAACP (National Association for the Advancement of Colored People) Legal Defense Fund's publication *An Even Chance* (Kickingbird and Charleston 1991).

The amendments that Congress passed to Title I required local school districts to establish a parent advisory committee (PAC) for every school that received funds. The PAC was to assist with planning, implementation, and evaluation of the Title I program in the school.

Despite the many factors that militated against development of Native American education, such as the inadequacy of legislation, the lack of a clear-cut national policy, and inefficiency of the BIA organization, the late 1960s did see growth and development. Native governments set themselves the goals to achieve greater authority in a number of areas affecting their life. Education was included in their goals. Also, it was during the 1970s and 1980s that federal legislation was directed at the elementary, secondary, and vocational schools and community colleges serving native communities.

THE SELF-DETERMINATION ERA

As mentioned in Chapter 2, toward the end of the 1960s a special senate subcommittee on Indian education was commissioned to study the current state of Native American education. In 1969, a report popularly known as the Kennedy Report indicated that native education was a "national tragedy" (U.S. Senate Special Subcommittee on Indian Education 1969). This report resulted in a change of government policy. What was to be known as the self-determination era was ushered in with the 1970 message of the President of the United States.

In his statement, Richard Nixon called for the implementation of policies that would enable the Native Americans to determine their own destiny. He called for the repeal of House Concurrent Resolution 108, which had set up termination as a policy. He advocated that there be tribal control and operation of federal programs. He requested that the sacred lands of the Taos Pueblo at Blue Lake be restored. He emphasized the need for economic development of the Native Americans through the Indian Financing Act of 1974 (25 U.S.C. 1451) as well as increased financial support for Indian health, assistance to urban Indians, the establishment of the Indian Trust Counsel Authority, and the appointment of an assistant secretary for Indian affairs.

The first response of Congress was the Indian Education Act in 1972. Later it passed the broader Indian Self-Determination and Education Assistance Act of 1975 (see further on). These actions by Congress led to discussion about the role of the federal, state, and native governments with respect to education issues. Even though Nixon had called for the repealing of the Termination Act, it was another eighteen years before Congress formally ended the termination policy. This was achieved by repealing House Concurrent Resolution 108 with the passage of the Indian Education Amendments of 1988, or Public Law 100–297 on 8 April 1988 (25 U.S.C. 5203, sec. 2001, Title V, Part B).

It was during the 1970s and the 1980s that the authority of tribal government was defined further, though there does not appear to have emerged a common understanding or clarification of the authority of native governments. Congress and the Supreme Court appear to have proceeded along divergent paths with respect to the power and authority of tribal governments. Generally, the two branches of the government seem to have been supportive of native education.

Various legislative acts, after the 1970 Indian policy statement by Nixon, led to an increase in the economic and social well-being of tribal members. Congress also admitted that the previous attempts at assimilation and termination were a failure. Through the passage of the Menominee Restoration Act in 1973, Congress formally rejected attempts to destroy or change the tribes.

Indian Education Act

The Indian Education Act of 1972 (Public Law 92–318) was a significant piece of legislation in regard to Native American education. The act provided for the funding of supplementary and innovative programs for Indian students both on reservations and in urban schools. The act also mandated that local parent committees be involved in all aspects of special native education grant projects at public schools and stressed the development of curricula that included culturally relevant materials for the different tribal groups.

The U.S. Office of Education was responsible for overseeing the disbursement of the funds. It was a stipulation of the act that public schools could not use the money for operational expenses. However, Native American schools could use the money as they needed. This act made it possible for native tribal and community members to fund special educational programs for their children. A 1975 amendment to the act required that to be eligible for monies, the school district had to show that projects were developed with the participation and approval of a parent advisory committee composed of parents of the children the program was to serve. Finally, Congress had established a legislative framework for native participation in programs that operated outside Indian country but served the education needs of native children. The intention of the act was to overcome the past attitudes of hostility that had tainted the relationships between native and state governments.

Initially $18 million was appropriated under the Indian Education Act. In addition, the Bureau of Indian Education within the Office of Education was established as well as the National Advisory Council on Indian Education. It was largely through the involvement of the Native American people that programs made possible by the act were successfully implemented. When the economic contractions of 1973 endangered these programs, Native American lawyers ensured the continuance of monies for the community-controlled programs.

American Indian Policy Review Commission

In 1975, Congress established the American Indian Policy Review Commission (AIPRC) (Public Law 93–580, 25 U.S.C. 174). The responsibility of the commission was to study the U.S. government's relationship with American Indians and to make legislative recommendations. The commission was charged with determining the nature and scope of necessary revisions in the policy and programs that had been developed to benefit American Indians. The committee made over 200 recommendations to Congress on how to improve Indian affairs (Trafzer 2000, 403).

Indian Self-Determination and Education Assistance Act

The Indian Self-Determination and Education Assistance Act of 1975 directed the Bureau of Indian Affairs (BIA) to contract services with the tribes rather than other non-Native agencies. The Congress directed that the quality of reservation life was to be improved by taking into account the tribal government as well as the customs and practices of the reservation. The BIA, instead of continuing a management role, was to move into an advisory one. Much of the federal funding still flows to the BIA, which has now turned its focus toward supporting and facilitating the involvement of Native Americans in their self-development as well as the development of their resources. One of the results of the change in focus of the BIA is that now approximately 95 percent of its employees are Native American, whereas in the 1930s there were very few Native Americans in the agency (Hanson, 1996, 3).

It was President Gerald Ford who signed into law the Indian Self-Determination and Education Assistance Act of 1975. However, with this administration, changes in Indian policy initiated by both the legislature and the executive branches slowed. The federal courts now took up the mantle of promoting Indian welfare and policies. The Supreme Court also became more assertive in rulings favoring self-determination and tribal sovereignty. In the case *Santa Clara Pueblo v Martinez,* the Court ruled that the Santa Clara Pueblo could deny membership to the child of a woman who had married outside the tribe even though children of men who married outside of the Pueblo could be enrolled. The Court made this ruling in support of a tradition that predated the Constitution. Other cases supporting the sovereignty of the tribes marked the era of the 1970s and 1980s.

Generally speaking, the next administration of Jimmy Carter also did little to promote Indian affairs. There were, however, two factors that were to have a notable effect on the Native American situation. The first involved upgrading the position of commissioner of Indian affairs to assistant secretary of interior for Indian affairs. The first to fill this new position was Forrest J. Gerard, who had worked in the Bureau of Indian Affairs. The significance of the appointment was that Forrest J. Gerard was a member of the Blackfeet tribe.

Gerard was to play an important role in urging Congress to pass the Indian Child Welfare Act in 1978. Before the welfare act, it was the practice of the state and county courts to place Indian children in non-Indian homes. In fact, they went so far as to give non-Indians preference in the hope that native children would be assimilated into European families and thus the European way of life. The Indian Child Welfare Act overturned the federal government's previous policy of forcibly and systematically taking Native children and placing them in a non-Indian environment either through boarding schools or adoption. The act established for the first time specific procedures for the adoption and placement of Native American children in foster care. There was a restriction on placing Native American children away from Native American adoptive or foster parents. If the children were to be placed in non-Native homes, the biological parents had to give their consent and it was also now possible for them to withdraw this consent.

The following administrations of Presidents Ronald Reagan and George H. W. Bush continued to uphold the principles of Indian self-determination. However, under both of these administrations federal funding to tribes was drastically cut. Furthermore, they recommended that the states and tribes pay for Indian programs. There were also comments from government officials that indicated a trend away from supporting Indian programs. Secretary of Interior James Watt referred to tribal governments as a form of socialism. Later President Reagan stated while on a visit to Moscow that the United States was mistaken to maintain Indian cultures. Essentially, Reagan and Watt wanted the Native Americans to be assimilated and did not support Native American sovereignty.

President Bill Clinton was more supportive of Indian self-determination. In 1994 he sponsored a White House conference for Native Americans. However, he did little to further American Indian sovereignty during his two terms. Even though he was in favor of open communication with tribes, he did not increase the overall budget for Indian affairs. He did, however, appoint Menominee leader Ada Deer as head of the Bureau of Indian Affairs in 1994, and his executive order in 1998 increased appropriations to encourage Indian children to finish high school and attend college (Trafzer 2000, 405).

Title XI of the Education Amendments Act

Title XI of the Education Amendments Act of 1978 (Public Law 95–561) promoted native self-determination. The law stated that it would be the policy of the Bureau of Indian Affairs to facilitate Indian control of Indian affairs in all matters relating to education. Additionally, the act directed the bureau to fund native schools according to the Indian school equalization formula. This formula was designed to achieve an equitable distribution of funds among schools.

Through the Indian School Equalization Program (ISEP) the federal government established direct funding to BIA and tribally operated schools. The funds were for primary and secondary education of Indian children but would not cover construction. The formula for funding schools is based on student units. Weights are allotted to each program or service and then multiplied by the average student number. Boarding schools receive a greater weight than nonresidential schools (Brescia, 1991, 8).

Another mandate of the act was uniform education standards for all BIA and contract schools. Teachers and other education personnel would no longer work within the federal civil service system but would contract directly with each school. Local school boards would control Native American education. Local BIA agency superintendent positions were created. The personnel in these positions were required to report directly to the Office of Indian Education in the central office in Washington. Through this reorganization education was removed from federal authority to the local BIA agency superintendents and the area offices.

The intent of the act was to promote native self-determination in education, which had not been implemented previously. However, federally funded native education still remains firmly controlled by the BIA. Furthermore, the bureaucratic administration of the ISEP formula created uncertainty, instability, and a general lack of adequate funding for federal Indian schools. In response, some tribes abandoned the federal system and developed community controlled public schools, such as on the Rocky Boys Reservation in Montana and the Zuni Reservation in New Mexico.

Indian Self-Determination and Education Assistance Act Amendments

As time passed, it became evident that the Indian Self-Determination and Education Assistance Act of 1975 was in need of revisions. In fall 1988 Congress added updated language to the law. Congress declared that it was committed to the maintenance of the government's relationship with individual Indian tribes and the Indian people and to an orderly transition from federal domination to a real self-determination policy. Indian people would be involved in the planning and implementation and administration of their programs and services.

Congress also indicated that the United States was committed to supporting and assisting Indian tribes in maintaining strong and stable tribal governments. These governments would be capable of administering quality programs and developing the economies of their respective communities (Public Law 100–472, October 5, 1988). Further amendments to the law went on to provide for support of experimental tribal self-governance projects.

Tribally Controlled Schools Act

In order to reinforce tribal control of schools, Congress passed the Tribally Controlled Schools Act of 1988. Congress affirmed that Native American children had special and unique educational needs, including programs to foster the linguistic and cultural aspirations of Indian tribes and communities. At the same time Congress outlined a national goal to provide the resources, processes, and structures that would help tribes and native local communities develop needed educational services and opportunities for Native American children. Congress stated its desire that Native American youth would achieve success and economic well-being.

The act reaffirmed that Congress was committed to the policies that supported its responsibilities for federal relations with the Indian Nations.

Reauthorization of the Indian Education Act

In 1988 President Reagan signed into law the Augustus F. Hawkins–Robert T. Stafford Elementary and Secondary School Improvement Amendments of 1988. He became the third president to reauthorize the Indian Education Act. These amendments were contained within the language of Public Law 100–297 and provided for maintenance of the Office of Indian Education and formula grants to school districts containing large native populations (Subpart 1). There were provisions for discretionary programs for native communities and organizations seeking to fund educational programs for native children (Subpart 2) and adults (Subpart 3). A fellowship program, and the continuance of the National Advisory Council on Indian Education, were also to be supported (Hatch 1991, 9).

SUMMARY

Sometimes the federal government or individuals have taken the leadership role in shaping policy for Native American education; at other times the Supreme Court has led the way. At times the treaties and laws are clearly embedded in prevailing attitudes. At other times legislation reshapes attitudes, for example, the change from termination to self-determination policies.

No matter what agency has taken the lead in official interactions with Native Americans, it is clear that the scene is continually changing. It is also clear that even though legislation may no longer promote attitudes of assimilation, there are still those who believe that Native Americans are singled out for special treatment. Many still do not understand what has happened to the American Indian in the settling of the land.

REFERENCES AND FURTHER READING

American Indian Law Review. 1973. Norman: University of Oklahoma Law School.

Brescia, W. 1991. "Funding and Resources for American Indian and Alaska Native Education." In *Indian Nations at Risk: Solutions for the 1990s.* Washington, DC: Department of Education.

Cadawalader, Sandra L., and Vine Deloria Jr. 1984. *The Aggressions of Civilization: Federal Indian Policy since the 1800s.* Philadelphia: Temple University Press.

Cohen, F. S. 1972 [1948]. *Handbook of Federal Indian Law.* Albuquerque: University of New Mexico Press.

Cohen, L. K. 1960. *The Legal Conscience: Selected Papers of Felix S. Cohen.* New Haven, CT: Yale University Press.

Congressional Record, 59th Congress, 1st Sess., sections 3122, 5041. Washington, DC: U.S. Government Printing Office.

Congressional Record, 100th Congress. Statement of Daniel K. Inouye, Chairman, Select Committee on Indian Affairs. Regarding the Activities of the Select Committee in the 100th Cong., sections 17391–17394. Washington, DC: U.S. Government Printing Office, November 10, 1988.

Costo, Rupert, and Jeanette Henry. 1977. *Indian Treaties.* San Francisco: Indian Historian Press.

DePuy, H. F. 1917. *A Bibliography of the English Colonial Treaties with the American Indians, Including a Synopsis of Each Treaty.* New York: Lenox Club.

Drummond, A. M. and R. Moody. 1953. "Indian Treaties: The First American Dramas." *Quarterly Journal of Speech* 39: 15–24.

Fixico, Donald L. 1991. *Urban Indians.* New York: Chelsea House.

Forbes, Jack D. 1981. *Native Americans and Nixon: Presidential Politics and Minority Self-Determination, 1969–1972.* Los Angeles: American Indian Studies Center, University of California at Los Angeles.

Getches, David J., and Charles F. Wilkinson. 1986. *Federal Law.* St. Paul: West Publishing.

Hanson, C. L. 1996. *From War to Self-Determination: A History of the Bureau of Indian Affairs.* Available from the American Studies Resources Centre website, Liverpool, UK, *www.americansc.org.uk.*

Hasse, Larry J. 1974. "Termination and Assimilation: Federal Indian Policy 1943–1961." Ph.D. diss., Washington State University.

Hatch, J. 1991. "American Indian and Alaska Native Adult Education and Vocational Training Programs: Historical Beginning, Present Conditions, and Future Directions." In *Indian Nations at Risk: Solutions for the 1990s.* Washington, DC: U.S. Department of Education.

Kappler, C. J. 1929. *Indian Affairs, Laws, and Treaties.* Washington, DC: U.S. Government Printing Office.

Kickingbird, K., and G. M. Charleston. 1991. "Responsibilities and Roles of Governments and Native People in the Education of American Indians and Alaska Natives." In *Indian Nations at Risk: Solutions for the 1990s.* Washington, DC: Department of Education.

Kickingbird, K., and L. Kickingbird. 1979. "A Short History of Indian Education, Part II." *American Indian Journal* 5, no. 9: 13–16.

Lynch, P. D., and Charleston, G. M. 1990. "The Emergence of American Indian Leadership in Education." *Journal of American Indian Education.* Tempe: Arizona State University Press.

Meyer, D. E. 1972. "We Continue to Massacre the Education of the American Indian." *Journal of American Indian Education.* Tempe: Arizona State University Press.

Mohr, W. H. 1993. *Federal Indian Relations, 1774–1778.* Philadelphia: University Press of Pennsylvania.

National Advisory Council on Education. 1982. *Indian Education: America's Unpaid Debt (8th Annual Report to the U.S. Congress).* Washington, DC: U.S. Government Printing Office.

O'Brien, Sharon. 1989. *American Indian Tribal Governments.* Norman: University of Oklahoma Press.

Otis, D. S. 1973. *The Dawes Act and the Allotment of Indian Lands.* Edited by Francis Paul Prucha. Norman: University of Oklahoma Press.

Philip, Kenneth R. 1972. *John Collier's Crusade for Indian Reform, 1920–1945.* In Leon Borden Blair, ed., *Essays on Radicalism in Contemporary America.* Austin, University of Texas Press.

Price, M. E. 1992. *Law and the American Indian: Readings, Notes, and Cases.* Indianapolis: Bobbs-Merrill Co.

Seaton, F. 1958. *Federal Indian Law.* Washington, DC: U.S. Government Printing Office.

Standing Bear, Luther. 1928. *My People the Sioux.* Edited by E. A. Brininstool. Boston: Houghton Mifflin.

Trafzer, C. E. 2000. *As Long as the Grass Shall Grow and Rivers Flow: A History of Native Americans.* Orlando, FL: Harcourt.

U.S. Commission on Civil Rights. 1975. *The Navajo Nation: An American Colony.* Washington, DC: U.S. Government Printing Office.

U.S. Congress. 1976. *American Indian Policy Review Commission, Final Report.* Washington, DC: Government Printing Office.

U.S. Congress. 1977. *American Indian Policy Review Commission, Task Force Five, Report.* Washington, DC: Government Printing Office.

U.S. Department of the Interior. 1877. *Report of the Indian Commissioner.* Washington, DC: U.S. Department of the Interior.

———. 1934. "Solicitors Opinion." In *Powers of Indian Tribes.* Washington, DC: Department of Interior, p. 55.

———. 1973. *Report on Audit of Johnson-O'Malley Contracts between the Bureau of Indian Affairs and the Oklahoma Department of Education, Oklahoma City, Oklahoma.* Washington, DC: Office of Survey and Review.

U.S. Indian Claims Commission. 1979. *Final Report of the United States Indian Claims Commission.* Washington, DC: U.S. Government Printing Office.

U.S. Senate. 1935. Report No. 1080, 73rd. Congress 2nd Session, presented by Senator Wheeler. Washington, DC: U.S. Government Printing Office.

U.S. Senate, Select Committee on Indian Affairs, 95th Congress, 2nd Session S.2502. 1978. *Hearings to Authorize the States and the Indian Tribes to Enter into Mutual Agreements and Compacts Respecting Jurisdiction and Governmental Operations in Indian Country. Tribal State Compact Act of 1978.* Washington, DC: U.S. Government Printing Office.

U.S. Senate Special Subcommittee on Indian Education. 1969. *Indian Education: A National Tragedy, a National Challenge.* Senate Report No. 91–501. Washington, DC: U.S. Government Printing Office.

U.S. Senate Special Committee on Investigation of the Select Committee on Indian Affairs. 1989. *A New Federalism for American Indians.* Senate Report 101–216, 101st Congress. Washington, DC: U.S. Government Printing Office.

Wroth, L. C. 1928. "The Indian Treaty as Literature." *Yale Review* 17: 749–766.

Chapter Five

✎ Issues and Strategies

Caleb Cheessehateaumuck was an Algonquian Indian who graduated from Harvard in 1665. Cheessehateaumuck was a brilliant student who was proficient in English, Latin, and Greek as well as his own native language. He died a short time after his graduation from a disease brought by white people to which he had no immunity. In many ways this story summarizes the relationship between Native Americans and their European conquerors. Though many native inhabitants benefited from their educators' efforts, many were torn from their culture and their families. Most suffered spiritually, emotionally, or physically (Wright 1991, 1).

During the 1960s and 1970s there was a greater sensitivity to education approaches for different groups. Educators, researchers, and policymakers became more conscious of the need to take into account those factors that make people different rather than trying to make everyone fit the same pattern. This chapter focuses on current issues in education and on recent research and recommendations made to promote success for Native Americans in the education system.

ASSUMPTIONS AND IDEOLOGIES

It is a basic assumption that education will equip all children with the skills and knowledge they need to function successfully within the society. In turn, it is the role and purpose of education to provide for the community in particular and the society at large members who will provide the resources that keep both viable (Garcia and Ahler, 1994, 13). Thus native children need an appreciation not only of the wider American culture but also of the culture of their particular village, tribe, or community.

The ideas that underpin much of Native American education can be summed up in the words of Herbert J. Benally. Benally, a Navajo Indian, stated that Navajo education should consist of an integrated, general curriculum focused on Navajo culture and address student character and moral development (Skinner 1991, 19). Gilbert Vigil, governor of the Tesuque Pueblo, reinforced these ideas, saying that no program, no matter how well funded or staffed, can be successful if it fails to incorporate and reflect the values of the community. Thus if American Indians fail to see their values reflected in the educational system, curriculum, and materials, they will see themselves as outsiders and lose their motivation to succeed. When education proceeds without references to Native Americans or illustrations and stories from their traditions and culture, these children receive the message that Indians and their ways do not count (Skinner 1991, 22).

The challenge for the education system, particularly for those institutions educating Native Americans or their teachers, is the development of an understanding and appreciation of Native Americans and their culture. The system is challenged not only to incorporate the culture and its language but also to promote, protect, and preserve them. Students who can identify with the school and its education programs have a better chance to achieve academic success and strengthen their cultural identities.

The Industrial Model

When one walks through a traditional high school, college, or university built in the 1950s, one is reminded of a factory. The long corridor with specialty classrooms on either side is reminiscent of the assembly line. The hierarchical management structures of the traditional school system mimic those of industry. The teacher answers to a principal who answers to the superintendent and then on to the school board, reflecting the industry arrangement of worker, supervisor, president, and board of directors (Berg and Ohler 1991, 301).

That students are often referred to as "products" of a school or school system, which indicates how the industrial era has shaped people's worldview. Another example is the tendency to keep increasing the size of high schools to achieve efficiency and economy of scale. Keeping in mind the language that refers to students as products of schools, one appreciates that in such a system teachers are the active ones and students are the passive materials to be shaped into the appropriate product. This approach thus encourages students to adopt passive modes of behavior.

Another aspect of the industrial model is that it posits low-context environments. In other words, in schools organized after this model, students have access to a minimum amount of background information. Reality is divided into discrete categories (Berg and Ohler 1991, 303), as opposed to the Native American's holistic view of reality. Native American students come from high-context environments saturated with information.

During the industrial era, science became the dominant, integrating view of reality. This view, which in turn led to a "monocultural, reductionist view of reality" (Berg and Ohler 1991, 305), is being challenged by multiple views of reality. The many ways of communicating, storing, and disseminating information support multiple views of the world, and these different views are central to an age of education supported and shaped by technology (McCracken 1989, 20, cited in Berg and Ohler, 1991, 305).

A Paradigm Shift

An education system based on an industrial mind-set is inadequate for the new era. Many of the recent task forces that have been established to study poor performance in the nation's schools often recommend that educators need to work harder at present educational practices. The order of the day is more testing and more drill and practice. However, Branson (1987, 15) maintains that schooling in its present form has reached its upper limits. Trying harder at a model of education that grew out of another era does not answer many of the challenges of today's world.

Berg and Ohler (1991, 304), quoting the work of Bramble, Mason, and Berg, present some of the paradigm shifts brought about by the new technologies: The present education philosophy based on the industrial age promotes uniformity and self-reliance, whereas the information paradigm supports individual difference and collective responsibility. Education in mathematics and communication skills for economic survival is stressed now, whereas the information era encourages giving students the skills to find, analyze, and evaluate data. The present education system develops linear and sequential thinking, whereas education for the information age develops nonlinear and multidimensional thinking. The general movement is away from hierarchical, linear thinking to multidimensional and multifaceted thinking with the teacher as facilitator rather than as controller of all knowledge.

A key person in the development of the school for the new information era is the administrator. However, administrators are often still trained in the traditional areas of law, finance, personnel management, and curriculum. Even when technology is discussed, it is often from the perspective of appropriate or useful hardware and software (Berg and Ohler 1991, 315). An education program that emphasizes flexibility and a consensus style of administration is more appropriate to the information era and to the education of Native Americans.

A new set of values would be encapsulated in a revised education for administrators. Relationships throughout the organization would be informal rather than formal, and the administrator would be a facilitator rather than a manager. Additionally, administration would ensure a two-way flow of information with a broadening rather than a converging focus. Instead of promoting a fixed organizational structure, the administrator would support a loose, decentralized way of changing and developing relationships. This flexibility of style and openness to change and divergent points of view are the values and attitudes that promote Native American education.

All students need to be proficient in the use of modern technologies so they can effectively access relevant materials as well as navigate in the mainstream culture. Educators also need to use technology to help address some of the specific challenges that Native American students face. Technology can help break down the tyranny of distance by enabling different tribes throughout the country to reach out to each other and strengthen cultural ties. It also brings to all students cultural information about the many tribes throughout the country (Berg and Ohler 1991, 319).

Present and emerging technologies challenge traditional views of education. In particular, the widespread and immediate access to information afforded by computer technology raises questions about the very structure of schools and curricula. For example, in the past, the college or university provided the latest in research and controlled the flow of information. Today, results of groundbreaking research are often available on the World Wide Web before they are reported in journals and long before they are part of textbooks.

Native American students and cultures have not been well served by the assimilation approaches of traditional U.S. schools. Changes in information technology present an ideal opportunity for educators to initiate reforms that could be beneficial to Native American students.

Assimilation versus Multiculturalism

Effective educators are conscious of the fact that assimilation into mainstream society has been the traditional goal in educating Native Americans. In order to maintain an integrative rather than an assimilative posture, teachers must encourage students to achieve economic independence, continuing education, and political involvement based on their own cultural backgrounds.

When one searches for a philosophy that would provide direction and guidance to support Native American education, one is led to the assumptions and goals of multicultural education. Multicultural education challenges the myths and premises fundamental to early forms of Euro-American education. Multicultural education highlights the diverse groups with different values, assumptions, and languages that make up U.S. society. The assimilation ideology of "melting pot" is not part of a philosophy that supports and values diversity (Garcia and Ahler, 1994, 20).

There are different multicultural models related to special student populations, but all embrace two major goals. The first is to meet the educational needs of culturally diverse students by recognizing that their cultural knowledge is worthwhile and by reinforcing and expanding on that knowledge. Diversity is celebrated, and those students who are not members of the American mainstream are valued as bringing another rich dimension to life. This goal is a direct response to the demands by American minority groups for educational opportunities historically denied them. There is no reason to presume, in meeting this goal, that students who are not members of the American mainstream are culturally deficient or deprived or will not be loyal Americans (Cummins 1994, 20–24).

A second goal of multicultural education is to promote cultural awareness and sensitivity among all students, that is, to promote appreciation of and respect for one's own and others' cultures. Initially, this particular goal was aimed especially at American mainstream students. The onus was put on them to learn to appreciate minority cultures in order for equity in education to be realized. However, it has become clear that this goal is appropriate for all cultural groups of students (Garcia and Ahler, 1994, 13).

It is important for all Americans to have as accurate, balanced, and complete a picture of the history of the country as possible. Without discussion about the achievements of Native Americans and other minority ethnic groups, the story is distorted. For example, how many people know that some native people helped write the Constitution and that a Native American was vice president of this country (Charles Curtis [1929–1933])? More balanced curricula would help nonnative students overcome their unfamiliarity with American Indians and Alaska natives and increase general respect for their contributions (Charleston and King, 1991, 8). At the postsecondary level, there is a paucity of multicultural and cross-cultural programs. Even where courses are offered, "culturally relevant curriculum" is poorly defined and articulated.

Desegregation: A Mixed Blessing

Desegregation has been a mixed blessing for Native American education. In many situations it has given native students access to more resources, but they have been isolated from their peers and have not had access to effective cultural programs and support services. The intent of the Supreme Court's decision in *Brown v Board of Education* was to provide all students with greater opportunities to share in resources that were not readily available in many schools. However, Native Americans are a tribal people, and their youth most often learn best when they are with a larger number of their tribal brothers and sisters. The effects of isolation are most keenly felt and seen in urban schools. Where possible and feasible, it behooves school districts to develop magnet programs that would not only encourage native students to come together but would also support them (Charleston and King, 1991, 13).

When Native American students are part of a school that pays no heed to their culture, the students may begin to take on the characteristics of disenfranchised youth. They can become fractious, apathetic, and hostile to the school environment. Yet it is often difficult for the school to obtain the resource materials appropriate for incorporation into the curriculum.

Until public schools are restructured to adequately meet the needs of native students, there must be continued local, state, and federal support for effective native alternative schools. The inability of many native young people to identify with the schools, their values and mission, results in their assuming the profile of other disadvantaged inner-city youth. There has been escalation in gang activity, violence, and use of weapons at younger and younger ages. Native communities are challenged to develop intervention strategies to reverse the trend and aid their youth in their journey through school.

LEARNING STYLES

According to Rita Dunn, learning style is the way that an individual concentrates on, absorbs, and retains new or difficult information or skills. Learning style should not be confused with the materials or methods of teaching that complement (or hinder) a person's learning style (Dunn 1983, 505).

A person's learning style is related to the way in which internal learning patterns are linked with the outside presentation of reality. There are debates in educational circles about the origin of a person's learning style—how much of it is culturally induced and how much is hereditary. Three components of learning style have been identified: ways of thinking, ways of feeling, and basic inherited tendencies. Of these three dimensions, the affective, or ways of feeling, is the least well understood; yet at all stages of learning, this component is highly influential (Pepper 1985).

Traditional Tribal Education

Native American children were taught and nurtured not only by parents but by the tribe as a whole. Education was a community activity and responsibility, as distinct from the tradition in Western society of focusing responsibility on educational institutions. Native children were taught at their own pace, and their achievements were considered the achievements of the family. When the children did well, they brought honor to their families.

Since learning in the tribe was a group activity, learning was part of the tribal environment. Children did not go off to school for scheduled hours during the day. Education was woven into the fabric of the daily life of the tribe. Skills and knowledge were passed on in a natural and nonthreatening manner.

After the student became proficient, he or she then became a mentor or teacher of the next group of students. Artisans, warriors, and healers passed on their knowledge and skills in a continuous cycle. This method of education served Native American tribes well until they came in contact with the greater technological advances of the Western world.

Tribal Education Meets Mainstream Education

As the Native American tribes were conquered or formed treaties with the federal government, their method of education was influenced by mainstream America. The government assumed responsibility for providing educational opportunities and resources for Native American students. As was mentioned earlier, one purpose of Native American education was to lessen the number of skirmishes that took place between the Indians and the settlers. The government thought that this aim could be achieved in part if Native Americans turned from hunting to farming so as ultimately to be assimilated into the mainstream.

Education in the traditional Native American setting occurs by example and not as a process of indoctrination. Elders serve as embodiments of both good and bad experiences. In witnessing the elders' failures as much as their successes, the young person is cushioned from becoming too enthusiastic or discouraged. In contrast, the mainstream population tends both to deify its heroes and to judge them harshly when they fail.

Typically, native cultures teach their children to learn through listening, thinking, and, when they feel comfortable enough to attempt the task, acting. The more common method of teaching in a Euro-American classroom is trial and error. This mode is the opposite of Native American methods. Many other students also find this way of learning difficult.

Because the child in native cultures is encouraged and reinforced as a worthy representative of the family, he or she does not dwell on individual accomplishments. In the environment of schools in mainstream America, this tendency not to acknowledge individual strengths can be a distinct disadvantage. (There is some benefit, of course, when blame is the issue, as responsibilty is spread over a much larger group.)

The home learning environment of many Native Americans is characterized by such factors as freedom of movement, learning through direct experience, and hands-on and activity-oriented learning. These learning models emphasize visual, spatial, and kinesthetic orientations. In contrast, in the typical school environment, free movement is significantly restricted, and indirect intellectual learning, which emphasizes verbal, mathematical, and logical orientations, is the norm.

Throughout the 1960s and 1970s, most researchers attributed the poor achievement of Native Americans to cultural differences. It was generally believed that students' poor performance was a result of the differences between learning styles in their homes and those in the school. To focus on this approach, researchers adopted the tools of anthropology. From the perspective of an ethnographer, they observed the different learning styles of different groups within the classroom and looked at how these students preferred to demonstrate their learning to others (Swisher and Deyhle 1994, 81).

Cooperative versus Competitive Learning

A body of recent ethnographic research on minority children reveals different reactions to cooperative and competitive situations. Native

American students are more likely to respond to a cooperative rather than a competitive environment. Within the tribal system an individual works not for his or her personal gain but for the good of the group. Native Americans prize consensus and cooperation.

Much of the evidence about cooperation versus competition is anecdotal. A. G. Miller and R. Thomas (1972) and Anthony Brown (1977) conducted studies with the Blackfeet and Cherokee to examine cooperative and competitive classrooms. They found that there were marked differences between Canadian Blackfoot children and Canadian white children while playing a game. This game allowed either competitive or cooperative behavior, but the rewards were kept for cooperative behavior.

In line with the fact that competition is a highly used motivator in schools, white children on the whole behaved competitively even when there was no reward for such behavior. The Blackfeet children were cooperative. Brown also found that Cherokee children tended to be more cooperative and less competitive than white American children.

For the Cherokee students, there was a negative relationship between cooperative behavior and high achievement. In other works, those students who were most cooperative had lower scores. In the Cherokee classroom, children closely followed traditional Cherokee norms. They maintained harmonious relations and, more important, held fast to standards of achievement that all children could meet (Brown 1977). Thus the high-ability students did not display their competence. One can conclude from this research that Native American students experience conflict in a competitive classroom. This research also confirms the findings of ethnographic studies that many Indian students avoid competition when they view it as unfair (Dumont 1972; Wax, Wax, and Dumont 1964).

Demonstrations of Learning

Education researchers and practitioners have conducted an onoing search for those instructional methods that address the relationship between how children learn to learn and how they are expected to demonstrate learning in the classroom. Researchers have shown that the way in which children acquire and display their learning is shaped and influenced by the cultural norms of their group as well as the socialization practices of that group (Cohen 1969). Mehan (1981, 51) acknowledges that students must know the appropriate way to demonstrate their learning.

Susan Philips (1972) conducted one of the most extensive studies of Native American students learning. She focused on the way the students from the Warm Springs Indian Reservation in Oregon participated and communicated. Philips observed that Indian children were reluctant to participate in large- and small-group recitations, although they were more talkative than non-Indian children when they initiated the interaction with the teacher or worked on student-led group projects. She concluded that their behavior could be explained by lack of support in their community for public social performance. Through observation, careful listening, supervised participation, and individualized self-correction and testing, Philips identified specific modes of learning in the Warm Springs Indian community.

Further ethnographic research has suggested that the reluctance to speak out publicly is not restricted to this group. Many Native American students are uncomfortable with the common schoolroom dynamic of the teacher dominating the classroom and calling on students to answer publicly.

A study that compared two Cherokee classrooms supported these findings (Dumont 1972). In one classroom, teacher-dominated recitations were the predominant mode of interaction. In this classroom the children were silent. In the other classroom the children were engaged and talked excitedly. In this classroom the students could choose when and how to participate. The teacher had encouraged the students to work in small groups on projects they had chosen.

The research by Philips and Dumont presents frameworks for analyzing Native American student interactions in the classroom. Their research indicates that many Indian children are more likely to participate actively and verbally in projects they choose and in those situations where they choose to participate. Following on from these observations is the fact that Native American children are less likely to actively participate in the classroom if they are called on unexpectedly. There is also evidence that Native American children are more likely to participate if they are answering from within the group or team.

Brewer (1977, 23) discusses the differences in learning and in the demonstration of that learning. For example, essential learning steps for Oglala Sioux children are observation, self-testing in private, and then demonstration of a task for approval. Native Americans in general do not find public mistakes a helpful way to learn (John 1972, 333).

The expectation that the Native American student will volunteer information or give answers to questions when such behavior is against the norms of the group is unreasonable. It is probably this value that one does not make a public display of his or her knowledge that has led to the stereotype of the "silent and unresponsive Indian child" (Swisher and Deyhle 1994. 90).

Strategies for Dealing with Different Learning Styles

Although it is not easy to identify learning styles, when they are considered in categories such as analytical or relational, dependent or independent, linear or global, general differences arise between Native Americans and nonnative students (Cazden 1982; Dumont 1972; Erickson and Mohatt 1982; Philips 1972, 1983; Van Ness, 1981). Native American students tend to process information in a global and relational way as distinct from a sequential and analytical manner.

Generally speaking, teachers use the style of teaching that grows out of their preferred way of learning. If there are no teachers whose style supports a student's learning style, that student is disadvantaged.

The more a teacher understands the assumptions and norms of a culture, and thus a child's motivations, the more she or he is able to adapt her or his teaching style to incorporate learning strategies that support the learning styles of the student. Such flexibility can be difficult for teachers whose education programs have not included analyses of cultural differences. Many teachers are to some extent still influenced by the notion of America as "the melting pot," which was part of the culture for so long.

A wide body of knowledge exists about bilingual education, native learning styles, and English-as-a-second-language (ESL) teaching techniques. Teachers of native students need to familiarize themselves with this literature. In addition, teachers of native students should have a cultural literacy specific to the tribal background of their students. Unfortunately, accredited teacher-education programs often offer only one multicultural course. By giving their blessing to a generic multicultural approach, these accredited programs actually stall progress in cultural literacy.

When one considers that the learning style of a Native American student is influenced by an environment and tradition that has little in common with a Western school, it is understandable that the Indian child may feel alienated. Teachers of native students cannot assume that their students will be interested in Western academic subject matter. They must constantly draw connections for their students between academic knowledge and its application to the real world. Additionally, teachers should use the active teaching strategies described by Jim Cummins (1989). Many of these strategies are experiential and interactive.

The discontinuity between home and school environments can be so great that Native American students experience a kind of culture shock that significantly affects their attitudes toward school (Cajete 2000, 154). A well-prepared teacher will not be surprised when children bring a different reaction to schoolwork than that generally accepted as characteristic of the majority (Leacock 1976). A desire to work cooperatively with one's classmates will not be interpreted as a lack of motivation.

Instructional strategies should include opportunities for Native American children to learn from their elders, work collaboratively in small groups, take into account the environment, and demonstrate their learning accomplishments in ways that are comfortable for them. Including Native American art, history, natural science, and literature in the curriculum will enhance the learning experience. Specific references to the historical experiences and cultures of regional Native American communities would add a further refinement (Skinner 1991, 3–5).

Recently, Indian education literature has moved away from the notion that Native American learners possess a particular learning style that is culturally determined. Instead, the emerging research shows that Native American students reflect all possible modes of learning. What does need to be remembered is that these learning modalities are mediated by a particular cultural orientation. Cultural orientation, especially in terms of language, continues to influence the learning and perceptions of Native American students (Cajete 2000, 155).

TEXTBOOKS AND OTHER LEARNING MATERIALS

One key element of most Native American cultures is an extended family structure that provides warmth, security, and self-esteem to the individual. In the Native American community, unlike in mainstream America, one does not have to achieve individuality by separating from one's family or extended family. In an assimilationist classroom, all examples of family structure are drawn from European readings and literature, which feature the nuclear family arrangement. The extended-family arrangement of the Native American is subtly denied through omission. By the same token, materials that may not be overtly racist but that refer almost exclusively to a particular cultural perspective certainly promote a cultural bias.

Many of the standard teaching materials, such as textbooks, have limited value for minority students (O'Neil 1979, 154). Not only are American textbooks largely inappropriate in cultural content for native students, they are also over-relied upon in most classrooms. There is evidence that teaching methods that rely less on textbooks work better with native students. In mathematics, this means that there needs to be a greater use of materials that can be manipulated. In science it means a laboratory approach that includes the natural environment. In reading it means whole language methods that support students in reading and studying literature from both the mainstream U.S. society and their native culture.

Even though there are more minority characters now depicted within the basic reading books used in schools, these books are still predominately about white people in a white culture. Even when minority characters are present, they are not within the minority culture but rather within the white culture. An analysis of stories in books typically used by first-grade students indicates that American Indian characters appear in only about 1 percent of the books (Reyhner 1994, 101).

Audrey Simpson-Tyson's (1978, 801) research on Crow Indian children confirms that reading and language activities for Indian students in the first grades of school need to contain many references to experiences, scenes, and objects in their daily lives. When there is congruence among the words students read and the words they hear in the family and the community, they are reinforced in their reading experience. Cummins's (1981, 42) review of research on bilingual education reinforces this perspective.

Indigenously developed curricula are also needed in schools. The tribe is the custodian of its language and culture and thus the best agent to translate these areas into educational materials (Charleston and King 1991, 6). Cultural materials with positive portrayals of Native American people help Native American children develop healthy cultural identities and have a positive influence on their education. There is no room for an assimilation approach in education that erodes students' confidence and pride in their heritage (Yellow Bird and Chenault 2000, 225).

David Gipp, president of the United Tribes Technical College in Bismarck, North Dakota, says, "The development of a culturally-relevant curriculum base by state education agencies is essential for the on-going promotion of curriculum reform toward multicultural education on a state-wide basis." North Dakota's centennial activities included a four-part native curriculum for primary, intermediate, junior high, and high school levels based on whole language approaches, student-centered objectives, and both traditional and contemporary context about American Indian culture. Gipp also suggests that "schools should be recognized for successfully integrating Indian cultural curriculum resources into the local system" (quoted in Skinner 1991, 17).

When considering the education of Native American students, one needs to refer to many of the strategies that are effective in the education of any ethnic group. Culturally compatible curricular materials and teaching methods, such as cooperative learning, support the learning style of Native American students. There is an opportunity for all those concerned with schools to introduce more understanding and more ethnically diverse materials and methods

GIFTED AND TALENTED PROGRAMS

Perhaps one of the most challenging areas for thought and discussion is gifted and talented Native American students in the education system. As with many minority groups, Native American students are under-represented in enrichment programs. As one studies the issues involved and reflects on the history of Native American education within the country, it becomes clearer as to why the education of gifted and talented Native American students is a problematic area. How are the students to be identified as gifted and talented? Are standardized tests to be used? If they are, is there not an inherent bias against Native American students? Does the system militate not only against the identification of gifted and talented Native American students but also against their success?

Even from the early days of attendance at boarding schools, many Native American students have tended to underperform because their teachers had low expectations for them. Education was seen primarily as the way to bring the Native American student to the level of the Western student. This attitude often led to overlooking Native American students' special talents. Thought was not usually given to the possibility that Native Americans would be good leaders or provide mainstream society with new and valuable insights (Tonmah 1991, 417). Native American prohibitions against outperforming one's peers, especially in the alien world of school, also acted as a deterrent to an individual native child's success (Tonemah 1991, 408).

Certainly there are gifted and talented Native American students, just as there are gifted and talented students in all cultures (Tonemah 1991, 407). The history of any group of people is replete with stories of those who displayed extraordinary vision, talent, and leadership. Within the Native American community, outstanding individuals were honored as leaders, holy ones, dancers, artisans, warriors, and so on (Tonemah 1991, 407). The outstanding members of the tribe took on the responsibilities of managing, directing, and promoting the welfare of the group by responding to the demands of the time.

Tonemah (1991, 408) asks the educational community, "Where are the gifted and talented Native American students?" He answers his question with the observation that what were typically perceived as outstanding qualities in the Native American community are now ignored by the educational community. Those behaviors that characterize "outstanding" Native American students are not encouraged by the Western school. Not only are these students denied opportunities to which they are entitled but society is deprived of talents to which it has a right.

Defining Giftedness

An important part of discussing the issue of gifted and talented students, not only among Native Americans students, is defining giftedness. Attempts to describe the construct of giftedness have not been successful (McShane 1989, quoted in Tonemah 1991, 2). Sternberg and Davidson (1986) discuss implicit and explicit theories and point to a subdivision of explicit theory into cognitive, developmental, and domain-specific theory. Tonemah (1991) quotes Davidson as describing giftedness as a construct that has been invented to reflect whatever society wants it to be! Such a definition does not inspire much confidence.

Other researchers have proposed a number of different definitions of giftedness. Renzulli (1986) defined giftedness as a three-ring construct of above-average ability, creativity, and task commitment. Gardner acknowledges that all societies want to identify those who are best suited to the positions of importance within the society, in other words, the gifted.

Assessing Giftedness

As long as there is disagreement about what giftedness is, there will be difficulty in assessing giftedness. There is a long tradition in American education of identifying those students who demonstrate a high level of "intelligence" as gifted and talented. Intelligence has become synonymous with giftedness. However, the very notion of intelligence is subject to changing definitions.

In the 1930s, women and minority groups debated the validity of intelligence tests. They claimed that there was an inherent bias within the construction of the tests, and this bias discriminated against them. During the first half of the twentieth century, the focus of testing for intelligence was on physics and in the next half, on molecular biology and genetics. Disciplines other than psychology may frame the question in the future. Questions to be examined, no doubt, will include the relationship between intelligence and genes and the ways intelligence is used in different cultural and social contexts (Gardner 1999, 213).

Researchers have identified specific gene clusters that control abilities such as reading. A future question may be whether there is a cluster of genes that controls performance on IQ tests. Another focus for researchers concerns the subtle interactions among different "intelligences," as outlined by Howard Gardner, in the accomplishment of complex and important tasks. Cross-cultural studies will be important, as they study the different emphases that are placed on functions within a particular ethnic group (Gardner 1999, 213).

Even though much controversy surrounds intelligence tests, they are still widely used because they are standardized. Tests such as the widely researched Stanford-Binet appear to offer a sense of security. This test and similar ones have been used to identify students who achieve scores toward the outer limits of a bell curve. These are the students identified as gifted and the ones most likely to do exceedingly well at school. Often many of these students come from homes having resources that enhance the learning experience of the students (Tonemah 1991, 410).

The intelligence tests used in the American education system to identify gifted students have relied heavily on students' skills in logic, mathematics, and language. Giftedness is defined more by what is assessed rather than by a clear definition or understanding of what one wants to assess. As Gardner (1999) suggests, there is an opportunity at this time to develop a view of intelligence and giftedness that takes into account not only intellectual skills but the way in which they are used in different circumstances. If we take these ideas and apply them within the school context, we can see that we need different tests for different racial and ethnic groups.

Gardner (1999, 17) points out that some students' reactions to an unknown test giver in an unfamiliar environment can militate against their success on the test. These anxieties can be further exaggerated when different ethnic and racial groups know that their intelligence is being measured (Gardner 1999, 17). Also, it should be clear that to identify a student as gifted and talented on the basis of one test is suspect. The researchers Tonemah and Brittan (1985) have demonstrated that current commercial tests developed to measure intelligence are really for use in large urban school districts. Most Native American students, however, attend schools in small rural districts. Tonemah and Brittan (1985) have developed the American Indian Gifted and Talented Assessment Model (AIGTAM).

Gardner states that it is an error for anyone to search for "pure" intelligence. The relationship between mathematical problem solving and good writing, which are more easily measured, and other tasks valued by society is "too modest to be useful" (1999, 207). It is important that in the assessment of intelligence and, by extension, giftedness, educators develop a more extensive and subtle form of testing than is currently being used. When there is agreement as to what is to be identified, researchers will need to work with the producers of commercial tests to develop assessment tools that are fair to the members of different ethnic and racial groups.

Colleges and universities also need to reevaluate their programs for the educators of the gifted and talented. It behooves these institutions to lead the way in developing gifted and talented programs that ensure appropriate representation of all ethnic groups. School districts need to keep abreast of research developments and ensure that their teachers already in service are kept up to date with new assessment instruments and education techniques.

Those behaviors that characterize the "outstanding" Native American student are not encouraged by the Western school. For example, individual creativity is often a mark of the gifted student, but the very organization of a typical school tends toward acceptance of the social mores of the dominant culture. Classrooms are generally arranged with the students in rows. They are required to march into school in silence and are strictly controlled while in school. This emphasis on conformity and control means that a Native American student who has qualities that identify him or her as gifted would be seen as different or even as nonconformist.

ACADEMIC FAILURE AND DROPOUT RATES

One of the disturbing facts presented by the National Center for Education Statistics (1989) is that American Indian and Alaskan native students have a dropout rate twice the national average. The 1969 Senate report *Indian Education: A National Tragedy, A National Challenge* documented the same dropout rates. Karen Swisher and John Tippeconnic report that although most Native Americans and Alaska Natives are successful at school, as a group, they have the highest dropout rate, about 36 percent (Swisher and Tippeconnic III, 2000, 297).

The problem of Native American students dropping out of school is not recent. As far back as the Carlisle Indian School (see Chapter 1), only a small percentage of students graduated. Approximately seven out of every ten native students both on the reservations and in cities graduate from high schools. Reports from the National Assessment of Educational Progress (NAEP) indicate that as early as the fourth grade, Native American students score below the national level in basic reading, math, and history (Cajete, 2000, 136).

Over the decades, educators and educational researchers have identified many factors responsible for the high rate of academic failure among the youth of minority groups. Some have pointed to genetic characteristics, racial segregation and discrimination, or cultural deprivation. Other studies have focused on the home environment, such as parents' income, and on students' school attendance.

Less attention has been given to the deficits of the schools and teachers. Often school factors can be more influential in causing native students to drop out. A number of critical factors have been identified in research on high student dropout rates across groups. These factors also apply to Native American dropout rates.

- Large schools
- Uncaring teachers
- Passive teaching methods
- Irrelevant curriculum
- Inappropriate testing
- Tracked classes
- Lack of parent involvement (Weis, Farrar and Petrie 1989).

Additional considerations are the approaches of remedial programs for students who fall behind in their work, teacher-training programs, and the effect of positive role models on Native American students.

Large Schools

There is evidence that large schools, especially comprehensive high schools with more than 1,000 students, create conditions that lead to high dropout rates. In the 1984 study *A Place Called School: Prospects for the Future*, John Goodlad (1984) criticized large schools for creating what he called factory-like environments that prevented teachers and other school staff from forming personal relationships with the students. Another study found that small classes and programs, low pupil-teacher ratios, program autonomy, and a supportive school environment decreased student dropout rates. It found that "many students who have not met with success in the regular school program have been alienated by a large, bureaucratic system that does not respond to their unique needs." (Sherman and Sherman 1990, 49). Smaller school size also allows a greater percentage of students to participate in extracurricular activities. Students participating in these activities, especially sports, tend to remain at school.

If students have a long bus trip to school, the dropout rate increases; when excessive travel is not required, drop out occurs less frequently (Platero et al., 1986). In rural areas, students are often required to take long bus rides to school. Those who miss the bus often cannot find alternative transportation, thus increasing their absenteeism. Long distances between homes and school also discourage parents from a more active role in school activities.

Unless large schools are restructured to create schools within schools and provide larger blocks of time so that individual teachers can form caring relationships with individual students, they will continue to create situations that lead to dropping out of school. It is difficult for caring teachers to interact with any one student long enough to know a student personally and to form the kind of supportive relationships when they have too little time or too many students. As mentioned earlier, another approach to this problem is the creation of Native American magnet schools to provide both the individual attention and culturally appropriate curriculum that native students need to succeed.

Uncaring Teachers

The importance of warm, supportive, and caring teachers is documented in the native student dropout research (Coladarci, 1983; Deyhle, 1989; Platero, et al. 1986). An ethnographic study done on Navajos and Utes, including both interviews with students and classroom observations, reports that students "complained bitterly that their teachers did not care about them or help them in school" (Deyhle, 1989, 39). This study also reports that "a little less than half of the Navajo and almost two-thirds of the Ute [students] felt school was not important for what they wanted to do in life" (42). Donna Deyhle finds that "when youth experienced minimal individual attention or personal contact with their teachers, they translated this into an image of teacher dislike and rejection" (39). Fewer native students report that "discipline is fair," that "the teaching is good," that "teachers are interested in students," and that "teachers really listen to me" than other racial or ethnic groups (National Report on Dropouts 1990, 43).

Native American students not only experience the anxiety associated with beginning a new year of school but often face a new culture and a new language. Caring teachers are willing to learn about their students and adjust their teaching to fit the pupils' cultural backgrounds. Such teachers recognize the different cultural heritage of students as a positive contribution to the class and not as another difficulty with which they must deal.

Two general educational development (GED) instructors note in supplemental testimony before the Inidan Nations at Risk Task Force hearings in Seattle that "those students who study for the GED examination often are experiencing for the first time instructors who are Native American themselves, and who truly acknowledge that they are intelligent human beings who are capable of learning and deserve to be treated with dignity and respect. For many, this is a new concept" (*Indian Nations at Risk* document 1991, 5).

A more complete account of how caring, individual attention affects students is given in Kleinfeld's 1979 study of St. Mary's School in Alaska. St. Mary's, a Catholic boarding school, was successful despite what would generally be considered inadequate funding. Judith Kleinfeld concluded from her study that the most important education at St. Mary's takes place not through teaching subject matter or technical skills but through communicating values and principles that endure in spite of the disorganizing pressures of cultural change. Direct teaching is only a small part of this communication. Rather, most of the transmission of values is embedded within the structure of student and staff relationships. The values are communicated above all through the intimate associations that develop at St. Mary's between teachers and their students (Kleinfeld 1979, 27–28).

St. Mary's volunteer teachers interact with students both in and out of the classroom. The school could be identified as "a village society with a structure of social relationships similar to that of the students' own communities" (Kleinfeld 1979, 34). St. Mary's students did not score higher on standardized test than graduates from other schools; however, the self-confidence gained from interacting with caring adults allowed them to master the college environment better and thus go on to graduate from college.

Rock Point Community School, another successful native school, reinforces some of Kleinfeld's conclusions. A study at this school found that Native American students are more successful when the teachers care about the community as well as their jobs. They view education from a more holistic standpoint than many other educators. For these teachers, subject matter is only part, and not necessarily the major part, of their work (Reyhner 1990).

It is common for students to find transitions difficult as they enter and proceed through their school days. For example, in fourth grade, teachers traditionally tend to move toward more formal textbook-oriented instruction. With the introduction of the textbook, the teacher moves to abstract, narrative descriptions. Too many native students fail to bridge the gap in moving from the more informal teaching methods of earlier grades to more formal methods involving textbooks, and it is only a matter of time before they drop out. Another transition point occurs at the completion of either the sixth or the eighth grade. Often, they transfer to large, factory-like secondary schools where, instead of working with a familiar group and one teacher, they must adjust to many different teachers and students (Reyhner 1991, 185). This change can lead to a sense of alienation; a feeling of loss may lead students to drop out of school. Dropout prevention must start at home and continue through early childhood education into high school and beyond as a community-wide effort. Caring teachers can help students successfully bridge the many transitions they face as they proceed through their schooling.

Recent educational reform movements has emphasized teachers being better prepared academically to teach students and incorporate them into the learning enterprise. Other reform movements recommend weeding out students who are bored and uninterested by subjecting them to tests and by applying more rigorous discipline. The nationwide emphasis on rigorous discipline rather than prevention has led to this country's number one ranking in the size of prison population. More people are incarcerated in the United States than in either the Soviet Union or the Union of South Africa (Reyhner 1992, 8). This attitude also influences the way in which the citizenry interacts with the schools and has a ripple effect on the teaching of Native American students. Teachers of native students need greater access to specialized training, native curriculum materials, and support services. The money will not be provided if society emphasizes discipline rather than education.

The personal development of a positive identity is an ongoing and cumulative process. The process begins in the home with the development of a bond of trust between parent and child. Self-confidence is nurtured as the child grows and interacts with other children and adults. To continue to build a positive and strong identity, the child needs ongoing reinforcement from adults (Erikson 1963), including teachers. Classroom messages that conflict with the home will confuse children and prevent the formation of strong self-concepts (Reyhner 1991, 180). Caring teachers give messages to developing native children that reinforce the value of their culture.

Teacher-Training Programs

Native parents testified many times about the need for more native teachers both to provide role models for their children and to share their unique cultural knowledge. Many changes that have been made in teacher-preparation programs and certification standards have aggravated rather than solved problems for recruiting more native educators. Increased certification standards are preventing native students from entering the teaching profession because the National Teachers' Examination and other tests are culturally biased and fail to measure native student strengths. The winter 1989 issue of the *Fair Test Examiner* reports that nearly 38,000 black, Latino, native, and other minority teacher candidates were barred from classrooms by teacher-competency tests. In addition, teacher-preparation and certification programs are culturally and linguistically planned according to the "one size fits all" ethic. The "size" is based on a middle-class, Western European cultural orientation.

One of the puzzles in the U.S. education process is that a native person can successfully complete four or more years of college and receive a bachelors degree at an accredited college or university and be denied a license to teach native students. This denial is predicated on one standardized examination that does not reflect native education at all. At the same time, a nonnative who has never seen a native student, never studied native history, language, or culture and who has a three-credit class in multicultural education that emphasized blacks and Hispanics can legally teach native students (Platero et al. 1986).

Current teacher-recruitment programs do not necessarily attract properly trained individuals, and do not prepare teachers to teach native students. Furthermore, once hired, teachers often get little in-service training on native curriculum and teaching methods. If the educational system does not nurture and value caring and competent teachers, it will not be able to recruit, much less retain, them.

Passive Teaching Methods

It is popularly assumed that students who drop out are already failing, but research on native students shows that the academic performance of dropouts is not significantly different from students who remain at school. Navajo students most frequently gave boredom with school as their reason for planning to drop out or for having dropped out. Forty-five percent of the Navajo dropouts were B or better students (Platero et al. 1986, Platero 1986).

That teaching methods promote passivity is not a new issue. The Meriam Report in 1928 reported that almost all schools had locked rooms or isolated buildings used as "jails" for unruly students and that in some schools native children were forced to maintain quietness. There was not an atmosphere of excitement and discovery.

Traditional transmission methods of teaching that focus on students sitting passively in class and memorizing information are in marked contrast with more experiential and interactive teaching methodologies, such as the explorer classroom (Cummins 1988). In the explorer classroom, students interact with their environment and with their peers and teachers as they learn from different areas in the room. Cummins's review of the research indicates that teachers who use transmission methods cause minority student failure, whereas experiential and interactive methods created conditions for minority student success. Unfortunately, most teacher-training programs emphasize the transmission model.

Other studies of native students show the same need for teachers to know more about the home culture of their students. Swisher and Deyhle (1989) have analyzed a number of these studies to show how teachers can improve the instruction of native students. Teachers who are not trained to teach native children, and most teachers today are not, tend to experience failure when they begin their career teaching native children. Many of these teachers often become discouraged and find other jobs, and the students are left to suffer from continued poor teaching. Changes in certification requirements are urgently needed. Teachers of native students should have specialized training in native education. This position is supported by data from the *Report on BIA Education*. These data show an extremely high turnover rate of Bureau of Indian Affairs (BIA) professional staff in comparison with nationwide figures for other teachers. Such turnover leads native students to have a lower opinion of their teachers than any other group (Report on BIA, 1988).

Inappropriate Curriculum

Many schools with Native American students are characterized by an inappropriate curriculum as well as poor teaching methods (Coladarci 1983). As mentioned in a previous section, the vast majority of textbooks are not written for native students. There are still reports that "too many textbooks are demeaning to minorities" (Senate Report 1989, 28). Testimony from the INAR Task Force hearings indicates that too often superficial attempts are made in schools to provide native curricula through a Thanksgiving unit or a Native American Day rather than developing a culture-based, culture-embedded curriculum that permeates both the school day and the school year. Extensive material exists to produce a culturally appropriate elementary and secondary curriculum for native students; however, there is little incentive for publishers to cater to the relatively small market that native students represent.

The wealth of information that could positively affect native students' understanding and self-concept is indicated by books such as Jack Weatherford's (1988) *Indian Givers: How the Indians of the Americas Transformed the World*. This information does not seem to be reaching native students at the elementary and secondary level.

Inappropriate Testing

Present-day education places immense reliance on standardized tests as a measure of the worth and accomplishments of the individual. Students preparing for college are made to feel that the task is a solitary one and that the measure of their potential is found in the entrance and qualifying tests they take. If teachers take advantage of the traditional approach of Native Americans, students will see themselves as part of larger groups and not isolated. Although it is not possible for teachers to change the entire education system, it is possible for them to make the classroom an understandable and secure place.

Most educators, if pressed, will admit that at best, tests measure only a potential to undertake successfully a certain course of study. If really challenged to explain the requirement of test scores, administrators sometimes concede that they require them simply because the forms they use for admission require them.

Standardized testing, with its flawed construction, produces built-in failure for many students (Oakes 1985, ch. 2; Bloom 1981). In addition to the built-in sorting function of standardized tests, they have a cultural bias. Some of the recommendations in *A Nation at Risk* (National Commission on Excellence in Education 1983) and other studies have hurt rather than helped native students. For example, the academic emphasis that uses tests to measure school success has led to more native students being held back a grade, which leads to dropping out as these students reach high school. The National Education Longitudinal Study of 1988 reports that 28.8 percent of native students has repeated at least one grade. This is the highest percentage of any racial or ethnic group reported (National Education Longitudinal Study, 1990, 9). The research on failing students indicates that retaining students in a grade for another year only creates more failures. Even retaining students in kindergarten does not help students who are having academic problems.

It is a thoughtless practice that leads school administrators and teachers to use the BIA-mandated California Test of Basic Skills (CTBS) and other standardized test scores. The results of these tests indicate that the present curriculum is not working. Administrators often do not realize that they are comparing the test scores of bilingual and culturally different students with those of monolingual (English-speaking) students. If they do acknowledge the differences, many times efforts to change the curriculum are focused on "teaching to the test" in order to show success. Thus the curriculum is based on whatever the standardized test covers rather than on the real needs of native students. Research indicates that it takes about six years for non-English-speaking students to achieve academic proficiency in English so that they can match the English-language test scores of students whose native language is English (Cummins 1988).

It is also only fair that achievement tests given to native students be aligned with what they are being taught in their schools (and not vice versa!). Cummins (1988) maintains that tests should be used to pinpoint student weaknesses. Using tests in this way would help students rather than leading to failure or to keeping them out of the teaching profession.

Low Expectations and Tracking

Yvonne and David Freeman (1988) have analyzed a number of bilingual programs. They found that the assumptions underpinning these programs could limit or enhance the programs' effectiveness. They found that educators have consistently devalued the store of knowledge and experience that native students bring to school and have not expected them to achieve success. Many programs promote drill and practice in the hope of overcoming perceived language deficiencies.

Schools have tended to use the deficit model of education in regard to indigenous children. This model is based on the belief that First Nations children have not had the necessary intelligence to be successful at school. There are remnants of such thinking when one hears such words as "at-risk" or "vulnerable" attached to Native American children. Such apparently caring language masks larger issues of a political nature that keep Native Americans in a subservient position (Yellow Bird and Chenault 2000, 202).

Tracking is the common practice in secondary schools used to divide the student body into high achievers, average achievers, and low achievers. A separate class is provided for each group. Tracking is often based on the questionable results of standardized testing. As was mentioned previously, tests often have hidden with them cultural biases toward minorities. Oakes (1985) describes the negative effect that tracking has in the nation's high schools. Black, Hispanic, and native students are disproportionately represented in the lower tracks, where they often receive a substandard education.

Native and other minority students are least likely to benefit from active teaching strategies because they are often shunted to low-track classes. High-track students have more dynamic learning activities and high-prestige subject matter. For example, students in the upper tracts of a class are more like to study Shakespeare in English classes than those in the lower tracks (Oakes 1985). In Deyhle's dropout study, students "spoke of the boredom of remedial classes, the repetition of the same exercises, and uninteresting subjects" (1989, 44).

Oakes (1985, 117) documents that in tracked classrooms "lower-class students are expected to assume lower-class jobs and social positions as adults." Furthermore, lower-class students often actively resist what they are taught in schools (120). Statistics from the National Education Longitudinal Study of 1988 show that less than 10 percent of native students score in the upper quartile of achievement tests in history, mathematics, reading, and science, whereas over 40 percent are in the lowest quartile. The low expectations of teachers for low-track students, already unsuccessful in school, make an already serious problem worse. The experiences of Jaime Escalante, as portrayed in the movie *Stand and Deliver*, illustrate that teachers who have high expectations for their students can be successful. These teachers bring their subjects alive for their students and expect high achievement in minority students, who are normally written off in the schools. Benjamin Bloom (1981) finds that given proper teaching, 90 percent of students can master classroom subject matter. The film also portrays some of the negative aspects of standardized testing. The Educational Testing Service officials assumed cheating when Hispanic students succeeded beyond the officials' expectations.

The Crossover Effect and Remedial Programs

As mentioned earlier, Native American students as early as the fourth grade score below the national level in basic reading, math, and history (Cajete, 2000, 136). Dehyle and Swisher suggest that at some time in school, Indian students who have been achieving at or above the level of their peers from the mainstream culture "cross over" and start to do poorly. This crossover effect is a well-known phenomenon among indigenous education scholars. Recent research suggests that the crossover effect does not exist in schools where there is a supportive atmosphere for indigenous cultures, identity, and languages (Yellow Bird and Chenault, 2000, 223).

Social workers can help students and school staffs understand the strengths of indigenous cultures and can aid school personnel in developing a helping lexicon for native students (Yellow Bird and Chanault

2000, 224). Social workers and educators can in turn collaborate with parents and the community to raise the level of consciousness about the crossover effect. Together, they can design supportive environments in the school and community that honor indigenous cultures.

Students who do not have the appropriate language skills are unable to keep up with their schoolwork. The response of the system has been to place such students in remedial classes where, although they may improve their reading skills, they fall behind in the subject area. Further, native students in remedial programs receive the clear message that they are behind their peers. The dilemma facing the teacher and the school system is how to help students improve their language skills in a way that does not keep them from progress in all subjects.

Too often, the school's remedial programs, with the best intentions, focus on finding the reasons for students' failure in their homes. The idea that native students are "culturally disadvantaged" or "culturally deprived" reflects a bias against Native Americans. Whenever these attitudes continue, educators will continue to look toward the home rather than to other factors that may cause students to drop out. Schools need to recognize and value what the native students learn at home. It is also important that students are not given a diluted curriculum. As pointed out earlier, when teachers do not challenge their students with a rigorous curriculum, students can easily become bored.

Chamot and O'Malley (1986) have developed a model of language development for students who have a limited proficiency in English. This model has been named the *Cognitive Academic Language Learning Approach (CALLA).* The principles embedded in the model call for teachers to aid students in their development of the English language through their work and involvement in mathematics, science, and other curricula areas. Teachers using the *CALLA* approach not only plan activities using culturally relevant materials; they also take into account the vocabulary students need for the lesson (Ovando, 1994, 228). Such a balanced approach improves students' understanding without resorting to remedial programs.

Two major studies (Deyhle 1991, Platero 1986) of native dropouts found that an orientation program that included traditional native studies was not a handicap in regard to school success. Additionally, *Navajo Students at Risk* stated, "The most successful students were for the most part fluent Navajo/English bilinguals" (Platero 1986, 6). Ruey-kin Lin (1990) reported that native college students who had traditional orientations outperformed those with modern orientations. However, ethnographic studies conducted in classrooms across the country since 1969 indicate that supplemental programs are not enough to solve the dropout problem. There is a need for schoolwide reform, as has been indicated in a recent Department of Education–sponsored study on dropout prevention (Sherman and Sherman 1990).

Lack of Parent Involvement

Often school staff say they want parent involvement but really want parents only to see that their children attend school and do their homework. Parent involvement also means educating parents about the function of the school and allowing parents real decisionmaking power about what and how their children learn. Such involvement serves to reflect parent and community values and to reduce cultural discontinuity between home and school. Many successful native schools are tribally controlled with native people as school board members, administrators, and teachers.

Restrictions on curriculum placed by states on public schools, and even the BIA on BIA-funded schools, limit the effectiveness of native parent involvement. State and BIA regulations force native schools to use curriculum and textbooks not specifically designed for native children and to employ teachers who, though certified, have no special training in native education.

Lack of Role Models

Researchers have looked beyond the schools and cultural disparities to ascertain what else might hinder or aid learning. According to Ogbu (1987, 312–334) it is critical that minority students have role models from their particular group who are successful within the larger society in order to accept the school and education as the means to their success. If members of a particular minority group are never able to be economically successful or are not part of the power structure, it is unlikely that students will be highly motivated. One can appreciate the cumulative effects of the lack of such role models coupled with a failure to take into account language and other cultural differences (Brown 1991, 1–4; Swisher and Deyhle, 1994, 82).

Reentry Strategies for Dropouts

The few good studies of native dropouts, such as *Navajo Students at Risk* (Platero et al., 1986), point out the nationwide need to systematically keep track of the number of native dropouts. These data are necessary because retention programs can be designed only when the extent of the problem is known. The new Montana TRACKS program outlines how states can begin the process. Many studies seriously overestimate and others seriously underestimate the extent of the dropout problem. These inaccuracies come about because schools do not know how many children have never entered school or whether a student, who appears to have dropped out has actually transferred to another school without notice. A regular-school-based retrieval program is most desirable, but alternative schools and general educational development (GED) programs also provide effective means to further the education of "at risk" native students.

CULTURAL PRESERVATION

Edward Benton-Banai (Swisher and Deyhle 1994, 81) is concerned with the social dysfunction among native families and communities. He believes that a culturally based curriculum is a means of revitalizing native cultural values and traditions and that this revitalization will in turn help minimize social dysfunction (Indian Nation at Risk Task Force 1990, 81).

David Gipp, president of United Tribes Technical College in Bismarck, North Dakota, testifies, "There is a need to encourage state education agencies and public schools to institutionalize commitments toward the cultural preservation of American Indian communities through state Indian Education policies" (Skinner 1991, 17). Minnesota, Montana, and Washington have adopted state policies that provide a foundation for progressive Indian education programs.

As the study of diverse cultures becomes more embedded within the curricula of all schools, attention needs to be given to the first citizens of the United States. More regional native heritage, cultural, and historical societies and learning centers should be established to help revitalize the values and traditions of native families and communities as a way of minimizing social dysfunction. The study of Native American language, law, history, culture, art, and philosophy is of utmost importance in those schools that have some or all Native American students. Understanding built on knowledge about the Native American heritage can do much to build pride among native youth and stabilize native communities.

SUMMARY

It is easy to assume that when students begin their first year at school they are starting school on an equal plane. This is not the case. Schools are predicated on the experience of those who establish, staff, and maintain them. Their values and way of doing things become strategies within the school context. Those who come from another culture are disadvantaged, as much of their time and energy is spent learning the new culture.

Though schools cannot be the perfect instrument for dealing with the differences among cultures, educators can establish, as early as possible, conditions that will ensure the success of Native American students. For many youngsters the first days of school are difficult even when all look alike, speak the same way, and identify with the materials that are presented. It is important that the school is culturally sensitive from the moment the student enters its doors. The better students' initial experiences, the more likely they will have long-term success.

All students bring with them to school a vast social, cultural, and linguistic repertoire of understandings and knowledge. A teacher who is successful builds on these understandings and additionally uses the techniques and processes through which the students learn. To be successful in teaching Native American students, teachers need to understand and consider the learning processes in American Indian settings (Brown 1991; McCarty and Schaffer, 1994, 117).

Generally speaking, those strategies that make for a good learning environment are applicable to teaching Native American students. As with all students, the Native American student needs content material that is age appropriate and incorporates concrete materials, shared experiences, and prior knowledge. It behooves teachers to remember that they need to educate the whole child and not be trapped in the narrow confines of disciplines that have shaped the educational process in the recent past. The foundation for learning should be the common experience of being human.

The dropout rate among Native American students indicates how important it is to look not only at individuals but also at structural issues. Solving problems on an individual level, using individual solutions, is important. Structural approaches aimed at reducing institutional racism and oppression are equally important (Yellow Bird and Chenault 2000, 202).

Some researchers believe that the school is the panacea for bringing about educational equity. Others believe that the school makes little difference. What is more, the importance of school is different for individuals. One can be sure, however, that an institution that takes up so much time in a young person's life is not without importance and influence (Swisher and Deyhle 1994, 81).

REFERENCES AND FURTHER READING

Allen, P.G. 1983. *Studies in American Indian Literature: Critical Essays and Course Designs.* New York: Modern Language Association.

Appleton, N. 1983. *Cultural Pluralism in Education.* New York: Longman.

Astin, A. W. 1982. *Minorities in American Higher Education.* San Francisco: Jossey-Bass.

Aukerman, R. C. 1981. *The Basal Reader Approach to Reading.* New York: John Wiley.

Banks, J. A. 1975. *Teaching Strategies for Ethnic Studies.* Boston: Allyn and Bacon.

Barnes, D. *From Communication to Curriculum.* Harmondsworth, UK: Penguin, 1976.

Bennett, C. I. 1985. *Comprehensive Multicultural Education: Theory and Practice.* Boston: Allyn and Bacon.

Bennett, W. J. 1986. *First Lessons: A Report on Elementary Education in America.* Washington, DC: Department of Education.

Berg, P., and J. Ohler. 1991. "Strategic Plans for Use of Modern Technology in the Education of American Indian and Alaska Native Students." In *Indian Nations at Risk: Solutions for the 1990s.* Washington, DC: Department of Education.

Biglin, J. E., and J. Wilson. 1972. "Parental Attitudes Toward Indian Education." *Journal of American Indian Education* 11, no. 3: 1–6.

Bloom, B. S. 1981. *All Our Children Learning.* New York: McGraw Hill.

Branson, R. K. 1987. "Why the Schools Can't Improve: The Upperlimit Hypothesis." *Journal of Instructional Development* 10, no. 4.

Brewer, A. 1977. "On Indian Education." *Integration* 15: 21–23.

Brown, A. D. 1977. An Examination of Age, Sex, and Cross-cultural Differences in Cooperation and Competition, and Relationship of the Two Variables in School Achievement. Ph.D. diss., City University of New York.

Brown, G. 1986. "Cross Cultural Self-Concept: The Best of Both Worlds." Selected papers from annual Mokakit Tribal Conference. Vancouver, BC: Mokakit Education Research Association.

Brown, R. D. 1973. *A First Language: The Early Stages.* Cambridge, MA: Harvard University Press.

Buckley, M. H. 1986. "When Teachers Decide to Integrate the Language Arts." *Language Arts* 63 (April).

Bullock, Anthony. 1975. *A Language for Life: Report of the Committee of Inquiry*

Appointed by the Secretary of State for Education and Science (Sir Anthony Bullock). London: Her Majesty's Stationery Office.

Bureau of Indian Affairs. 1988. *Report on BIA Education: Excellence in Indian Education through the Effective School Process*. Washington, DC: Office of Indian Education Programs, BIA.

Butterfield, R. A. 1983. "The Development and Use of Culturally Appropriate Curriculum for American Indian Students." *Peabody Journal of Education* 61, no. 1: 49–66.

Caine, R., and G. Caine. 1997. *Education on the Edge of Possibility*. Alexandria, VA: Association for Supervision and Curriculum Development.

Cajete, G. 1994. *Look to the Mountain: An Ecology of Indigenous Education*. Durango, CO: Kivaki Press.

Cazden, C. B. 1982. "Four Comments." In P. Gilmore and A. Glatthkorn, eds., *Children in and out of School*. Washington, DC: Center for Applied Linguistics.

Chamot, A. U. and J. M. O'Malley. 1985. "Using Learning Strategies to Understand Secondary Science Presentations." In *Delivering Academic Excellence to Culturally Diverse Populations*. Teaneck, NJ: Fairleigh Dickinson University Press, pp. 33–34.

———. 1986. *A Cognitive Academic Learning Approach: An ESL Content-based Curriculum*. Rosslyn, VA: National Clearinghouse for Bilingual Education.

Cohen, R. A. 1969. "Conceptual Styles, Cultural Conflict, and Nonverbal Tests of Intelligence." *American Anthropologist* 71: 828–856.

Coladarci, T. 1983. "High-school Dropouts among Native Americans." *Journal of American Indian Education*, 23, no 1: 15–22.

Collier, V. P., and W.P. Thomas. 1989. "How Quickly Immigrants Become Proficient in School English." *The Journal of Educational Issues of Language Minority Students* 5 (Fall).

Cummins, J. 1981. "The Role of Primary Language Development in Promoting Education Success for Minority Students." In *Schooling and Language for Minority Students: A Theoretical Framework*. Los Angeles: Evaluation, Dissemination, and Assessment Center, California State University.

———. 1988. *Empowering Minority Students*. Sacramento: California Association for Bilingual Education.

———. 1994. "The Empowerment of Indian Students." In Jon Reyhner, ed., *Teaching American Indian Students*. Norman: University of Oklahoma Press.

Dehyle, D. 1983. "Measuring Success and Failure in the Classroom: Teacher Communications about Tests and the Understandings of Young Navajo Students." *Peabody Journal of Education* 61, no. 1: 67–85.

———. 1989. "Pushouts and Pullouts: Navajo and Ute School Leavers." *Journal of Navajo Education* 6, no. 2: 36–51.

Dumont, R. V. 1972. "Learning English and How To Be Silent: Studies in Sioux and Cherokee Classrooms." In C. Cazden, V. John, and D. Hymes, eds., *Function of Language in the Classroom.* New York. Teachers College Press.

Dunn, Rita. 1983. "Learning Style and Its Relation to Exceptionality at Both Ends of the Spectrum." *Exceptional Children* 49, no. 6: 496–506.

Eberhard, D. K. 1989. "American Indian Education: A Study of Dropouts." *Journal of American Indian Education* 29, no. 1: 32–40.

Erickson, F., and G. Mohatt. 1982. "Cultural Organization of Participation Structures in Two Classrooms of Indian Students." In G. Spindler, ed., *Doing the Ethnography of Schooling.* New York: Holt, Rhinehart, and Winston.

Erikson, E. H. 1963. *Childhood and Society,* 2nd ed. New York: W. W. Norton.

Freeman, Yvonne, and David Freeman. 1988. *Bilingual Learners: How Our Assumptions Limit Their World.* Tucson: University of Arizona Press.

Garcia, R. L., and J. G. Ahler. 1994. "Indian Education: Assumption, Ideologies, Strategies." In J. Reyhner, ed., *Teaching American Indian Students.* Norman: University of Oklahoma Press.

Gardner, H. 1999. *Intelligence Reframed: Multiple Intelligences for the 21st Century.* New York: Basic Books.

Gilliland, H. 1995. *Teaching the Native American.* 3rd ed. Dubuque, IA: Kendall/Hunt.

Gipp, D. 1991. *Testimony to Indian Nations at Risk Task Force.* Washington, D.C.: U.S. Department of Education.

Gipp, D., and S. Fox. 1991. "Promoting Culturing Relevance in American Indian Education." *Education Digest,* 57, no. 3: 58–64.

Goodlad, J. 1984. *A Place Called School: Prospects for the Future.* New York: McGraw Hill.

Hakes, J. A., et al. 1980. *Curriculum Improvement for Pueblo Indian Students: A Pilot Study.* ERIC No. ED 190 283. Albuquerque, NM: All Indian Pueblo Council.

Hayes, S. A. 1990. "Educational Innovation at Lunimi." *Journal of American Indian Education* (May).

John, V. P. 1972. "Styles of Learning—Styles of Teaching: Reflections on the Education of Navajo Children." In C. Cazden, D. Hymes, and V. P. John, eds., *Functions of Language in the Classroom.* New York: Teachers College Press.

Kitano, M. K. 1991. "A Multicultural Perspective on Serving the Culturally Diverse Gifted." *Journal for the Education of the Gifted* 151: 4–19.

Kleinfeld, J. 1972. *Effective Teachers of Indian and Eskimo High School Students.* ERIC No. ED 302 364. Fairbanks, AK: University of Alaska, Institute of Social, Economic and Government Research, Center for Northern Educational Research.

————. 1979. *Eskimo School on the Andreafsky: A Study of Effective Bicultural Education.* New York: Praeger.

Kuhn, T. 1970. *The Structure of Scientific Revolutions,* 2d ed. 2 vols. Chicago, IL: University of Chicago Press.

Leacock, E. 1976. "The Concept of Culture and Its Significance for School Counselors." In J. I. Roberts and S. K. Akinsany, eds., *Schooling in the Cultural Context.* New York: David McKay.

Lin, R-L.1990. "Perception of Family Background and Personal Characerististics among Indian College Students." *Journal of American Indian Education,* 29, no. 3: 19–28.

Lipka, J. M. 1989. "A Cautionary Tale of Curriculum Development in Yup'ik Eskimo Communities." *Anthropology and Education Quarterly* 20, no. 3: 216–231.

Locust, C. 1988. "Wounding the Spirit: Discrimination and Traditional American Indian Belief Systems." *Harvard Education Review* 58, no. 3: 315–330.

Love, R. K. 1998. Art as Developmental Theory: The Spiritual Ecology of Learning and the Influence of Traditional Native American Education. Ph.D. diss., University of New Mexico.

McCracken, T. 1989. *Between Language and Silence: Postpedagogy's Middle Way: Part I: The Text.* Educational Resources Information Center (ERIC) ED 307630.

Meriam, L., ed. 1928. *The Problem of Indian Administration.* Baltimore, MD: Johns Hopkins University Press.

Miller, A. G., and R. Thomas. 1972. "Cooperation and Competition among Blackfoot Indian and Urban Canadian Children." *Child Development.* 43: 1104–1110.

National Center for Education Statistics. 1989. *Analysis Report: Dropout Rates in the United States: 1988* (NCES 89–609). Washington, DC: Office of Educational Research and Improvement, U.S. Department of Education.

————. 1990. *National Education Longitudinal Study of 1988: A Profile of the American Eighth Grader* (NCES 90–458). Washington, DC: Office of Educational Research and Improvement, U.S. Department of Education.

National Commission on Excellence in Education. 1983. *A Nation at Risk: The Imperative for Educational Reform.* Washington, DC: U.S. Government Printing Office.

Oakes, J. 1985. *Keeping Track: How Schools Structure Inequality.* New Haven, CT: Yale University Press.

Ogbu, J. U. 1987. "Variability in Minority School Performance: A Problem in Search of an Explanation." *Anthropology and education Quarterly* 18, no. 4: 312–334.

————. 1992. "Understanding Cultural Diversity and Learning." *Education Researcher* 21, no. 8: 5–14.

O'Malley, E., ed. 1992. *American Indian Education Handbook.* Sacramento, CA: State Department of Education, American Indian Education Unit.

O'Neil, F. 1979. "Multiple Sources and Resources for the Development of Social Studies Curricula for the American Indian." In *Multicultural Education and the American Indian.* Los Angeles: American Indian Studies Center, University of California at Los Angeles, pp. 153–156.

Oros, T. 1993. "A Prescription of Success." *Winds of Change* 8, no. 3: 48–51.

Ovando, C. J. 1994. "Science." In J. Reyhner, ed., *Teaching American Indian Students.* Norman: University of Oklahoma Press.

Pepper, F. C. 1985. *Understanding Indian Students: Behavioral Learning Styles.* Portland, OR: Northwest Regional Educational Laboratory.

Philips, S. U. 1972. "Participant Structures and Communicative Competence: Warm Springs Children in Community and Classrooms." In Courtney B. Cazden, Dell Hymes, and Vera P. Johns, eds., *Functions in the Classroom.* New York: Teachers College Press, pp. 370–394.

———. 1983. *The Invisible Culture: Communication in Classroom and Community on the Warm Springs Indian Reservation.* New York: Longman.

Piatt, B. 1990. *Only English? Law and Language Policy in the United States.* Albuquerque: University of New Mexico Press.

Platero, P. R., E. A. Brandt, G. Witherspoon, and P. Wong. 1986. *Navajo Students at Risk: Final Report for Navajo Area Student Dropout Study.* Window Rock, AZ: Navajo Division of Education, Navajo Nation.

Ramirez, M., III, and A. Castanda. 1974. *Cultural Democracy, Bicognitive Development, and Education.* New York: Academic Press.

Renzulli, J. S. 1986. "The Three-ring Conception of Giftedness: A Developmental Model for Creative Productivity." In J.S. Renzulli, ed., *The Triad Reader.* Mansfield Center, CT: Creative Learning Press.

Reyhner, J. 1991. "Plans for Dropout Prevention and Special School Support Services for American Indian and Alaska Native Students." In *Indian Nations at Risk: Solutions for the 1990s.* Washington, DC: U.S. Department of Education.

Reyhner, J., and J. Eder. 1989. *A History of Indian Education.* Billings, MT: Native American Studies, Eastern Montana College.

Sanders, D. 1987. "Cultural Conflicts: An Important Factor in Academic Failure of American Indian Students." *Journal of Multicultural Counseling and Development* 18, no. 15: 81–89.

Scollon, R., and S. B. Scollon. 1981. *Narrative, Literacy, and Face in Interethnic Communication.* Norwood, NJ: Ablex.

Sherman, R. Z., and J. D. Sherman. 1990. *Dropout Pevention Strategies for the 1990.* Washington DC: Pelavin Associates.

Shonerd, H. 1990. "Recruiting and Retaining Native Americans in Teacher Education." ERIC No. ED 331 686.

Silentman, I. 1995. "Revaluing Indigenous Language Resources through Language Planning." *Bilingual Research Journal* 1, no. 1: 179–182.

Simpson-Tyson, Audrey K. 1978. "Are Native American First Graders Ready to Read?" *The Reading Teacher* 31, no. 7: 798–801.

Skinner, L. 1991. "Teaching through Traditions: Incorporating Native Languages and Cultures into Curricula." In *Indian Nations at Risk: Solutions for the 1990s.* Washington, DC: Department of Education.

St. Germiane, R. 1995. "Bureau Schools Adopt Goals 2000." *Journal of American Indian Education* 35, no. 1: 39–43.

Steele, C. L. 1986. Mokawk Cultural Perspectives: A Curriculum Database of Mohawk Cross-Cultural Curriculum. Ph.D. diss., State University of New York at Albany.

Sternberg, R. J., and J. E. Daridson, eds. 1986. *Conceptions of Giftedness.* New York: Cambridge University Press.

Swisher, Karen. 1984. "Comparison of Attitudes of Reservation Parents and Teachers toward Multicultural Education." *Journal of American Indian Education* 23, no. 3: 1–10.

Swisher, Karen, and Donna Deyhle. 1989. "The Styles of Learning Are Different, but the Teaching Is Just the Same: Suggestions for Teachers of American Indian Youth." *Journal of Navajo Education* (August): 1–14.

———. 1994. "Adapting Instruction to Culture." In J. Reyhner, ed., *Teaching American Indian Students.* Norman: University of Oklahoma Press.

Swisher, Karen G., and John W. Tippeconnic III. 1986. "Research to Support Improved Practice in Indian Education." In Karen G. Swisher and John W. Tippeconnic III, eds., *Next Steps: Research and Practice to Advance Indian Education.* Charleston, WV: Clearinghouse on Rural Education and Small Schools.

Thornton, R. 1978. "American Indian Studies as an Academic Discipline." *American Indian Culture and Research Journal* 2, no. 3–4: 10–18.

Tippeconnis, J. W., III. 1983. "Training Teachers of American Indian Students." *Peabody Journal of Education* 61, no. 1: 6–15.

———. 1990. "American Indians: Education, Demographics, and the 1990s." In G. E. Thomas, ed., *U.S. Race Relations in the 1980s and 1990s: Challenges and Alternatives.* New York: Hemisphere.

Tippens, D. J., and N. F. Dana. 1992. "Culturally Relevant Alternative Assessment." *Science Scope* 15, no. 6: 50–52.

Tonemah, S. 1991. "Gifted and Talented American Indian and Alaska Native Students." In *Indian Nations at Risk: Solutions for the 1990s.* Washington, DC: U.S. Department of Education.

Tonemah, S., and M. Brittan. 1985. *American Indian Gifted and Talented Assessment Model (AIGTAM).* Norman, OK: American Indian Research & Development.

U.S. Senate Special Subcommittee on Indian Education. 1969. *Indian Education: A National Tragedy; A National Challenge.* Senate Report No. 91–501. Washington, DC: U.S. Government Printing Office.

U.S. Senate Special Committee on School Performance. 1989. *Helping Schools Succeed at Helping All Children Learn.* Fairbanks, AK: Fifteenth Alaska Legislature.

Van Ness, H. 1981. "Social Control and Social Organization in the Alaskan Athabaskan Classroom: A Microethnography of 'Getting Ready' for Reading." In H. T. Trueba, G. P. Gutherie, and K. Hu-Pei, eds., *Culture and the Bilingual Classroom.* Rowley, MA: Newbury House.

Wax, M., R. Wax, and R. V. Dumont. 1964. "Formal Education in an American Indian Community." *Social Problems* 11: 95–96.

Weatherford, J. 1988. *Indian Givers: How the Indians of the Americas Transformed the World.* New York: Fawcett Columbine.

Weis, L., E. Farrar, and H. Petrie, eds. 1989. *Dropouts from School: Issues, Dilemmas, and Solutions.* Albany: State University of New York Press.

Wright, B. 1991. "American Indian and Alaska Native Higher Education: Toward a New Century of Academic Achievement and Cultural Integrity." In *Indian Nations at Risk: Solutions for the 1990s.* Washington, DC: U.S. Department of Education.

Yellow Bird, M. J., and V. Chenalut, V. 1986. "The Role of Social Work in Advancing the Practice of Indigenous Education: Obstacles and Promises in Empowerment-Oriented Social Work Practice." In Karen G. Swisher and John W. Tippeconnic III, eds. *Next Steps: Research and Practice to Advance Indian Education.* Charleston, WV: Clearinghouse on Rural Education and Small Schools.

Chapter Six

✌ The Basics: Language, Math, and Science

This chapter builds on the issues explored in Chapter 5 in considering three specific curriculum areas. Language and literacy are key components in building a solid foundation for further education. Math and science are also very important for the success of Native American students and their experience of education.

LANGUAGE

All children who do not have a learning disability learn language. The words and the language they acquire and master are specific to the ethnic group into which they are born. Most impressive, apart from the fact that language is universal, is the ease with which children learn this complex symbolic system.

When children master the language of the group to which they belong, they master not only the words and sounds but also the way in which their group constructs sentences. As they understand the words and the way in which sentences are constructed, they are able to respond to and interact with other people in their group.

Development of Language Skills

The development of language skills by children is not haphazard but follows a natural order. This order and sequence have been demonstrated as similar across a number of different language and cultural groups (Brown 1991, 2; Dualy, Burt, and Krahen 1982; Lindfors 1987; McCarty and Shaffer, 1994, 120). A broad outline of this development shows the movement from mostly nonverbal to verbal expressions. Children's first words are most often tied to a desire for something to happen. At this time in their development, they can comprehend much more than they can say, although it is not possible for a researcher to determine the extent of a child's knowledge through merely observing and noting speech production (Brown 1991, 1–2).

Children move from words to short, simple sentences to longer and more complex ones. As they become older and gain more experience, they are able to move beyond the present tense to express remembrances and possibilities. Typically, these stages of development do not happen at the same time for all children. Differences in their grasp of the language mirror the differences among all people in regard to their learning and understanding.

Children practice and make mistakes, are corrected, and try again. Throughout the process, they draw on the context of the culture in which they live (McCarty and Shaffer 1994, 120). Thus children are able to learn and master basics of language or language construction in a natural setting without the interventions of teachers or curricula.

Language and Writing

In American society, children are surrounded by words on billboards, labels, advertisements, building signs. They are immersed in words not only as sounds but also as written symbols (Brown 1991, Hudelson 1989, Smith, 1988). Most children achieve this level of sophistication in language by the age of four or five. They do it without a structured curriculum, hours of drill and practice, and without being able to analyze sentence structure.

Associated with learning language is the development of some level of writing. Oral and written language development are intertwined in the sense that the written word can extend and enhance the meaning of the spoken word and vice versa (Goodman 1986). T. L. McCarty and Rachel Shaffer (1994 115–116) studied Tohono O'odham first-graders as well as Navajo high school students.

A cursory review of the literature indicates that the achievement of Native American students is below the norm in reading, language arts, science, social studies, and mathematics. Gerald Brown (1991) maintains that these students are not successful in school because they have not been able to grasp the language of schools, or cognitive academic language, well enough to access the other subjects of the curriculum. In recent times there has been a focus on instructional strategies that concentrate on using modified subject matter. The teacher guides the students to achieve academic competence, or the ability to learn through English rather than merely communicate in English (Brown 1991, 11; Chamot 1985).

It is important to start at a very basic level in developing strategies for teaching reading and language arts and to apply these strategies from the child's first days of school. Unfortunately, relatively few teachers are well prepared to teach Native American students, and few opportunities exist for this kind of training (Brown 1991, 26).

Key Aspects of Reading

Three key factors influence the act of reading. They are the *text,* the *language,* and the *schema* within the text (Brown 1991, 12). The text carries a message. This message may relate to the experience of the students or may be totally foreign to them. The text also reflects the understandings and knowledge of the author. A nineteenth-century text carries a set of meanings totally different from meanings in a twenty-first-century text.

The language chosen by the author, that is, the words and the arrangement of those words, determine how easy or difficult the text is to read. The words and their arrangement may vary from the simple to the complex and abstract.

A schema determines how one responds to the text and is based on one's experience. When one reads or hears a story, for example, the words evoke different associations for different people. People develop particular images and concepts in relation to such objects as pencils and books, such places as home and school, and such abstract ideas as patriotism and loyalty. Brown (1991) delineates three different forms of schemata: content, script, and structure.

- The content schema is the sum of the student's current knowledge.
- The script schemata refers to the different roles the student has performed or has observed family, community members, or friends performing. A student has a memory store of many scripts, and if these do not relate to the script within the text, the text will be incomprehensible. Personal scripts are culturally specific and intimately related to the socio-economic status, lifestyle, gender, and age of the reader.
- Students also bring a structure schema to their interaction with texts. This schema is a particular way of organizing their world. The experiences of previous reading and story-telling provide the bases for the structure schema. The more the stories that the students are required to read are in harmony or have a similar structure, the easier it is for them to read and understand the text. Thus teachers should ensure that texts for Native American students are congruent with their experiences.

Cognitive Academic Language Learning Approach

Native American students bring different degrees of English-language proficiency to their formal education. Many come to school with what is referred to as "reservation English" or "village English." They have used this language to communicate with family, peers, and other community members, and it has helped them shape their identity and understand the world about them.

The native limited English proficiency (LEP) student may need special consideration in regard to daily assignments and testing. As with all LEP students, native LEP students may need more time to complete assignments. It is important for the teacher to assess if the students in their early years at school understand the language that is used for testing.

Today, most Native American students speak only English, though, a minority still understand their native language. Thinking first in their native language and then translating into English is no longer the case among most of these students. The reverse, thinking in English and trying to find a word or situation in their native language, is now the norm.

Traditionally, American education has been textbook driven, requiring students to have a good grasp of academic English. Because so many Native American students continue to score below the norm, it appears fair to say that schools are not able to effectively provide them with the level of language proficiency they need (Brown 1991, 1; Fox 1986, 1988, 1990).

Students may have the oral English skills to communicate with their peers on the playground. However, they may not have acquired the skills necessary to use language in the academic situation (Brown 1991, 12). Brown states (1991, 11) that it is imperative that Native American students develop cognitive academic language proficiency (CALP) in addition to basic interpersonal communication skills (BICS). As formulated by Cummins (1984), these constructs refer, respectively, to the English language as it is used in the schools and the use of the English language to successfully interact with others. Cummins (1981) reported that even a though a student may attain proficiency in interpersonal communication, she or he may need from five to seven years to achieve proficiency in academic language skills.

As discussed in Chapter 5, Chamot and O'Malley (1986) have developed a model of language development named the cognitive academic language learning approach (CALLA). With this model teachers aid students in their development of the English language through their work and involvement in mathematics, science, and other curricula areas. The CALLA approach helps students increase their language proficiency without falling behind in other subject areas and thus keeps them from the discouragement of remedial programs

English as a Second Language

Research shows that after a language is learned, it forms the primary foundation for learning subsequent languages. When students are involved in learning a second language, they engage in subconscious processes that help them develop a facility with the new language. The better they grasp their first language, the better, generally speaking, they grasp their second language (Ovando and Collier 1994, 58–61).

People typically learn a new language in two ways—through unconscious acquisition or through a more conscious process. The most natural way to learn a language involves no formal teaching but rather immersion in the environment in which the particular language is spoken. The other method requires formal study focused on the structure and syntax of the new language. The student is involved in learning grammatical rules, correctness of form, and other technical matters (Ovando and Collier 1994, 62).

Stephen Krashen (1982) has developed a model for the acquisition of a second language. Because the developmental stages of learning a second language so closely resemble those of acquiring the first language, he postulated that mastery of the second language is mostly subconscious. In other words, one develops facility with the second language through using the language and being exposed to its use by others. He makes the point that learning a second language solely through the use of rules of syntax and sentence construction, that is, learning it consciously, has a limited effect.

A great deal of research supports the proposition that using relevant subject matter, presenting it in the student's primary language, and coupling that with appropriate English-language input is the most effective way to teach English as a second language (Cummins 1989, 1990; Krashen and Biber 1988; McCarty and Shaffer 1994, 122; Moll and Diaz 1987; Hakuta 1986; Tikunoff 1985; Crawford 1989; Watahomigie and Yamamoto 1987). By taking this approach the teacher takes advantage of the intellectual resources that students have already developed. Failure to use students' resources puts them at a serious disadvantage (Krashen and Biber 1988).

Another important factor in the development of a second language is students' attitude toward the people who speak this language. If

Native American students sense that their teachers respect their primary language and desire to help them achieve a mastery of English, they will be positively influenced. Furthermore, if teachers of Native American students engage positively while teaching the second language, there is a greater likelihood of success. According to Krashen's affective filter hypothesis, students are more likely to be open to the new language and thus develop fluency more quickly if their filter is low. Native American students with a high filter will be inhibited from learning the language.

Krashen hypothesizes that students acquire fluency more readily when they are exposed to interaction with the language at or somewhat above their level of proficiency. Teachers who base interactions on previous knowledge while challenging students to extend their understandings and ensuring a safe environment for experiment will provide the atmosphere for language acquisition.

It may appear, while students are absorbing what they have learned, that they are not advancing in their grasp of the language. More likely, they are building their competence in the new language through active listening and self-correction. As important as challenging students is making sure that they understand the import of the texts that are a little beyond their present competence. This understanding motivates them to advance and acquire new skills (Brown 1991, 4–5).

Krashen (1982) and Brown (1991) emphasize four key environmental factors for Native American students acquiring academic English:

- The learning process in communicating in the new language should focus on the content rather than the form.
- One-way communication and limited two-way communication are most beneficial. In the restricted two-way communication, the student listens and has the freedom to respond when ready in a nonverbal way or in his or her tribal language.
- Acquisition of the second language is enhanced by using the materials and engaging in the activities that are mentioned in the discussions.
- Students learn the language better if they are able to talk and interact with their peers, especially if there are peers who are fluent in the second language. Students find it less desirable to practice their skills with parents or teachers. They also prefer to talk with peers from their own ethnic group.

As mentioned, even though students may demonstrate high levels of verbal competence in a language, they may still not have the skills that enable them to cope with the academic environment. In addition to learning a second language, students must learn to follow schedules, make use of textbooks, and participate in the general activities and routines of the classroom. Some Native American students would benefit from appropriate ESL (English as a second language) instruction. Such instruction needs to support both interpersonal language skills and cognitive academic language skills.

Many ESL programs require a listen-and-repeat, or an audiolingual, approach. The teacher uses specially scripted drills that cue the students. Sometimes students are required to imitate the teacher, at other times to respond to the teacher's cues. When students reply, the teacher praises or corrects them. When the emphasis is on grammar, students are required to memorize and recite idioms and word forms and understand the rules governing sentence structure. These approaches are weak because they take language out of its natural context of communication. Students are able to learn language in a far more complex context than these approaches support (Brown 1991; McCarty and Shaffer 1994, 118).

The Role of Language in Preserving Culture

Language is perhaps the most critical element in revitalizing and maintaining culture. It is the tool used to access the values and meanings embedded within society. Language embodies and protects the group's unique ethnicity, symbols, culture, and history. Steven Pratt (Osage) believes that language can revitalize culture. He takes the same position as James Banks, who believes language and culture are two sides of the same coin (Banks 1988, 261). If the language disappears, the "glue" that holds the group together is dissolved, and the cord that ties the past to the present is severed (Banks 1988, 262). Indeed, at this time there are a number of Native American languages that could well disappear and never be spoken again, such as Shoshoni. To help remedy this situation, Pratt, an Osage elder, and his colleague Hazel Lohah Harper advocate instruction in native languages.

Acknowledgment and use of the native language also contributes to the self-esteem of native children. Through the practice of the school, they will experience the valuing of their culture through the valuing of their language (Brown 1991, 1; Charleston and King 1991, 7). Because the federal government was the agency that initiated and supported the policy of assimilating Native Americans, it would seem logical that the government undertake and support measures that would help remedy the harm of its earlier programs.

Schools and universities that have a second-language requirement also have leadership roles. They could not only accept a native
language but also encourage a tribal language as the language of choice.
In Native American schools the requirement of a European language de-
values the importance of the native language. If Native American students are not encouraged to study their language, they should at least be
allowed this pursuit

MATH AND SCIENCE

*Everybody Counts—A Report to the Nation on the Future of Mathemat-
ics Education* states that three out of four students stop studying mathematics before they are equipped with the skills they need for college
or careers (National Research Council 1989, 1–3). This deficiency is
more acute among Native American students. However, many of the
difficulties they have in mastering mathematics, and consequently science, probably have less to do with the ability to process mathematical
ideas than with the way mathematics and the sciences are taught
(Davison 1994, 241). Typically, the approaches of many teachers are
not in keeping with the ways in which Native American students
process information.

During the compilation of the report *Indian Nations at Risk* (Department of Education 1991), some common themes emerged in relation to mathematics and science. Many of those who provided written
testimonies for the report emphasized the need to acknowledge Native
American cultures and to teach native students in ways that build on
their strengths (Preston 1991, 1).

The need for reform in the teaching of mathematics and science
was a key theme in the report *Indian Nations at Risk*. Consistently, U.S.
students have scored below other industrial nations. Other reports have
confirmed these low scores, among them *A Nation at Risk* (National
Commission on Excellence in Education 1983), *Educating Americans for
the 21st Century* (National Science Board Commission on Pre-college
Education in Mathematics, Science and Technology 1983), and the previously mentioned *Everybody Counts—A Report to the Nation on the Future of Mathematics Education* (National Research Council 1989). If
mainstream students are having difficulties, it is likely that the problem
is more acute for those students having problems fitting into the traditional school.

Until about the third grade, Native American students are close in
achievement to other students (Leap, 1988, De Avila 1988). From this

time on, Native American students begin to drop behind many mainstream students in mathematics and science. Significant factors that influence the students' achievements are the language deficit, cultural differences between home and school cultures, and the excessive reliance in schools on abstraction (Davison 1994, 242). American Indians and Alaskan natives are more successful in learning when educational material takes advantage of their spatial and visual strengths (More 1989, Preston 1991, 2).

The American Association for the Advancement of Science (AAAS) prepared a document titled *Recommendations for the Improvement of Science and Mathematics for American Indians* (19) High school teachers are advised to teach science using an "ethnoscientific" approach. Ethnoscience is a field of study that attempts to delineate within a particular culture its patterns of perception, classification, and thought. Within the context of American Indian cultures, Gregory Cajete defines ethnoscience as "the methods, thought processes, mind sets, values, concepts, and experiences by which Native American groups understand, reflect, and obtain empirical knowledge about the natural world" (1986, 1). For example, in a lesson dealing with frogs, the subjective reaction (positive or negative) to touching the frog will be derived not only from students' individual personalities but also from their cultural backgrounds.

The AAAS also recommends use of a bilingual instruction modality when students have a strong preference for their native language. The final piece of advice is that teachers should actively recruit American Indian students for programs in science and technology (Green and Brown 1976). These recommendations raise three important issues in the improvement of science instruction for Native American students. How can educators achieve an effective balance between the traditional, home learning experiences of the students and the formal science curriculum? Which language should be the language of choice in the science curriculum? With regard to the more vigorous recruiting of Native American students for science and technology, what is the place of science teaching within the whole school curriculum for American Indians? (Davison 1994, 223).

Science as a Second Language

As was mentioned previously, the language that is first learned forms the primary foundation for the learning of subsequent languages. If one takes the position that science is a special kind of language for communicating information about nature, then the method of learning a language has an important implication for teaching and learning science. Science can be learned the same way young children naturally acquire a language system, that is, by immersion in an environment that is acquisition-rich in the language of science. Students can also learn new science constructs in the same way that new words and forms of a language are learned. For example, ideas and structures from the arts, humanities, or social sciences can be integrated into the presentation of science (Cajete 2000, 51).

Ideally, both home and school offer many opportunities to develop and apply this learning process. The more interesting and involving the material, the more the child is likely to learn. If the material comes from the known world of the child, then he or she has a familiar base from which to work. Familiarity is particularly important when leading the child to consider a new concept or idea.

Concrete Teaching Materials

Students from many non-Western cultures do not find the problems that are used in mathematics classes relevant to them (Saxe 1982). The reason can be linked to the fact that in the first three years of life, children have a great curiosity, and parents educate their children based on their own cultural stories. The word problems used in traditional Western classrooms are often based on white experience.

The challenge for teachers is to continue to nurture this natural curiosity. Many theories have been developed on how to keep students involved in learning. One of the important aspects of effective teaching is a focus on individual needs (More 1989).

When teaching mathematics, particularly in the earlier years, the use of materials that can be manipulated has been found to be most effective (Preston 1991, 3; Suydam and Weaver 1975). The use of hands-on materials helps those students whose primary learning mode is kinesthetic rather than abstract. Research shows (Burns 1975, 1986) that when students learn through the manipulations of real objects, they are able to retain their learning more easily. They need to be led from the concrete to pictorial representations and then to symbolic understandings. If students make these transitions successfully, they are better able to transfer their learning and understanding from one situation to another (Preston 1991, 3; Suydam, 1986). For a long time, educators have advocated the use of concrete aids in education (Brownwell 1935; Burns, 1986; Montessori 1965; Piaget 1952; Reys 1971; Davison 1994).

The use of concrete materials also lessens anxiety in the learning situation. Any class is composed of many different types of students, so the real challenge for the teacher is to appeal to the different learning styles through different learning materials and programs. An activity-centered approach in working with Indian students is one of the best ways to handle different learning styles. There is emerging evidence that students who are taught through the use of concrete materials will be more successful in their continuing education. This observation is supported by Indian students' preference for geometric tasks. Furthermore, the evidence suggests that Native American students can succeed in English-language mathematics if the problems make sense in terms of the way the students process information (Davison 1994, 248). The diversity of Native Americans themselves provides many opportunities for the development of a variety of learning materials, especially in mathematics and science.

Using Stories

A considerable number of schools in which Native American students are educated are located in isolated rural areas. Teachers in these schools face the daily challenge of not having ready access to the resources they need. However, a technique that is readily available to the teacher is storytelling. Storytelling has been traditionally used as a way of education among American Indians and Alaskan natives.

Native American students who do well in the basic functions of addition, subtraction, multiplication, and division often fail when it comes to solving word problems. These students may benefit from developing their own stories that call for mathematical reasoning. For example, how much flour would a family have to bring to a celebration to make a particular number of loaves of fried bread? By using occasions and events that are familiar to the students, teachers are able to approach mathematics in a way that lessens the potential of Native American students developing a fear of the subject area (Preston 1991, 5). The integration of reading, writing, conversing, and mathematics is supported by the whole language approach to education (Davison 1994, 249).

Rational versus Holistic Science

In mainstream education, a rational scientific view of the world is central. From the earliest days of missionary education to the days of BIA boarding-school education to the present, replacing the "primitive" beliefs of Native Americans with the "correct" beliefs of science has been an integral part of the school's curriculum. Most science educators have determined that if non-Western explanations of natural phenomena do not fit the Western scientific framework, they are not scientific. This approach to science discounts other perceptions, which may take into account data-collection methods that are different from those traditionally espoused in rationalistic science. The Western orientation has caused much conflict in Native American families, communities, and schools (Cajete 2000, 146).

A student from a traditional Indian background might be more inclined to see a scientific problem from a holistic point of view. A student from the majority culture might be more interested in breaking down the problem into its smallest components. These worldviews are variously termed. For example, the holistic view has been referred to as simultaneous processing and the Western view as sequential or analytical (Das, Kirby, and Jarman,1979, quoted in Preston 1991, 2). More (1989) uses the terms field-dependent, or relational, as opposed to field-independent, or analytical (More also says American Indians are more conscious of other people [More 1986, 10–11]). Maruyama and Harkins (as cited in Cajete 1986) state that American Indian systems tend to be more mutual and qualitative, whereas Western classification systems tend to be more hierarchical and quantitative. Western systems also tend to see cause-and-effect relationships as unidirectional, linear phenomena, whereas Indian thought patterns tend to allow for many possible directions in cause and effect. The interrelationships are emphasized. As Cajete explains, a given "cause and effect cannot be isolated from other causes and effects with which they share a holistic relationship within a system" (1986, 6).

Spirit and Reason: The Vine Deloria, Jr., Reader (1999, 140) gives an example of the relational Native American worldview. If a young Indian child sees an animal, it suggests to her or him that there are other life forms nearby. These related animals can be useful to the tribe and to the other animals in the area. For the Native American, nothing appears in isolation. All life is interrelated. The idea of interrelationship can form the base of a science curriculum.

Cajete (2000, 144) points out that in Native American society, learning how to hunt is a programmed sequence of observations and experiences.

1. Learning via mythology, listening, and observation the habits of the animal to be hunted
2. Learning via observation, intuition, and reasoning how to track, read appropriate signs, and stalk the animal
3. Learning via a mind-set the appropriate respect and ritual that is to be extended to the animal

4. Learning via an ecological ethic and technology how to care properly for the carcass of the animal
5. Learning how to utilize fully the various parts of the animal

All of these processes require a variety of teaching techniques that range from formal instruction to learning by doing. They must take place within a particular contextual framework necessary for conveying these forms of knowledge (Cajete 2000, 144). This process points to possible areas of discord between European American and Native American approaches to science education.

A Bicultural Approach

Native American students have different personal identities as tribal members and different levels of bicultural understandings and capabilities. A bicultural approach to science education allows students to continue to learn and live within the context of both their native and the mainstream cultures. This approach can result in positive attitudes toward science and a reaffirmation of students' tribal identities. Additionally, the bicultural approach to science instruction can go a long way toward providing a bridge between the different worldviews of a tribe and mainstream science.

The typical ways students learn science include such processes as investigation, discovery, experimentation, observation, defining, relating, comparing, inference making, communication, and classification (Holt 1977). It appears that regardless of the level of scientific sophistication, as they interact with their environment, people use some or all of these processes to develop their survival technologies.

A number of Native American students can be classified as being English dominant in their language usage. Others have encountered in their homes and communities varying degrees of traditionalism in native language use and in interpreting the natural world. Some identify strongly with both the cultural and linguistic revitalization of their particular tribal group. It is important for a teacher to know and understand these factors because they have important ramifications in teaching science. Students who identify closely with their tribal roots can be strongly motivated to learn about science and its role in relation to some aspects of their tribal heritage.

As Cole and Scribner point out, the way people perceive and classify their environment varies across cultures (1974, 5). Given differences between Native American and Western science, teachers are faced with how best to develop a science program. Teachers need to be mindful that there is both an ideal and a realistic implementation of any approach to education. If teachers begin with the premise that teaching is a communicative art, they can apply methods found in the research to be effective by building a language base to explain the complexities encountered in the classroom (Cajete 2000, 148).

Many activities that are already an integral part of American Indian cultures can be applied to formal science education. Native American children, like all children, bring with them to school knowledge, skills, and experiences that can be related to the school's curriculum. For example, Indian children may have had firsthand experience with raising cattle or bison, growing wheat and corn. These experiences can be used as the foundation from which to study other areas of science, for example, ecology, climate, geology, and genetics.

The task of the teacher becomes one of creating an acquisition-rich, science-process environment. To achieve such an environment, teachers can take students on field trips museums and to different ecosystems in the local area. National and state parks also provide a multitude of different opportunities for the study of science in a natural setting. Hands-on activities with materials from the kitchen, laundry, and other areas of the house can alert students to science as a process taking place all around them. Teachers are challenged to present science as both a discipline and a cultural system of thought (Ovando and Collier 1994, 163).

Differing scientific worldviews do not necessarily mean mutually exclusive approaches to formal science lessons. Rather than taking an approach that supports either Western scientific thought or the Native American view of science, the school science curriculum would be enriched by embracing both views. Native Americans' experience of science education can be enhanced when the school builds on the home cultures of the students who, in turn, are introduced to the approaches of Western science (Ovando, 1994, 226). Just as learning a new language provides a valuable perspective on the culture of a particular people, so science provides a valuable perspective on culture. A unique and valuable learning opportunity is provided when teachers compare the Native American view of science with the Western view. Such an approach can broaden the perspectives of both groups of students and liberate them from a single cultural viewpoint (Cajete, 2000, 151).

G. Guthridge in an article titled "Eskimos Solve the Future" (1986), describes how he uses the students' own cultural frame of reference to solve future problems. Guthridge trained teams of students from Gambell, Alaska, to compete in the Future Problem Solving Program. The steps involved in this model were originally designed with a Western mind-set and required a great deal of verbal interaction among the students. Guthridge, however, accepted the students' use of their own communication style and pace until it felt comfortable and necessary to move toward more verbal articulation of ideas. He credits the Gambell students' success in coming up with highly imaginative solutions to future problems to the flexibility in approach. Students used learning strategies that had served their hunting ancestors well for millennia. At the same time, they acquired skill in using Western problem-solving techniques that they might someday apply to local issues. Regarding the Western worldview versus the native worldview, Guthridge tells his students that "the human brain is nothing more—and nothing less—than an efficient computer. Why not give it two types of software?" (1986, 72).

SUMMARY

Teachers need to view the diversity of Native Americans themselves as resources that provide many opportunities for the development of a variety of learning materials, especially in mathematics and science. All children benefit when they are given the opportunity to work with materials and situations that come from their experiences. All students need to be taught in ways that build on their strengths.

REFERENCES AND FURTHER READING

Almprese, J. A., W. J. Erianger, and N. Brigham. 1989. *No Gift Wasted: Effective Strategies for Educating Highly Able, Disadvantaged Students in Mathematics and Science.* Washington, DC: Department of Education.

Anderson, H.O. 1990. "The NCTM Curriculum and Evaluation Standards for School Mathematics: A Science Educator's Perspective." *School Science and Mathematics* 90, no 6: 544–549.

Attneave, C. 1977. "The Wasted Strengths of American Indian Families." In Steven Unger, ed., *The Destruction of Indian Families.* New York: Association on American Indian Affairs.

Bad Wound, E. 1991. "Teaching to Empower: Tribal Colleges Must Promote Leadership and Self Determination in Their Reservation." *Tribal College Journal* 3, no. 1: 15–19.

Banks, J. A. 1975. *Teaching Strategies for Ethnic Studies.* Boston, MA: Allyn and Bacon, 1975.

———. 1988. *Multiethnic Education: Theory and Practice.* 2nd ed. Boston, MA: Allyn and Bacon.

Baratta-Lorton, M. 1976. *Mathematics Their Way.* Menlo Park, CA: Addison-Wesley.

Baruth, L. G., and M. Lee Manning. 1992. "Understanding Native American Children and Adolescents." In M. Lee Manning, ed., *Multicultural Education of Children and Adolescents.* Boston, MA: Allyn and Bacon.

Bearden, L. J., W. A. Spencer, and J. C. Moracco. 1989. "A Study of High School Dropouts." *The School Counselor* 27: 113–120.

Bennet, C. I. 1986. *Comprehensive Multicultural Education: Theory and Practice.* Boston, MA: Allyn and Bacon.

Brophy, J. E. 1990. *Effective Schooling for Disadvantaged Students, Better Schooling for the Children of Poverty: Alternatives to Conventional Wisdom.* Washington, D.C. U.S. Department of Education.

Brown, G. L. 1991. "Reading and Language Arts Curricula in Elementary and Secondary Education for American Indians and Alaska Natives." In *Indian Nations at Risk: Solutions for the 1990s.* Washington, DC: Department of Education.

Bruner, J. S. 1996. *The Culture of Education.* Cambridge, MA: Harvard University Press.

Burns, M. 1975. *The I Hate Mathematics Book.* Boston: Little, Brown.

———. 1986. "Teaching 'What to Do' in Arithmetic vs. 'What to do and Why.'" *Educational Leadership* 43: 34–48.

Butterfield, R. A. 1995. *A Monograph for Using and Developing Culturally Appropriate Curricula for American Indian Students.* Portland, OR. Northwest Regional Education Laboratory.

Cajete, G. 1986. *Ethnoscience: A Native American Perspective.* Phoenix, AZ: Native American Science Education Association Conference.

———. 1986. Science: A Native American Perspective—A Culturally Based Science Education Curriculum. Ph.D. diss., International College.

———. 1994. *Look to the Mountain: An Ecology of Indigenous Education.* Durango, CO: Kivaki Press.

———. 2000. "The Native American Learner and Bicultural Science Education." In Karen G. Swisher and John W. Tippeconnic III, eds., *Next Steps: Research and Practice to Advance Indian Education.* Charleston, WV: Clearinghouse on Rural Education and Small Schools.

Carter, F. 1986. *The Education of Little Tree.* Albuquerque: University of New Mexico Press.

Chamot, A. U. 1985. "English Language Development through a Content-based Approach." In *Issues in English Language Development.* Rosslyn, VA: National Clearinghouse for Bilingual Education.

Charleston, G. M. and G. L. King. 1991. *Indian Nations at Risk Task Force: Listen to the People.* Washington, DC: Department of Education.

Cole, M., and S. Scribner. 1974. *Culture and Thought: A Psychological Introduction.* New York: John Wiley.

Crawford, J. 1989. *Bilingual Education: History, Politics, Theory, and Practice.* Trenton, NJ: Crane.

Cummins, J. 1984. *Bilingualism and Special Education: Issues in Assessment and Pedagogy.* San Diego, CA: College Hill.

———. 1989. "Empowering Minority Students: A Framework for Intervention." *Harvard Educational Review* 56, no 1: 18–36.

———. 1990. "Language Development among Aboriginal Children in Northern Communities." Report prepared under contract with the government of the Yukon for presentation at the Circumpolar Education Conference, Umea, Sweden.

Das, J. P., J. Kirby, and R. F. Jarman. 1979. *Simulataneous and Successive Cognitive Processes.* New York: Academic Press.

Davison, D. M. 1994. "An Ethnomathematics Approach to Teaching Language Minority Students." In Jon Reyhner, ed., *Effective Language Education Practices and Native Language Survival.* Choctaw, OK: Native American Language Issues.

———. 1994. "Mathematics." In J. Reyhner, ed., *Teaching American Indian Students.* Norman: University of Oklahoma Press.

De Avila, E. A. 1988. "Bilingualism, Cognitive Function, and Language Minority Group Membership." In Rodney R. Cocking and Jose P. Maestre, eds., *Linguistic and Cultural Influences on Learning Mathematics.* Hillsdale, NJ: Erlbaum.

Deloria, Vine Jr. 1990. "Transitional Education." *Winds of Change* (winter).

———. 1991. "Higher Education and Self-Determination." *Winds of Change* 6, no. 1: 18–25.

———. 1999. *Spirit and Reason: The Vine Deloria, Jr. Reader.* Golden, CO: Fulcrum.

Department of Education. 1991. *Indian Nations at Risk: Solutions for the 1990s.* Washington, DC: Department of Education.

Dodd, J. M., et al. 1995. "American Indian Student Retention." *NASPA Journal* 33, no. 1: 72–78.

Dualy, H., M. Burt, and S. Krashen. 1982. *Language Two.* New York: Oxford University Press.

Dunn, R. 1983. "Learning Styles and Their Relation to Exceptionality at Both Ends of the Spectrum." *Exceptional Children* 49, no. 6: 496–506.

FairTest. 1995. *Implementing Performance Assessments: A Guide to Classroom, School and System Reform.* Cambridge, MA: National Center for Fair and Open Testing.

Feest, C. F. 1980. *Native Arts of North America.* New York: Oxford University Press.

Fox, S. 1986. "The Whole Language Approach to Language Arts for the Indian Student." In Jon Reyhner, ed., *Teaching the Indian Child: A Bilingual Multicultural Approach.*. Billings, MT: Eastern Montana College Press.

———. 1988. "A Whole Language Approach to Communication Skills." In Hap Gilliland, ed., *Teaching the Native American*. Billings, MT: Council for Indian Education.

———. 1990. "Literacy for the American Indian: A Case Study in the Intergenerational Transfer of Cognitive Skills." In Thomas Sticht, ed., *Applied Behavior and Cognitive Skills*. San Diego, CA: Ablex.

Fuchs, E., and R. J. Havighurst. 1972. *To Live on This Earth: American Indian Education*. Garden City, NY: Doubleday.

Garrod, A., and C. Larimore, eds. 1997. *First Person, First Peoples: Native American Graduates Tell Their Life Stories*. New York: Cornell University Press.

Gilliland, H. 1995. *Teaching the Native American*. 3rd ed. Dubuque, IA: Kendall/Hunt.

Glasser, W. 1986. *Control Theory in the Classroom*. New York: Harper and Row.

Glatthorn, A. A. 1987. *Curriculum Renewal*. Alexandria, VA: Association for Supervision and Curriculum Development.

Goodman, K. S. 1986. *What's Whole in Whole Language*. Richmond Hill, ON: Scholastic.

Green, R., and J. W. Brown. 1976. *Recommendations for the Improvement of Science and Mathematics Education for American Indians*. Washington, DC: American Association for the Advancement of Science.

Greenbaum, P. E. 1985. "Nonverbal Differences in Communication Style between American Indian and Anglo Elementary Classrooms." *American Education Research Journal* 22, no. 1: 101–115.

Guthridge, G. 1986. "Eskimos Solve the Future." *Analog* (April): 67–72.

Hakuta, K. 1986. *Mirror of Language: The Debate on Bilingualism*. New York: Basic Books.

Heth, C., and S. Guyette. 1985. *Issues for the Future of American Indian Studies: A Needs Assessment and Program Guide*. ERIC No. ED 316 374. Los Angeles: University of California at Los Angeles, American Indian Studies Center.

Holt, B. 1977. *Science with Young Children*. Washington, DC: National Association for the Education of Young Children.

Hudelson, S. 1989. *Write On: Children Writing in ESL*. Englewood Cliffs, NJ: Center for Applied Linguistics and Prentice Hall Regents.

Huff, D. 1997. *To Live Heroically: Institutional Racism and American Indian Education*. Albany: State University of New York Press.

Johnson, D. W., and T. T. Johnson. 1987. *Learning Together and Alone*. 2nd ed. Englewood Cliffs, NJ: Prentice-Hall.

Justiz, M. J., ed. 1994. *Minorities in Higher Education*. ERIC No. ED 372 716. Phoenix: Oryx Press.

Krashen, S. D. 1981. *Second Language Acquisition and Second Language Learning.* New York: Pergamon Press, 1981.

———. 1981. "Bilingual Education and Second Language Acquisition Theory." In *Schooling and Language Minority Students: A Theoretical Framework.* Los Angeles: Evaluation, Dissemination, and Assessment Center, California State University, pp. 52–79.

———. 1982. *Principles and Practice in Second Language Acquisition.* New York: Pergamon Press.

———. 1982. "Theory versus Practice in Language Training." In R. W. Blair, ed., *Innovative Approaches to Language Teaching.* Rowley, MA: Newbury House.

———. 1983. "Newmark's 'Ignorance Hypothesis' and Current Second Language Acquisition Theory." In S. Cass and L. Selinker, eds., *Language Transfer in Language Learning.* Rowley, MA: Newbury House.

———. 1984. *Writing : Research, Theory, and Application.* New York: Pergamon Press.

———. 1985. *Inquiries and Insights: Selected Essays.* Haywood, CA: Alemany.

Krashen, S., and D. Biber. 1988. *On Course: Bilingual Education's Success in California.* Sacramento: California Association for Bilingual Education.

Leap, W. L. 1979. "American Indian English and Its Implications for Bilingual Education." In J. Alatis, ed., *International Dimensions of Bilingual Education.* Washington, DC: Georgetown University Press.

———. 1981. "American Indian Language Maintenance." In B. I. Siegel, ed., *Annual Review of Anthropology.* Palo Alto: Annual Reviews.

———. 1988. "Assumptions and Strategies Guiding Mathematics Word Problem-solving by Ute Indian Students." In Rodney R. Cocking and Jose P. Maestre, eds., *Linguistic and Cultural Influences on Learning Mathematics.* Hillsdale, NJ: Erlbaum.

Lindfors, J. W. 1987. *Children's Language and Learning.* 2d ed. Englewood Cliffs, NJ: Prentice Hall.

McCarty, T. L., and R. Schaffer. 1994. "Language and Literacy Development." In Jon Reyhner, ed., *Teaching American Indian Students.* Norman: University of Oklahoma Press.

———. 1994. "Language and Literacy in Native American Classrooms." In Jon Reyhner, ed., *American Indian Education: History, Research, Theory, and Practice.* Norman: University of Oklahoma Press.

Moll, L. C., and S. Diaz. 1987. "Change as the Goal of Educational Research." *Anthropology and Education Quarterly* 18: 300–311.

Montessori, M. 1965. *Dr. Montessori's Own Handbook.* New York: Schocken.

More, A. J. 1989. "Native Indian Learning Styles: A Review for Researchers and Teachers." *Journal of American Indian Education* (August): 15–28.

National Commission on Excellence in Education. 1983. *A Nation at Risk: The*

Imperative for Educational Reform. Washington, DC: Government Printing Office.

National Research Council. 1987. *Everybody Counts: A Report to the Nation on the Future of Mathematics Education.* Washington, DC: National Academy Press.

Native Education Initiative, Regional Educational Laboratory Network. 1995. *Promising Programs in Native Education.* ERIC No. ED 385 420. Palatka, FL: South Eastern Regional Vision for Education.

Neihardt, J. G., and Black Elk. 1961. *Black Elk Speaks: Being the Life Story of a Holy Man of the Oglala Sioux.* New York: W. Morrow, 1932; reprint, Lincoln: University of Nebraska Press.

Nel, J. 1994. "Preventing School Failure: The Native American Child." In *Preventing School Failure.* Washington, DC: Heldref.

Ogbu, J. U. 1992. "Understanding Cultural Diversity and Learning." *Educational Researcher* 21, no. 8: 5–14.

Okebbukola, P. A. 1986. "The Influence of Preferred Learning Styles on Cooperative Learning in Science." *Science Education* 70, no. 5: 509–517.

Ovando, C. J. 1994. "Science." In Jon Reyhner, ed., *Teaching American Indian Students.* Norman: University of Oklahoma Press.

Ovando, C. J., and V. P. Collier. 1985. *Bilingual and ESL Classrooms.* New York: McGraw-Hill.

Palsano, E. L. 1993. *We the . . . First Americans.* Washington, DC: U.S. Department of Commerce.

Pepper, F. C. 1985. *Understanding Indian Students: Behavioral Learning Styles.* Portland, OR: Northwest Regional Educational Laboratory.

Piaget, J. 1952. *The Child's Concept of Numbers.* New York: Humanities Press.

Preston, V. 1991. "Mathematics and Science Curricula in Elementary and Secondary Education for American Indian and Alaska Native Students." In *Indian Nations at Risk: Solutions for the 1990s.* Washington, DC: Department of Education.

Ramirez, M., and A. Castenada. 1974. *Cultural Democracy, Bicognitive Development, and Education.* New York: Academic Press.

Reys, R. E. 1971. "Considerations for Teaching Using Manipulative Materials." *Arithmetic Teacher* 18: 552.

Rutter, M., B. Maughan, P. Mortimore, and J. Ouston. 1979. *Fifteen Thousand Hours: Secondary Schools and their Effects on Children.* Cambridge, MA: Harvard University Press.

Saxe, G. B. 1982. "Culture and the Development of Numerical Cognition: Studies among the Oksapmin of Papua New Guinea." In Charles J. Bainerd, ed., *Children's Logical and Mathematical Cognition.* New York: Springer-Verlag.

Steward, R. J. 1993. "Two Faces of Academic Success: Case Studies of American

Indians on a Predominantly Anglo University Campus." *Journal of College Student Development* 34, no. 3: 191–196.

Suydam, M. N. 1986. "Manipulative Materials and Achievement." *Arithmetic Teacher* 33: 10–32.

Suydam, M. N., and F. Weaver. 1975. "Research on Learning Mathematics." In J. N. Payne, ed., *Mathematics Learning Early Childhood.* Reston, VA: National Council of Teachers of Mathematics.

Swisher, K. G. 1994. "American Indian Learning Styles Survey: An Assessment of Teacher Knowledge." *Journal of Educational Issues of Language Minority Students* 13: 59–77.

———. 1996. "The Haskell Indian Nations University Model for Elementary Teacher Education." *American Indian Quarterly* 20, no. 1: 83–90.

Tafoya, T. 1989. "Coyote's Eyes: Native Cognition Styles." *Journal of American Indian Education* (August): 29–42.

Talbot, S. 1994. "Indian Students and Reminiscences of Alcatraz." *American Indian Culture and Research Journal* 18, no. 4: 93–102.

Tikunoff, R. 1984. *An Emerging Description of Successful Bilingual Instruction: Executive Summary of Part I of the Significant Bilingual Instructional Features Study.* San Francisco: Far West Laboratory.

Trueba, H. T. 1988. "Culturally Based Explanations of Minority Students' Academic Achievement." *Anthropology and Education Quarterly* 19, no. 3: 270–287.

U.S. Department of Education, Office of Education Research and Improvement. 1997. *Assessment of Student Performance.* Washington, DC: U.S. Department of Education.

Verano, J., and D. Ubelaker. 1992. *Disease and Demography in the Americas.* Washington, DC: Smithsonian Institution Press.

Wade, E. 1986. *The Arts of the North American Indian: Traditions in Evolution.* New York: Hudson Hills Press in association with Philbrook Art Center, Tulsa.

Watahomigie, L. J., and A. Y. Yamamoto. 1987. "Linguistics in Action: The Hualapai Bilingual/Bicultural Education Program." In Donald Stull and Jean J. Schensul, eds., *Collaborative Research and Social Change: Applied Anthropology in Action.* Boulder, CO: Westview Press, pp. 77–98.

White House Conference on Indian Education. 1992. *Final Report of the White House Conference on Indian Education.* ERIC No. ED 353 124. Washington, DC: Government Printing Office.

Whiteman, H.V. 1978. "Native American Studies, the University, and the Indian Student." In T. Thompson, ed., *The Schooling of Native America.* Washington, DC: American Association of Colleges for Teacher Education.

Chapter Seven

•◦ Associations, Organizations, and Tribal Entities

AMERICAN INDIAN ORGANIZATIONS

American Indian Archaeological Institute (AIAI)
38 Curtis Rd.
P.O. Box 1260
Washington Green, CT 06793-0260
Phone: (203) 868-0518
Fax: (203) 868-1649

Provides information on the Northeastern woodlands tribes of the United States including a 2000 volume library and museum center.

American Indian College Fund (AICF)
217 E. 85th St., Ste. 201
New York, NY 10028
Phone: (212) 988-4155
(800) 776-3863
Fax: (212) 734-5118

Helps fund tribally controlled colleges.

American Indian Council of Architects and Engineers (AICAE)
11675 S.W. 66th Ave.
Portland, OR 97223
Phone: (503) 639-4914
Fax: (503) 620-2743

Represents American Indian-owned firms on a national level. Encourages students in the field.

American Indian Culture Research Center (AICRC)
Box 98
Blue Cloud Abbey

Marvin, SD 57251
Phone: (605) 432-5528

Aids in educating the non-Indian public about the philosophy of Native American people and assists in rebuilding communities.

American Indian Curricula Development Program
United Tribes Technical College
3315 University Drive
Bismarck, ND 58501

Produces curricula and teacher guides relevant to Indian and non-Indian students in grades K–12.

American Indian Graduate Center (AIGC)
Montgomery Blvd., NE, Ste. 1-B
Alburquerque, NM 87109
Phone: (505) 881-4584

Provides scholarship assistance.

American Indian Health Care Association (AIHCA)
245 E. 6th St., Ste. 499
St. Paul, MN 55101
Phone: (612) 293-0233

Assists urban healthcare centers in management and education.

American Indian Heritage Foundation (AIHF)
6051 Arlington Blvd.
Falls Church, VA 22044
Phone: (202) 463-4267

Educates non-Indians on cultural heritage of Native Americans. Maintains a museum and 250 volume library.

American Indian Higher Education Consortium (AIHEC)
513 Capitol Court NE. Ste. 100
Washington, DC 20002
Phone: (202) 544-9289
Fax: (202) 544-4084

Organization of tribally controlled colleges in the United States and Canada.

American Indian Historical Society (AIHS)
1493 Masonic Avenue
San Francisco, CA 94117
Phone: (415) 626-5235

Offers support for educational and cultural programs.

American Indian Library Association (AILA)
American Library Association
50 E. Huron St.
Chicago, IL 60611

Dedicated to providing assistance to Native Americans in library services.

American Indian Registry for the Performing Arts (AIRPA)
1717 N. Highland, Ste. 614
Los Angeles, CA 90028
Phone: (213) 962-6574

Organization of American Indian performers and technical personnel in the entertainment field.

American Indian Research and Development (AIRD)
2424 Springer Dr., Ste. 200
Norman, OK 73069
Phone: (405) 364-0656
Fax: (405) 364-5464

Seeks to improve the quality of education for the gifted Native American student.

American Indian Science and Education Center
1085 14th St., Ste. 1506
Boulder, CO 80302
Phone: (303) 492-8658

Provides educational assistance and maintains a 1500 volume library.

American Indian Science and Engineering Society (AISES)
1085 14th St., Ste. 1506
Boulder, CO 80302
Phone: (303) 492-8658
Fax: (303) 492-7090
aiseshq@spot.colorado.edu

Motivates students to pursue graduate studies in the field. Offers scholarships.

Americans for Indian Opportunity (AIO)
3508 Garfield St. NW
Washington, DC 20007
Phone: (202) 338-8809

Helps in establishing self-help programs in education, health, housing, job development and training opportunities.

Americans for Restitution and Rightings of Old Wrongs (ARROW, Inc.)
1000 Connecticut Ave., NW, Ste. 1206
Washington, DC 20036
Phone: (202) 296-0685

Seeks to improve standard of living for Native Americans.

Association of American Indian Physicians (AAIP)
10015 S. Pennsylvania, Bldg. D
Oklahoma City, OK 73159
Phone: (405) 692-1202

Organization of American Indian Physicians that encourages Native youth in the health profession.

Association of Community Tribal Schools (ACTS)
c/o Dr. Roger Bordeaux
616 4th Ave., W.
Sisseton, SD 57262-1349
Phone: (605) 698-3112

Advocates Indian self-determination and tribally controlled schools.

Association on American Indian Affairs (AAIA)
245 5th Avenue
New York, NY 10016
Phone: (212) 689-8720

Provides legal and technical assistance to tribes in education, health, and economic development.

Cherokee National Historical Society (CNHS)
P. O. Box 515
Tahlequah, OK 74465
Phone: (918) 456-6007

Preserves history and tradition of the Cherokee people and assists in educating the general public.

Choctaw Heritage Press

Mississippi Band of Choctaw Indians
Route 7, Box 71
Philadelphia, MS 39350

This press specializes in materials of an authentic nature that deal with the Mississippi Band of Choctaw Indians. The compasny also rents video tapes.

Coalition for Indian Education (CIA)

3620 Wyoming Blvd. NE, Ste. 206
Albuquerque, NM 87111
Phone: (505) 275-9788

Organization of Native American educators working to provide quality education.

Concerned American Indian Parents (CAIP)

CUHCC Clinic
2016 16th Ave., S.
Minneapolis, MN 55404
Phone: (612) 627-6888

Seeks to improve racist conditions that face Native American children.

Council for Indian Education (CIE)

517 Rimrock Rd.
Billings, MT 59102
Phone: (406) 252-7451

Seeks to improve education for Native Americans.

Council for Native American Indians (CNAIP)

280 Broadway, Ste. 316
New York, NY 10007
Phone: (212) 732-0485

Organization of individuals interested in philosophy and teachings of the earlier indigenous groups. Conducts research.

Council of Energy Resource Tribes (CERT)

1999 Broadway, Ste. 2600
Denver, CO 80202
Phone: (303) 297-2378

Provides technical assistance to tribes owning energy resources.

Daybreak Star Press
Daybreak Star Cultural/Educational Center
Discovery Park
P.O. Box 100
Seattle, WA 98199

Offers materials ranging from preschool through high school level.

First Nations Development Institute (FNDI)
69 Kelley Road
Falmouth, VA 22405
Phone: (703) 371-5615

Helps tribes achieve self-sufficiency by promoting economic development and commercial enterprise.

Gathering of Nations
P. O. Box 75102, Sta. 14
Albuquerque, NM 87120-1269
Phone: (505) 836-2810

Promotes the expression of Native American culture and religion.

Indian Arts and Crafts Association (IACA)
La Veta Drive NE, Ste. B
Albuquerque, NM 87108
Phone: (505) 265-9149

Promotes, preserves, protects the understanding of authentic American Indian arts and crafts.

Indian Country Press
202 Walnut
Irving Park Offices
St. Paul, MN 55102

Indian Country Press produces and distributes educational publications associated with the Red School House of St. Paul.

Minneapolis Public Schools
Planning, Development, and Evaluation Department
807 Northeast Broadway
Minneapolis, MN 55413

A staff of Native curriculum writers, housed within the Minneapolis Public School system has produced an array of materials ranging from language arts to arts and crafts

Navajo Curriculum Center Press
Rough Rock Demonstration School
Star Route One
Rough Rock, AZ 86503

This press publishes a wide variety of materials designed to preserve the artistic and cultural heritage of the Dineh/Navajo Nation.

University of Arkansas at Little Rock
Dept. of English
2801 S. University Ave.
Little Rock, AR 72204
Phone: (501) 569-3160

Promotes research concerning the American Native Press.

GOVERNMENT AGENCIES

Bureau of Indian Affairs
Office of Education
1849 C Street, NW
Washington, DC 20240-0001
Phone: (202) 219-3711
Fax: (202) 501-1516
www.oiep.bia.edu

The Bureau of Indian Affairs (BIA) Indian School Equalization Program (ISEP) funds tribally and BIA-operated day schools, boarding schools, and dormitories. These monies can be used for instruction, including blingual instruction; boarding and dormitory expenses; exceptional-student education; transportation; intense counseling for students in residence; school maintenance and repairs; school board training; and prekindergarten expenditures (Brescia 1991, 8).

The BIA program for the Institutionalized Handicapped is required to provide services and special education for students with disabilities at no cost to parents. It also provides funds to each school board to train board members in such areas as fiscal management, philosophy of education, and the legal aspects of school and board membership.

Additionally the BIA has programs that fund students' transportation and the technical-support program. In the technical support program the BIA provides assistance to the director, Office of Indian Education Programs along with technical assistance, training, and advice to local school boards and other Native community members (Brescia 1991, 9).

The adult education program of the BIA provides Native Americans with the resources to complete high school and prepare for the General Education Development Test. Generally those adults who have had less than five years of formal schooling are eligible for the adult-education programs.

Indian Health Service Scholarship Program
12300 Twinbrook Parkway, Suite 100
Rockville, MD 20852
Phone: (301) 443-6197
Fax: (301) 443-6048
www.hqe.his.gov

The Health Professions Scholarship Program provides financial assistance for American Indian and Alaska Native (Federally recognized only) students only enrolled in health professions and allied health profession programs. With this program, there are service obligations and payback requirements that the recipient incurs upon acceptance of the funding.

U.S. Department of Education
Through the Department of Education, institutions of higher education as well as native governments and organizations may negotiate grants or contracts for in-service training for teaching and administering special education projects for native students. In addition, native students may apply for fellowships to continue their education at the graduate level. National Workplace Literacy grants are open to institutions of higher learning, schools, businesses, private industry, state and local education agencies, and labor organizations. The money from these grants pays for the federal portion of adult-education programs that teach literacy skills to workers.

Learning Technologies Division
555 New Jersey Avenue, NW
Washington, DC 20208-5544
Phone: (202) 219-2097
Fax: (202) 208-4042
www.ed.gov/prog_info/StarSchools

The Learning Technologies Division operates the Star Schools Program. The Program provides for telecommunication partnerships with local school districts, state departments of education, public broadcasting entities and other public and private organizations. The grants are for telecommunications projects to encourage improved instruction in mathematics, science, foreign languages, vocational education, and other subjects to serve underserved populations. The Star Schools Program is one of the largest and most successful public and private partnerships for delivering distance education. The program provides for access for technology, telecommunications equipment and instructional programs.

The Star Schools projects deliver distance education courses and services using such technologies as satellite delivery systems, open broadcasts, cable, and the Internet. Through this program schools have access to instructional programming, including hands-on science and mathematics, algebra, calculus, physics, advanced placement courses, foreign language courses, workplace skills, and life skills programs. Instructional programs serve K–12 students and adult learners, including limited English-proficient students and disabled students and adult learners.

Office of Bilingual Education and Minority Languages Affairs (OBEMLA)
330 C St. SW
Washington, DC 20202
Phone: (202) 205-5463
Fax: (202) 205-8737
www.ed.gov/offices/OBEMLA

Office of Elementary and Secondary Education
400 Maryland Ave, Rm. 3E223, FOB-6
Washington, DC. 20202-6140
Phone: (202) 260-9198
Fax: (202) 205-5630
www.ed.gov/EdRes/EdFed/EdTechCtrs.htm

Office of Postsecondary Education (OPE)
1990 K St., NW
Washington, DC 20006-8500
Phone: (202) 502-7777
Fax: (202) 502-7681
www.ed.gov/offices/OPE

U.S. Department of the Interior

Vocational education money was allocated through the secretary of interior in 1956. These funds can be used to develop vocational training programs for Native Americans who reside on or near reservations. Programs that are funded under this scheme include on-the-job training, vocational and guidance counseling, apprenticeships, and institutional training. Contracts may be established with federal, state, and local government agencies as well as with a private school that is authorized to provide vocational education or training. Funds are allocated to federally recognized tribes and Alaska native villages (Brescia 1991, 11).

Library resources funds are available to offer or increase the quality of library services to Native Americans on or near reservations. Money from the program can be used for purchase of library materials and the training of library staff. Grants are made to Native American governments and Alaska.

White House Initiative on Tribal Colleges and Universities
330 C St., S.W. Room 4050 MES
Washington, DC 20202
Phone: (202) 260-5714
Fax: (202) 260-5702
www.hqe.his.gov

PRIVATE FUNDING SOURCES

Bush Foundation
332 Minnesota Street, East 900
St. Paul, MN 55101
Phone: (651) 227-0891
Fax: (651) 297-6481
www.bushfoundation.org

Ford Foundation
320 East 43rd St
New York, NY 10017
Phone: (212) 573-5000
Fax: (212) 573-3677
www.fordfoundation.org

Kellogg Foundation
One Michigan Avenue East
Battle Creek, MI 49017-4058
Phone: (616) 968-0413
Fax: (616) 968-0413
www.wkkf.org

National Science Foundation
Mathematics and science grant money has been set aside by the National Science Foundation Program for Partnerships in Education for Mathematics, Science, and Engineering. Local education entities can apply for grants to improve the quality of instruction, to award scholarships, and to purchase equipment for these areas.

PROFESSIONAL ORGANIZATIONS

American Education Research Association (AERA)
1230 17th St.
Washington, DC 20036-3078

Association for the Study of American Indian Literatures (ASAIL)
Department of English
Fort Lewis College
Durango, CO 81301

Council on Anthropology and Education (CAE)
1703 New Hampshire Ave. NW
Washington, DC 20009

D'Arcy McNicke Center for the History of the American Indian
Newberry Library
60 W. Walton St.
Chicago, IL 60610

ERIC Clearinghouse on Rural Education and Small Schools (ERIC/CRESS)
Appalachia Educational Laboratory
P.O. Box 1348
Charleston, WV 25325
http://ercir.syr.edu/plweb-cgi

International Reading Association (IRA)
800 Barksdale Rd.
P.O. Box 8139
Newark, DE 19714-8139
Phone: (302) 731-1600

Haulapai Bilingual Academic Excellence Program
P.O. Box 138
Peach Springs, AZ 86434
Phone: (602) 769-2202

Joint Committee for Languages (JNCL)
300 Eye St. NE
Washington, DC 20002
Phone: (202) 546-7855

National Association for Bilingual Education (NABE)
1220 L Street NW, Suite 605
Washington, DC 20005-4018
Phone: (202) 898-1829

National Council of Teachers of English (NCTE)
1111 Kenyon Rd.
Urbana, IL 61801

Native American Language Issues (NALI)
P.O. Box 963
Choctaw, OK 73020

Native American Research Information Service
American Indian Institute
555 Constitution Ave.
Norman, OK 73037

Teachers of English to Speakers of Other Languages (TESOL)
1600 Cameron St., Suite 300
Alexandria, VA 22314-2705
(703) 836-0744

TRIBAL COLLEGES IN THE UNITED STATES

Bay Mills Community College
12214 West Lakeshore Drive
Brimley, MI 49715

Blackfeet Community College
P.O. Box 819
Browning, MT 59417

Cankdeska Cikana Community College
P.O. Box 269
Fort Totten, ND 58335

College of Menominee Nation
P.O. Box 1179
Keshena, WI 54135

Crownpoint Institute of Technology
P.O. Box 849
Crownpoint, NM 87313

Diné College
P.O. Box 126
Tsaile, AZ 86556

D-Q University
P.O. Box 409
Davis, CA 95617

Dull Knife Memorial College
P.O. Box 98
Lame Deer, MT 59043

Fond du Lac Tribal and Community College
2101 14th Street
Cloquet, MN 55720

Fort Belknap College
P.O. Box 159
Harlem, MT 59526

Fort Berthold Community College
P.O. Box 490
New Town, ND 58763

Fort Peck Community College
P.O. Box 398
Poplar, MT 59255

Haskell Indian Nations University
155 Indian Avenue
Lawrence, KS 66046-4800

Institute of American Indian Arts
83 Avan Nu Po Road
Santa Fe, NM 87505

Keweenaw Bay Ojibwa
Community College
107 Bear Town Rd
Baraga, MI 49908

Lac Courte Oreilles Ojibwa Community College
13466 West Trepania Road
Hayward, WI 54843

Leech Lake Tribal College
6530 U.S. Highway 2 NW
Cass Lake, MN 56633

Little Big Horn College
1 Forest Lane
Crow Agency, MT 59022

Little Priest Tribal College
P.O. Box 270
Winnebago, NE 68071

Nebraska Indian Community College
P.O. Box 428
Macy, NE 68039

Northwest Indian College
2522 Kwina Road
Bellingham, WA 98226

Oglala Lakota College
P.O. Box 490
Kyle, SD 57752

Salish Kootenai College
P.O. Box 117
Pablo, MT 59855

Sinte Gleska University
P.O. Box 490
Rosebud, SD 57570

Sisseton Wahpeton Community College
P.O. Box 689, Agency Village
Sisseton, SD 57262

Si Tanka College/Huron University
P.O. Box 220
Eagle Butte, SD 57625

Sitting Bull College
1341 92nd Street
Fort Yates, ND 58538

Southwestern Indian Polytechnic Institute
9169 Coors NW
Albuquerque, NM 87184

Stone Child College
RR1, Box 1082
Box Elder, MT 59521

Turtle Mountain Community College
P.O. Box 340
Belcourt, ND 58316

United Tribes Technical College
3315 University Drive
Bismarck, ND 58504

White Earth Tribal and Community College
210 Main Street South
P.O. Box 478
Mahnomen, MN 56557

TRIBAL CONTACTS AND STATE-RECOGNIZED TRIBES

Alabama (6)

Contact Ms. Darla F. Graves, Executive Director, Alabama Indian Affairs Commission, One Court Square, Suite 106, Montgomery, AL 36104, (334) 242-2831

Tribes: Echota Cherokee, MaChis Lower Creek, Mowa Choctaw, Northeast Alabama Cherokee, Southeast Alabama Cherokee, Star Muskogee Creek.

Connecticut (3)

Contact Mr. Ed Sarabia, Indian Affairs Coordinator, Office of Indian Affairs, 79 Elm St., Hartford, CT 06106-5127, (860) 424-3066

Tribes: Golden Hill Paugussett (R), Paucatuck Eastern Pequot (R), Schagticoke (R).

Georgia (3)

Contact Mr. Robert Giacomini, Director of State Data and Research Center, 250 14th St. NW, Rm 543, Atlanta, GA 30318, (404) 894-9416

Tribes: Georgia Eastern Cherokee, Cherokee of Georgia, Lower Muskogee Creek (R), Tama Tribal Town.

Louisiana (5)

Contact Ms. Pat Arnold, Deputy Director of Indian Affairs for Louisiana, 1885 Wooddale Blvd, 12th Floor, Baton Rouge, LA 70806, (225) 922-220

Tribes: Choctaw-Apache of Ebarb (TDSA), Caddo Tribe, Clifton Choctaw (TDSA), Four Winds Cherokee, United Houma Nation (TDSA).

Massachusetts (5)

Contact Ms. Janice Falcon, Commission of North American Indian Center of Boston, 105 S. Huntington Ave., Jamaica Plain, MA 02130, (617) 727-6394

Tribes: None. There is no mechanism in place in this state for Indian tribes to petition for state recognition.

Michigan (3)

Contact Ms Karen Kay, Michigan Commission on Indian Affairs, Michigan Department of Civil Rights, Victor Bldg, Suite 700, 201 N. Washington Square, Lansing, MI 48913, (517) 373-0654

Tribes: Burt Lake Band of Ottawa and Chippewa Indians, Grand River Band of Ottawa Indians, Swan Creek Black River Confederate Tribe.

Montana (1)

Contact Mr Wyman J. McDonald, Office of Indian Affairs, State Capital, Rm 202, P.O. Box 200801, Helena, MT 59620-0801, (406) 444-3702

Tribes: Little Shell Chippewa Tribe.

New Jersey (3)

Contact Chief Roy Crazy Horse, Chairman, New Jersey Commission on American Indian Affairs, Rankokus Indian Reservation, P.O. Box 225, Rancocas, NJ 08703, (609) 777-0883

Tribes: Nanticoke Lenni-Lenape, Powhatan Renape (R), Ramapough Mountain (TDSA).

New York (2)

Contact Mr. Patrick Kehoe, Assistant Counsel, State of New York Executive Chambers, Rm 214, Albany, NY 12224, (518) 474-2294

Tribes: Shinnecock (R), Poospatuck (R).

North Carolina (9)

Contact Mr. Gregory Richardson, Executive Director, NC Commission of Indian Affairs, 217 W. Jones Street, Raleigh, NC 27603, (919) 733-5998

Tribes: Coharie (TDSA), Haliwa-Saponi (TDSA), Lumbee (TDSA), Meherrin (TDSA), Indians of Person County, Waccamaw-Siouan (TDSA), Cumberland County Association for Indian People, Guilford Native American Association, Metrolina Native American Association.

Oklahoma (1)

Contact Ms. Barbara Warner, Oklahoma Indian Affairs Commission, (405) 521-3828

Virginia (8)

Contact Ms Thomasina Jordon, Chair, Virginia Council of Indians, 3008 Russell Rd., Alexandria, VA 22305, (804) 786-7765

Tribes: Chickahominy Indian Tribe (TDSA), Chickahominy Eastern Band (TDSA), Monacan Indian Nation, Nansemond Indian Tribe, Rappahannock Indian Tribe, Upper Mattaponi Tribe, Mattaponi Indian Tribe (R), Pamunkey Indian Tribe (R).

West Virginia (1)

Contact Joanna Wilsin, The Cultural Center, 1900 Kanawha Blvd., Charleston, WV 25305-0300, (304) 558-0220

Tribes: Appalachian American Indians of West Virginia
Source: U.S. Census Bureau, 2001.

TRIBES OF THE UNITED STATES

The following list of 336 tribal entities is taken from the *Federal Register,* vol. 65, no.49, 13 March 2000.

Tribes in the Contiguous States

Absentee-Shawnee Tribe of Indians of Oklahoma
Agua Caliente Band of Cahuilla Indians of the Agua Caliente Indian
     Reservation, California
Ak Chin Indian Community of Marciopa (Ak Chin) Indian Reservation,
     Arizona
Alabama-Coushattta Tribes of Texas
Alabama-Quassarte Tribal Town, Oklahoma
Altural Indian Rancheria, California
Apache Tribe of Oklahoma
Arapahoe Tribe of the Wind River Reservation, Wyoming
Aroostook Band of Micma Indians of Maine
Assiniboine and Sioux Tribes of the Fort Peck Indian Reservation, Montana
Augustine Band of Cahuilla Mission Indians of the Augustine
     Reservation, California
Bad River Band of the Lake Superior Tribe of Chippewa Indians of the
     Band River Reservation, Wisconsin
Barona Group of Capitan Grande Band of Mission Indians of the
     Barona Reservation, California

Bay Mills Indian Community of the Sault Ste. Marie Band of Chippewa
Indians, Bay Mills Reservation, Michigan
Bear River Band of the Rohnerville Rancheria, California
Berry Creek Rancheria of Maidu Indians of California
Big Lagoon Rancheria, California
Big Pine Band of Owens Valley Paiute Shoshone Indians of the Big Pine
Reservation, California
Big Sandy Rancheria of Mono Indians of California
Big Valley Band of Pomo Indians of the Big Valley Rancheria, California
Blackfeet Tribe of the Blackfeet Indian Reservation of Montana
Blue Lake Rancheria, California
Bridgeport Paiute Indian Colony of California
Buena Vista Rancheria of Me-Wuk Indians of California
Burns Paiute Tribe of the Burns Paiute Indian Colony of Oregon
Cabazon Band of Cahuilla Mission Indians of the Cabazon
Reservation, California
Cachil DeHe Band of Wintun Indians of the Colusa Rancheria, California
Caddo Indian Tribe of Oklahoma
Cahuilla Band of Mission Indians of the Cahuilla Reservation,
California
Cahto Indian Tribe of the Laytonville Rancheria, California
Cahto Indian Tribe of Oklahoma
Campo Band of Diegueno Mission Indians of the Campo Indian Reser-
vation, California
Capitan Grande of Diegueno Mission Indian of the Campo Indian
Reservation, California
Catawba Indian Nation (aka Catawba Tribe of South Carolina)
Cayuga Nation of New York
Cedarville Rancheria, California
Chemeheuvi Indian Tribe of the Chemeheuvi Reservation, California
Cher-Ae Heights Indian Community of the Trinidad Rancheria,
California
Cherokee Nation, Oklahoma
Cheyenne-Arapaho Tribes of Oklahoma
Cheyenne River Sioux Tribe of the Cheyenne River Reservation, South
Dakota
Chickasaw Nation, Oklahoma
Chichen Rancheria of Me-Wuk Indians of California
Chippewa-Cree Indians of the Rocky Boy's Reservation, Montana
Chitimacha Tribe of Louisiana
Choctaw Nation of Oklahoma
Citizen Potawatomi Nation, Oklahoma

Cloverdale Rancheria of Pono Indians of California
Cocopah Tribe of Arizona
Coeur D'Alene Tribe of the Coeur D'Alene Reservation, Idaho
Cold Springs Rancheria of Mono Indians of California
Colorado River Indian Tribes of the Colorado River Indian Reservation,
    Arizona and California
Comanche Indian Tribe, Oklahoma
Confederated Salish and Kootenai Tribes of the Flathead Reservation,
    Montana
Confederated Tribes and Bands of the Yakama Indian Nation of the
    Yakama Reservation, Washington
Confederated Tribes of the Chehalis Reservation, Washington
Confederated Tribes of the Colville Reservation, Washington
Confederated Tribes of the Coos, Lower Umpqua, and Siuslaw Indians
    of Oregon
Confederated Tribes of the Goshute Reservation, Nevada and Utah
Confederated Tribes of the Grand Ronde Community of Oregon
Confederated Tribes of the Siletz Reservation, Oregon
Confederated Tribes of the Umatilla Reservation, Oregon
Confederated Tribes of the Warm Springs Reservation, Oregon
Coquille Tribe of Oregon
Cortinal Indian Rancheria of Wintun Indians of California
Coushatta Tribe of Louisiana
Coyote Valley Band of Pomo Indians of California
Crow Creek Band of Umpqua Indians of Oregon
Crow Creek Sioux Tribe of the Crow Creek Reservation, South Dakota
Crow Tribe of Montana
Cuyapaipe Community of Diegueno Mission Indians of the Cuyapaipe
    Reservation, California
Death Valley Timbi-Sha Shoshone Band of California
Delaware Nation, Oklahoma (formerly Delaware Tribe of Western
    Oklahoma)
Delaware Tribe of Indians, Oklahoma
Dry Creek Rancheria of Pomo Indians of California
Duckwater Shoshone Tribe of the Duckwater Reservation, Nevada
Eastern Band of Cherokee Indians of North Carolina
Eastern Indian Colony of Pomo Indians of the Sulphur Bank
    Rancheria, California
Elk Valley Rancheria, California
Ely Shoshone Tribe of Nevada
Enterprise Rancheria of Maidu Indians of California
Flandreau Santee Sioux Tribe of South Dakota

Forest County Potawatomi Community of Wisconsin Potawatomi
    Indians, Wisconsin
Fort Belknap Indian Community of the Fort Belknap Reservation of
    Montana
Fort Bidwell Indian Community of the Fort Bidwell Reservation of
    California
Fort Independence Indian Community of Paiute Indians of the Fort
    Independence Reservation, California
Fort McDermitt Paiute and Shoshone Tribes of the Fort McDermitt
    Indian Reservation, Nevada and Oregon
Fort McDowell Mohave-Apache Community of the Fort McDowell
    Indian Reservation, Arizona
Fort Mojave Indian Tribe of Arizona, California, and Nevada
Fort Sill Apache Tribe of Oklahoma
Gila River Indian Community of the Gila River Indian Reservation,
    Arizona
Grand Traverse Band of Ottawa and Chippewa Indians of Michigan
Greenville Rancheria of Maidu Indians of California
Grindstone Indian Rancheria of Wintun-Wailaki Indians of California
Guidiville Rancheria of California
Hannahville Indian Community of Wisconsin Potawatomie Indians of
    Michigan
Havasupai Tribe of the Havasupai Reservation, Arizona
Ho-Chunk Nation of Wisconsin (formerly known as the Wisconsin
    Winnebago Tribe)
Hoh Indian Tribe of the Hoh Indian Reservation, Washington
Hoopa Valley Tribe, California
Hopi Tribe of Arizona
Hopland Band of Ponwa Indians of the Hopland Rancheria, California
Houlton Band of Maliseet Indians of Maine
Hualapai Indian Tribe of Hualapai Indian Reservation, Arizona
Huron Potawatomi, Inc., Michigan
Inaja Band of Dieguено Mission Indians of the Inaja and Cosmit
    Reservation, California
Ione Band of Miwok Indians of California
Iowa Tribe of Kansas and Nebraska
Iowa Tribe of Oklahoma
Jackson Rancheria of Me-Wuk Indians of California
Jamestown S'Klallam Tribe of Washington
Jamul Indian Village of California
Jena Band of Choctaw Indians, Louisiana
Jicarilla Apache Tribe of Jicarilla Apache Indian Reservation, New Mexico

Kaibab Band of Paiute Indians of the Kaibab Indian Reservation, Arizona
Kalispel Indian Community of the Kalispel Reservation, Washington
Karuk Tribe of California
Kashia Band of Pomo Indians of the Stewarts Point Rancheria, California
Kaw Nation, Oklahoma
Keweenaw Bay Indian Community of L'Anse and Ontonagon Bands of Chippewa Indians of the L'Anse Reservation, Michigan
Kialegeee Tribal Town, Oklahoma
Kickapoo Tribe of Indians of the Kickapoo Reservation in Kansas
Kickapoo Tradition Tribe of Texas
Kickapoo Tribe of Oklahoma
Kiowa Indian Tribe of Oklahoma
Klamath Indian Tribe of Oregon
Kootenai Tribe of Idaho
La Jolla Band of Luiseno Mission Indians of La Jolla Reservation, California
Lac Courte Oreilles Band of Lake Superior Chippewa Indians of the Lac Courte Oreilles Reservation of Wisconsin
Lac du Flambeau Band of Lake Superior Chippewa Indians of the Lac du Flambeau Reservation of Wisconsin
Lac Vieux Desert Band of Lake Superior Chippewa Indians of Michigan
Las Vegas Tribe of Paiute Indians of the Las Vegas Indian Colony, Nevada
Little River Band of Ottawa Indians of Michigan
Little Traverse Bay Bands of Odawn Indians of Michigan
Los Coyotes Band of Cahuilla Mission Indians of the Los Coyotes Reservation, California
Lovelock Paiute Tribe of the Lovelock Indian Colony, Nevada
Lower Brule Sioux Tribe of the Lower Brule Reservation, South Dakota
Lower Elwha Tribal Community of the Lower Elwha Reservation, Washington
Lower Sioux Indian Community of Minnesota, Mdewankanton Sioux Indians of the Lower Sioux Reservation in Minnesota
Lummi Tribe of Lummi Reservation, Washington
Lytton Rancheria of California
Makah Indian Tribe of the Makah Indian Reservation, Washington
Manchester Band of Pomo Indians of the Manchester-Point Area Rancheria, California
Manzanita Band of Diegueno Mission Indians of the Manzanita Reservation, California

Mashantucket Pequot Tribe of Connecticutto here alpha
Match-e-be-nash-she-wish Band of Potawatomi Indians of Michigan
Mechoopda Indian Tribe of Chico Rancheria, California
Menominee Indian Tribe of Wisconsin
Mesa Grande Band of Diegueno Mission Indians of the Mesa Grande
　　　Reservation, California
Mescalero Apache Tribe of Mescalero Reservation, New Mexico
Miami Tribe of Oklahoma
Miccosukee Tribe of Indians of Florida
Middletown Rancheria of Pomo Indians of California
Minnesota Chippewa Tribe, Minnesota (Six component reservations:
　　　Bois Forte Band [Nett Lake]; Fond du Lac Band; Grand Portage
　　　Band; Leech Lake Band; Mille Lacs Band; White Earth Band)
Mississippi Band of Choctaw Indians, Mississippi
Moapa Band of Paiute Indians of the Moapa River Indian Reservation,
　　　Nevada
Modoc Tribe of Oklahoma
Mohegan Indian Tribe of Connecticut
Mooretown Rancheria of Maidu Indians of California
Morongo Band of Cahuilla Mission Indians of the Morongo
　　　Reservation, California
Muckleshoot Indian Tribe of the Muckleshoot Reservation,
　　　Washington
Muscogee (Creek) Nation, Oklahoma
Narrangansett Indian Tribe of Rhode Island
Navajo Nation, Arizona, New Mexico, and Utah
Nez Percé Tribe of Idaho
Nisqually Indian Tribe of the Nisqually Reservation, Washington
Nooksack Indian Tribe of Washington
Northern Cheyenne Tribe of the Northern Cheyenne Indian
　　　Reservation, Montana
Northfork Rancheria of Mono Indians of California
Northwestern Band of the Shoshoni Nation of Utah (Washakie)
Oage Tribe, Oklahoma
Oglala Sioux Tribe of the Pine Ridge Reservation, South Dakota
Omaha Tribe of Nebraska
Oneida Nation of New York
Oneida Tribe of Wisconsin
Onondaga Nation of New York
Otoe-Missouria Tribe of Indians, Oklahoma
Ottawa Tribe of Oklahoma
Paiute Indian Tribe of Utah

Paiute-Shoshone Indians of the Bishop Community of the Bishop
    Colony, California
Paiute-Shoshone Indians of the Lone Pine Community of the Lone
    Pine Reservation, California
Paiute-Shoshone Tribe of the Fallon Reservation and Colony, Nevada
Pala Band of Luisenao Mission Indians of the Pala Reservation,
    California
Pakenta Band of Nomlaki Indians of California
Pascua Yaqui Tribe of Arizona
Passamaquoddy Tribe of Maine
Pauma Band Luiseno Mission Indians of the Pauma and Yuima
    Reservation, California
Pawnee Nation of Oklahoma
Pechanga Band of Luiseno Mission Indians of the Pechanga
    Reservation, California
Penobscot Tribe of Maine
Peoria Tribe of Indians of Oklahoma
Picayune Rancheria of Chukshansi Indians of California
Pinoleville Rancheria of Pomo Indians of California
Pit River Tribe, California (includes Big Bend, Lookout, Montgomery
    Creek, and Roaring Creek Rancheria and XL Ranch)
Poarch Band of Creek Indians of Alabama
Pokagon Band of Potawatomi Indians of Michigan
Ponca Tribe of Nebraska
Ponca Tribe of Indians of Oklahoma
Port Gamble Indian Community of the Port Gamble Reservation,
    Washington
Potter Valley Rancheria of Pomo Indians of California
Prairie Band of Potawatomi Indians, Kansas
Prairie Island Indian Community of Minnesota Mdewakanton Sioux
    Indians of Prairie Island Reservation, Minnesota
Pueblo of Acoma, New Mexico
Pueblo of Cochiti, New Mexico
Pueblo of Isleta, New Mexico
Pueblo of Jemez, New Mexico
Pueblo of Laguna, New Mexico
Pueblo of Nambe, New Mexico
Pueblo of Picuris, New Mexico
Pueblo of Pojoaque, New Mexico
Pueblo of Sandia, New Mexico
Pueblo of San Felipe, New Mexico
Pueblo of San Ildefonso, New Mexico

Pueblo of San Juan, New Mexico
Pueblo of Santa Ana, New Mexico
Pueblo of Santa Clara, New Mexico
Pueblo of Santo Domingo, New Mexico
Pueblo of Taos, New Mexico
Pueblo of Tesuque, New Mexico
Pueblo of Zia, New Mexico
Puyallup Tribe of the Puyallup Reservation, Washington
Pyramid Lake Paiute Tribe of the Pyramid Lake Reservation, Nevada
Quapaw Tribe of Indians, Oklahoma
Quartz Valley Indian Community of the Quartz Valley Reservation of
      California
Quechan Tribe of the Fort Yuma Indian Reservation, California and
      Arizona
Quileute Tribe of the Quileute Reservation, Washington
Quinault Tribe of the Quinault Reservation, Washington
Ramona Band or Village of Cahuilla Mission Indians of California
Redding Rancheria, California
Red Cliff Band of Lake Superior Chippewa Indians of Wisconsin
Red Lake Band of Chippewa Indians of the Red Lake Reservation,
      Minnesota
Redwood Valley Rancheria of Pomo Indians of California
Reno-Sparks Indian Colony, Nevada
Resighini Rancheria, California (formerly known as the Coast Indian
      Community of Yurok Indians of the Resighini Rancheria)
Rincon Band of Luiseno Mission Indians of the Rincon Reservation,
      California
Robinson Rancheria of Pomo Indians of California
Rosebud Sioux Tribe of the Rosebud Indian Reservation, South
      Dakota
Round Valley Indian Tribes of the Round Valley Reservation, California
      (formerly known as the Covelo Indian Community)
Rumsey Indian Rancheria of Wintun Indians of California
Sac and Fox Nation of Missouri in Kansas and Nebraska
Sac and Fox Nation, Oklahoma
Sac and Fox Tribe of Mississippi in Iowa
Saginaw Chippewa Indian Tribe of Michigan, Isabella Reservation
Salt River Pima-Maricopa Indian Community of the Salt River
      Reservation, Arizona
Samish Indian Tribe, Washington
San Carlos Apache Tribe of the San Carlos Reservation, Arizona
San Juan Southern Paiute Tribe of Arizona

San Manual Band of Serrano Mission Indians of the San Manual
  Reservation, California
San Pasquel Band of Diegueno Mission Indians of California
Santa Rosa Band of Cahuilla Mission Indians of the Santa Rosa
  Reservation, California
Santa Rosa Indian Community of the Santa Rosa Rancheria, California
Santa Ynez Band of Chumash Mission Indians of the Santa Ynez
  Reservation, California
Santa Ysabel Band of Diegueno Mission Indians of the Santa Ysabel
  Reservation, California
Santee Sioux Tribe of the Santee Reservation of Nebraska
Sauk-Suiattle Indian Tribe of Washington
Sault Ste. Marie Tribe of Chippewa Indians of Michigan
Scotts Valley Band of Pomo Indians of California
Seminole Nation of Oklahoma
Seminole Tribe of Florida, Dania, Big Cypress, Brighton, Hollywood,
  and Tampa Reservations
Seneca-Cayuga Tribe of Oklahoma
Seneca Nation of New York
Shakopee Mdewakanton Sioux Community of Minnesota (Prior Lake)
Sheep Ranch Rancheria of Me-Wuk Indians of California
Sherwood Valley Rancheria of Pono Indians of California
Shingle Springs Band of Miwok Indians, Shingle Springs Rancheria
  (Verona Tract), California
Shoalwater Bay Tribe of the Shoalwater Bay Indian Reservation,
  Washington
Shoshone-Bannock Tribes of the Duck Valley Reservation, Nevada
Shoshone Tribe of the Wind River Reservation, Wyoming
Sisseton-Whapeton Sioux Tribe of the Lake Traverse Reservation, South
  Dakota
Skokomish Indian Tribe of the Skokomish Reservation, Washington
Skull Valley Bank of Goshute Indians of Utah
Smith River, Rancheria, California
Snoqualmie Tribe, Washington
Soboba Band of Luiseno Mission Indians of the Soboba Reservation,
  California
Sokagon Chippewa Community of the Moe Lake Band of Chippewa
  Indians, Wisconsin
Southern Ute Indian Tribe of the Southern Ute Reservation, Colorado
Spirit Lake Tribe, North Dakota (formerly known as Devil's Lake Sioux
  Tribe)
Spokane Tribe of the Spokane Reservation, Washington

Squaxin Island Tribe of the Squaxin Island Reservation, Washington
St. Croix Chippewa Indians of the St. Croix Reservation, Wisconsin
St. Regis Band of Mohawk Indians of New York
Standing Tock Sioux Tribe of North and South Dakota/Stockbridge-
    Munsee Community of Mohican Indians of Wisconsin
Stillaguamish Tribe of Washington
Summit Lake Paiute Tribe of Nevada
Suquamish Indian Tribe of the Port Madison Reservation, Washington
Sycuan Band of Diegueno Mission Indians of California
Table Bluff Reservation-Wiyot Tribe of California
Table Mountain Rancheria of California
Te-Moak Tribes of Western Shoshone Indians of Nevada (Four
    constituent bands: Battle Mountain Band, Elko Band, South
    Fork Band, and Wells Band)
Thlopthlocco Tribal Town, Oklahoma
Three Affiliated Tribes of the Fort Berthold Reservation, North Dakota
Tohono O'odhan Nation of Arizona
Tonawanda Band of Seneca Indians of New York
Tonkawa Tribe of Indians of Oklahoma
Tonto Apache Tribe of Arizona
Torres-Martinez Band of Cahuilla Mission Indians of California
Tulalip Tribes of the Tulalip Reservation, California
Tule River Indian Tribe of the Tule River Reservation, California
Tunica-Biloxi Indian Tribe of Louisiana
Tuolumne Band of Me-Wuk Indians of the Tuolomne Rancheria of
    California
Turtle Mountain Band of Chippewa Indians of North Dakota
Tuscarora Nation of New York
Twenty-Nine Palms Band of Luiseno Mission Indians of California
United Auburn Indian Community of the Auburn Rancheria of
    California
United Keetoowah Band of Cherokee Indians of Oklahoma
Upper Lake Band of Pomo Indians of Upper Lake Rancheria of
    California
Upper Sioux Indian Community of the Upper Sioux Reservation,
    Minnesota
Upper Skagit Indian Tribe of Washington
Ute Indian Tribe of the Uintah and Ouray Reservation, Utah
Ute Mountain Tribe of the Ute Mountain Reservation, Colorado, New
    Mexico, and Utah
Utu Utu Gwaitu Paiute Tribe of the Benton Paiute Reservation,
    California

Viejas (Baron Long) Group of Captain Grand Band of Mission Indians
of the Viehas Reservation, California
Walker River Paiute Tribe of the Walker River Reservation, Nevada
Wampanoag Tribe of Gay Head (Aquinnah) of Massachusetts
Washoe Tribe of Nevada and California (Carson Colony, Dresslerville
Colony, Woodfords Community, Stewart Community, and
Washoe Ranches)
White Mountain Apache Tribe of the Fort Apache Reservation, Arizona
Wichita and Affiliated Tribes (Wichita, Keechi, Waco, and
Tawakonie), Oklahoma
Winnebago Tribe of Nebraska
Winnemucca Indian Colony of Nevada
Wyandotte Tribe of Oklahoma
Yankton Sioux Tribe of South Dakota
Yavalpai-Apache Nation of the Camp Verde Indian Reservation,
Arizona
Yavapai-Prescott Tribe of the Yavapai Reservation, Arizona
Yerington Paiute Tribe of the Yerington Colony and Campbell Ranch,
Nevada
Yomba Shoshone Tribe of the Yomba Reservation, Nevada
Ysleta Del Sur Pueblo of Texas
Yurok Tribe of the Yurok Reservation, California
Zuni Tribe of the Zuni Reservation, New Mexico

Native Entities Recognized by the Federal Government within the State of Alaska

Agdaagux Tribe of King Cove Angoon Community Association
Akiachak Native Community
Akiak Native Community
Alatna Village
Algaaciq Native Village (St. Mary's)
Allakaket Village
Anvik Village
Arctic Village (See Native Village of Venetie Tribal Government)
Asa'carsarmiut Tribe (formerly Native Village of Mountain Village)
Atqasuk Village (Atkasook)
Beaver Village
Birch Creek Tribe (formerly listed as Birch Creek Village)
Central Council of the Tlingit and Haida Indian Tribes
Chalkyitsik Village
Chickaloon Native Village

Chilkat Indian Village (Klukwan)
Chilkoot Indian Association (Haines)
Chinik Eskimoo Community (Golovin)
Chuloonawick Native Village
Circle Native Community
Craig Community Association
Curyung Tribal Council (formerly Native Village of Dillingham)
Douglas Indian Association
Egegik Village
Eklutna Native Village
Ekwok VillageEmmonak Village
Evansville Village (aka Bettles Field)
Gulkana Village
Holy Cross Village
Hoonah Indian Association
Hughes Village
Huslia Village
Hydaburg Cooperative Association
Igiugig Village
Inupiat Community of the Arctic Slope
Iqurmuit Traditional Council (formerly Native Village of Russian Mission)
Ivanoff Bay VillageKaktovik Village (aka Barter Island
Galena Village (aka Louden Village)
Healy Lake Village
Kenaitze Indian Tribe
Ketchikan Indian Corporation
King Island Native Community
Klawock Cooperative Association
Knik Tribe
Kokhanok Village
Koyukuk Native Village
Lesnoi Village (aka Woody Island)
Levelock Village
Lime Village
Manly Hot Springs village
Manokotak Village
Matove Village of Aleknagik
Matove Village of Buckland
McGrath Native Village
Mentasta Traditional Council (formerly Mentasta Lake Village)
Metlakathla Indian Community, Annette Island ReserveNaknek Native
    Village

Native Village of Akhiok
Native Village of Akutan
Native Village of Ambler
Native Village of Atka
Native Village of Barrow Inupiat Traditional Government (formerly
        Native Village of Borrow)
Native Village of Belkofski
Native Village of Brevig Mission
Native Village of Cantwell
Native Village of Chanega (aka Chenega)
Native Village of Council
Native Village of Deering
Native Village of Ekuk
Native Village or Ellim
Native Village of Chistochina
Native Village of Chitina
Native Village of Chuathbaluk (Russian Mission, Kuskokwim)
Native Village of Diomede (aka Inalik)
Native Village of Eagle
Native Village of Eek
Native Village of Hamilton
Native Village of Hooper Bay
Native Village of Kanatak
Native Village of Karluk
Native Village of Kasigluk
Native Village of Kiana
Native Village of Kipnuk
Native Village of Kivalina
Native Village of Kluti Kaah (aka Copper Center)
Native Village of Kobuk
Native Village of Kongiganak
Native Village of Kotzebue
Native Village of Koyuk
Native Village of Kwigilingok
Native Village of Kwinhagak (aka Quinhagak)
Native Village of Larsen Bay
Native Village of Marshall (aka Fortuna Ledge)
Native Village of Mary's Igloo
Native Village of Mehoryuk
Native Village of Minto
Native Village of Nanwalek (aka English Bay)
Native Village of Napaimute

Native Village of Napakiak
Native Village of Nelson Lagoon
Native Village of Nightmute
Native Village of Nikolski
Native Village of Noatak
Native Village of Nuiqsut (aka Nooiksut)
Native Village of Nunapitchuk
Native Village of Ouzinkie
Native Village of Paimiut
Native Village of Perryville
Native Village of Pilot Point
Native Village of Pitka's Point
Native Village of Point Hope
Native Village of Point Lay
Native Village of Port Graham
Native Village of Port Heiden
Native Village of Port Lions
Native Village of Ruby
Native Village of Saint Michael
Native Village of Savoonga
Native Village of Scammon Bay
Native Village of Selawik
Native Village of Shaktoolik
Native Village of Sheldon's Point
Native Village of Shungnak
Native Village of Stevens
Native Village of Tanana
Native Village of Tatitlek
Native Village of Tazlina
Native Village of Teller
Native Village of Tetlin
Native Village of Timtitioal
Native Village of Tununak
Native Village of Tyonek
Native Village of Unalakleet
Native Village of Unga
Native Village of Venetie Tribal Government (Arctic Village and Village
    of Venetie)
Native Village of Wales
Native Village of White Mountain
Nenana Native Association
Newhalen Village

New Stuyahok Village
New Koliganek Village Council (formerly Koliganek Village)
Newtok Villag
Nikolai Village
Ninilchik Village
Nome Eskimo Community
Nondalton Village
Northway Village
Nulato Village
Nunakauyarmiut Tribe (formerly Native Village of Toksook Bay)
Organized Village of Grayling (aka Holikachuk)
Organized Village of Kake
Organized Village of Kasaan
Organized Village of Kwethluk
Organized Village of Saxman
Orutsaramuit Native Village (aka Bethel)
Oscarville Traditional Village
Pauloff Harbor Village
Pedro Bay Village
Petersburg Indian Association
Pilot Station Traditional Village
Platinum Traditional VillagePortage Creek Village (aka Ohgsenakale)
Pribilof Islands Aleut Communities of St. Paul and St. George Islands
Qagan Tayagungin Tribe of Sand Point Village
Qawalangin Tribe of Unalaska
Rampart Village
Saint George Island (Prigilof of Islands Aleut Communities of St. Paul
       and St. George Islands)
Saint Paul Island
Seldovia Village Tribe
Shageluk Native Village
Sitka Tribe of Alaska
South Naknek Village
Stebbins Community Association
Takotna Village
Tellida Village
Traditional Village of Togiak
Tuluksk Native Community
Twin Hills Village
Ugashik Village
Umkumiute Native Village
Village of Afognak

Village of Alakanuk
Village of Anaktuvuk Pass
Village of Aniak
Village of Atmautluak
Village of Bill Moore's Slough
Village of Clark's Point
Village of Crooked Creek
Village of Dot Lake
Village of Iliamna
Village of Kalskag
Village of Kaltal
Village of Kotlik
Village of Lower Kalskag
Village of Ohogamiut
Village of Old HarborVillage of Red Devil
Village of Salamatoff
Village of Sleetmute
Village of Solomon
Village of Stony River
Village of Tanacross
Village of Venetie (See Native Village of Venetie Tribal Government)
Village of Wainwirhgt
Wrangell Cooperative Association
Yakutat Tlingit Tribe
Yupiit of Amdreasfski

Chapter Eight

✏️ Print and Nonprint Resources

PRINT RESOURCES

In this chapter the reader is presented with a selection of written materials and nonprint resources that allow a deeper exploration into a number of the issues that have been presented throughout this book. The selected resources, which are in no way exhaustive, are in their way an indication of the complexity of Native American education. It is also obvious that one is not dealing with a Native American culture but rather with many different groups and many complex issues. In its own way the list of selected resources provides an insight into the many different aspects of education of Native American students that have been raised.

The teacher in the early part of the twentieth century would have been amazed that there were so many issues associated with Native American education. Essentially, until that time, Native American education was viewed from the perspective of assimilation. From the early 1960s onward there has been a general change with an emphasis on understanding cultural differences within society at large and in education. These changes have had their effects on Native Americans themselves. They have taken a greater interest in strengthening their cultures, languages, and stories and adapting education so that it strengthens their heritage and traditions.

Articles and Reports

Aboriginal Committee, Community Panel, Family and Children's Services Legislation Review in British Columbia. 1992. "Liberating Our Children, Liberating Our Nations: Report of the Aboriginal Committee, Community Panel, Family and Children's Services Legislation Review in British Columbia." Victoria, BC: Author.

American Indian Policy Review Commission. 1976. "Report on Indian Education." Washington, DC: Government Printing Office.

American School Counselor Association. 1993. "The School Counselor and Cross/Multicultural Counseling: The Position of the American School Counselor Association, Revised." Alexandria, VA: American School Counselor Association.

Association of Community Tribal Schools. 1997. "Our Children, Our Schools, Our Tribes: Thirty Years of Local Control of Indian Education, 1966–1996." ERIC No. ED 395 740. Sisseton, SD: Association of Community Tribal Schools.

Birchard, B. 1970. "Attitudes toward Indian Culture and Its Incorporation in the School Curriculum: Students, Parents, Teachers, and Community Leaders—Perceptions of Indian Education." Series IV, No. 10, Final Report, National Study of American Indian Education. ERIC No. ED 047 879. Washington, DC: Bureau of Research, Office of Education.

Blanchard, Joseph D. 1972. "Measurement and Testing Considerations for Native American Education." ERIC no ED 075 457.

Boyer, P. 1997. "Native American Colleges: Progress and Prospects." Princeton, NJ: Carnegie Foundation for the Advancement of Teaching.

Brescia, W. 1991. "Funding and Resources for American Indian and Alaska Native Education." In *Indian Nations At Risk: Solutions for the 1990s.* Washington, DC: Department of Education.

"A Compilation of Federal Education Laws. Volume II: Elementary and Secondary Education, Individuals with Disabilities, and Related Programs as Amended through December 31, 1990." Prepared for the Use of the Committee on Education and Labor. U.S. House of Representatives, 102nd Congress, first sess. ERIC no. ED 338 383.

Deyhle, D. 1983. "Measuring Success and Failure in the Classroom: Teacher Communication about Tests and the Understanding of Young Navajo Students." *Peabody Journal of Education* 61(1): 67–85, 1983.

Dister, David C. 1984. "Native Americans and Education." *Nature Study* 38, no. 1 (September): 15–16.

"Education and the Native American." 1987. ERIC no. ED 313 232. Charleston, WV: ERIC.

Hall, McClellan. 1995. "SI-YUU-DZE: Service Learning in Native Schools." *Journal of Emotional and Behavioral Problems* 3, no. 4: 34–36.

Henderson, James C. 1991. "Minority Student Retention." *New Directions for Community Colleges* 19, no. 2 (Summer): 47–55.

Irizarry, R. A. and Torres, J. A. 1980. "Native American Education Program: Title IV, Indian Education Act, 1979–1980." Final Evaluation Report, Project 5001-42-04201. ERIC no. ED 395 738. Charleston, WV: ERIC.

Marshall, John D. 1985. "A Glance at the Evolution of Native American Education: From Christianization to Self-Determination." ERIC no. ED 257 593.

McCoy, Mclody L. 2000. "Federal Indian Law and Policy Affecting American Indian and Alaska Native Education." Indian Education Legal Support Project "Tribalizing Indian Education." ERIC no. ED 459 031. Boulder, CO: Native American Rights Fund.

Oliver, Christopher. 1996. "The Internal Colonialism Model: What the Model Has Done to the Education of Native Americans." ERIC no. ED 396 883.

Reyhner, Jon, ed. 1986. "Teaching the Indian Child: A Bilingual/Multicultural Approach." ERIC no. ED 283 628.

Simonelli, Richard. 1993 "The Path of Native American Education: Where Tradition and Technology Meet." *Technos* 2, no. 3 (Fall): 12–17.

Stokes, Sandra M. 1997. "Curriculum for Native American Students: Using Native American Values." *Reading Teacher* 50, no. 7 (April): 576–584.

Wells, R. N., Jr. 1989. "The Forgotten Minority: Native Americans in Higher Education." ERIC no. ED 317 346.

Zickrick, M. 1992. "Indian Education: Student Incentive and Tuition Equalization Grants." Issue Memorandum 92-7. ERIC No. ED 356 938. Pierre, SD:Legislative Research Council.

Books

Cleary, L. M,. and T. D. Peacock. 1998. *Collected Wisdom: American Indian Education.* Boston: Allyn and Bacon.

This book is the result of a research project consisting of interviews with over sixty Indian and non-Indian teachers of Native American students working on or near nine reservations across the United States as well as fifty teachers in Australia and Costa Rica.

Costo, Rupert, and Jeannette Henry, eds. 1970. *Textbooks and the American Indian.* San Francisco: Indian History Press.

This book is a valuable resource as it evaluates over 150 textbooks in use in both the public and BIA schools. American history, geography, state and regional history, and world history are among the topics evaluated.

Dejong, D. H. 1993. *Promises of the Past: A History of Indian Education in the United States.* Golden, CO: North American Press.

This book gives the reader an historical overview of the education of the American Indian. There are excerpts of such documents as court decisions, government reports, and letters from commissioners of Indian affairs. Topics covered include the early experiences of Indian children, treaty negotiations, the work of missionaries, boarding schools, government schools,the role of public schools, and significant reports such as the Meriam and Kennedy Reports.

Delgado, V. 1997. "Interview Study of Native American Philosophical Foundations in Education." Ph.D. diss., University of North Dakota.

The author explores the philosophies of five native elders. They tell their stories in relation to their experiences of learning, knowledge acquisition, and development of their particular philosophical background. The study explores the need for the oral philosophies of Native Americans to complement formal educational philosophies.

Fedullo, M. 1992. *Light of the Feather: Pathways through Contemporary Indian America.* New York: Morrow.

The author describes his experiences in Indian schools in Montana, New Mexico, and Arizona as he encouraged Indian students to write poetry.

Gilliland, H. 1999. *Teaching the Native American.* 4th ed. Dubuque, IA: Kendall/Hunt.

This book emphasizes the need to use students' backgrounds to promote self-esteem, self-control, and the involvement of parents in education. There is also information on creative writing, whole language, and the teaching of native languages as well as on developing reading and computer skills.

Hirschfelder, Arlene B. 1982. *American Indian Stereotypes in the World of Children: A Reader and Bibliography.* Metuchen: NJ: Scarecrow Press.

Presents evidence from a number sources about common articles that indicate attitudes of children, and detail the images of Indians in children's stories and textbooks.

May, S. 1999. *Indigenous Community-Based Education.* Clevedon, UK: Multilingual Matters.

The editor has gathered essays describing the efforts of indigenous people to end the sort of school that seeks to assimilate indigenous people and deny their language and culture. The study reflects the work of people in Australia, Europe, New Zealand, and North and South America, Northern Arizona University Indigenous Studies Publications:

1. *Learn in Beauty: Indigenous Education for a New Century.* A collection of eleven papers presented at the Second Annual Learn in Beauty Conference held in Flagstaff, Arizona, June 2000.
2. *Revitalizing Indigenous Languages.* A collection of eleven papers from the Fifth Annual Stabilizing Indigenous Languages Symposium held in Louisville, Kentucky, May 1998.
3. *Teaching Indigenous Languages.* A collection of twenty-five papers from the Fourth Annual Stabilizing Indigenous Languages Symposium "Sharing Effective Language Renewal Practices" held at Northern Arizona University in Flagstaff, Arizona, May 1997.
4. *Stabilizing Indigenous Languages.* The proceedings of the First and Second Stabilizing Indigenous Languages Symposia at the Center for Excellence in Education, Northern Arizona University, Flagstaff, Arizona, 1997.

Peshkin, A. 1997. *Places of Memory: Whiteman's Schools and Native American Communities.* Mahwah, NJ: Erlbaum.

The author enlarges on the cultural discontinuity theory to explain the academic failure of Native American students. Peshkin spent a year in observation at a well-funded boarding school serving New Mexico's Pueblo Indians. The parents of the students were supportive of education, and the teachers were also well prepared for their profession; still, the students' academic performance was indifferent.

Reyhner, Jon, ed. 1994. *Teaching American Indian Students.* Norman: University of Oklahoma Press.

A valuable resource, this book provides the reader with information on a wide range of topics that are helpful for those who educate American Indian students. The book provides a precise summary of research on Native American education as well as providing teachers with practical help and guidance.

Rhodes, R. 1994. *Nurturing Learning in Native American Students.* Hotevilla, AZ: Sonwai Books.

The reader is provided with a student- and community-centered approach to educating Native American students. The student is presented as an active learner and the educators as the ones who facilitate and coach their students. The book encourages teachers to view the school from the perspectives of its students and their communities. Contains practical recommendations for educators of Native American students.

Spring, J. 1994. *The American School, 1642–1993.* 3rd ed. New York: Mc-Graw Hill.

This book details the history of education from an alternative perspective and encourages critical thinking. The author analyses those forces within society that shape education. Policies that have shaped the lives of Native Americans and other ethnic groups within the United States are explored and discussed.

Stedman, Raymond William. 1982. *Shadows of the Indian: Stereotypes in American Culture.* Norman: University of Oklahoma Press.

A study of racial and cultural stereotyping is presented with reproductions of historic painting, engravings, and other drawings. There is a lengthy bibliography of books, periodicals, and newspapers.

Swisher, Karen G., and John W. Tippeconnic III, eds. 1999. *Next Steps: Research and Practice to Advance Indian Education.* Huntington, WV: Chapman Printing.

All the contributors to this book are Native American. They explore Native American education today and what it should be in the future. The book is composed of four sections: the past and present foundation of Indian education, issues associated with the curriculum, the college and university experience, and the next steps for research.

Books for Youth

Ancona, G. 1993. *Powwow.* New York: Harcourt Brace.

This book of photographs focuses on the four kinds of dancers—traditional, fancy, grass, and jingle-dress. Texts and photos are interwoven to explain the customary clothing, the different styles of the dances, and the pride and honor associated with the different rituals.

Andrews, J. 1999. *Very Last First Time.* New York: MacMillan.

Eva, an Inuit girl, lives along Ungava Bay in northern Canada. During the winter the people of this area search for mussels ons the seabed. Today, Eva climbs through the ice hole for the first time by herself.

Baylor, B. 1987. *When Clay Sings.* New York: Macmillan.

This book celebrates the lives and thoughts of the ancient people whose pottery can still be found in the desert of the American Southwest. Children attempt to imagine the lives that took place in the desert they see as their own.

Benchley, N. 1972. *Small Wolf.* New York: Harper and Row.

In this book *Small Wolf* meets settlers on the island of Manhattan. The reading is simple while the plots are more complicated for the independent reader. This is an I Can Read Book Level 3.

Bruchac, J. 1999. *Between Earth and Sky: Legends of Native American Sacred Places.* New York: Brace.

The author takes the readers on a tour of Native American sacred places. At each location, Bruchac relates the legend of the location. The book celebrates geographic location as well as the beauty of nature and the beauty within each person.

Cohen, C. L. 1988. *The Mud Pony.* New York: Scholastic.

A traditional Skidi Pawnee tale retold by Caron Lee Cohen. A poor boy becomes a powerful leader when Mother Earth turns his mud pony into a real one, but after his pony turns back to mud, he must find his own strength.

George, J. C. 1987. *The Talking Earth.* New York: Harper Trophy.

Billie Wind is a girl torn between two worlds: the modern world of pollution, nuclear war, and development, which threatens the earth and world of her tribe, the Seminole People.

Girlion, B. 1990. *Indian Summer.* New York: Scholastic.

This book deals with the adjustments Joni has to make when she finds herself living on a modern "Woodlands" (Iroquois) reservation in upstate New York over a summer.

Goble, P. 1998. *Adopted by the Eagles: A Plains Indian Story of Friendship and Treachery.* New York: Simon and Schuster.

White Hawk and Tall Bear are Kolas sharing a sacred friendship. Both men fall in love with the same woman. Tall Bear is betrayed by his friend and left to die on a ledge. However, the Great Spirit hears Tall Bear's cries, and eagles come to the rescue.

Goble, P. 1994. *Buffalo Woman.* New York: Bradbury Press.

A young hunter takes out his bow against a buffalo drinking from a stream. However, before he can use his bow the buffalo is transformed into a beautiful woman. The young hunter brings the woman home and marries her. The story continues as the woman meets the young hunter's relatives.

Hobbs, W. 1989. *Bearstone.* New York: Atheneum.

Bearstone is set along Colorado's Continental Divide. Cloyd, a fourteen-year-old youth, is sent to work for an old rancher. Cloyd finds a turquoise bearstone, which leads to the beginning of his adventure and to learning about the history of the area.

Indians of North America. New York: Chelsea House.

A new series of 53 books about Native American tribes written especially for young adults. Scholars discuss significant place of American Indian tribes in our society.

Kroeber, T. 1973. *Ishi: Last of His Tribe.* New York: Bantam.

In the 1900s a small band of Californian Indians in the Yahi tribe lived in hiding. In time the members of the tribe died until there was a single survivor, a man who is known as Ishi.

Luenn, N. 1990. *Nessa's Fish.* New York: Atheneum.

When her grandmother falls ill during an ice-fishing expedition, Nessa calls on the teachings of her people to protect the ailing woman and save their catch of fish.

Morgan, W. 1988. *Navajo Coyote Tales.* Santa Fe: Ancient City.

These six tales come directly from the Navajo and are translated into English. They recount the Coyote's meetings with Rabbit, Fawn's Stars, Crow, Snake, Skunk, Woman and Horned Toad.

Moroney, L. 1989. *Baby Rattlesnake.* San Francisco: Children's Book Press.

Preschoolers will relate to the main character as he struggles with self-control and aggressive urges. Baby Rattlesnake wants a rattle of his own. His troubles begin when he goes into the desert to scare someone with his rattle.

Nelson, S. D. 1999. *Gift Horse: A Lakota Story.* New York: Harry N. Abrams.

This book is an introduction to nineteenth-century Native American life on the Great Plains. It is a coming-of-age story.

Parish, Peggy. 1988. *Good Hunting, Blue Sky.* New York: Harper and Row.

Little Indian Blue Sky is not able to secure meat using his new bow and arrow, but when a wild boar charges, Blue Sky rides it into the village.

Scott, J. C. 1995. *Native Americans in Children's Literature.* Phoenix, AZ: Oryx Press.

A valuable resource for language arts teachers, this book provides synopses and critiques of over 100 books. In the appendix are ideas for the teacher on incorporating Native American children's literature into the curriculum.

Journals

The Aboriginal Child at School: A National Journal for Teachers of Aborigines. Department of Education, University of Queensland, St. Lucia, Queensland, Australia.

American Indian Culture and Research Journal. American Indian Studies Center, 3220 Campbell Hall, University of California, Los Angeles, CA 90024.

American Indian Quarterly. Native American Studies, University of Nebraska Press, 901 North 17th St., Lincoln, NE 68588-0520.

Canadian Journal of Native Education. First Nations House of Learning, 6365 Biological Sciences Road, University of British Columbia, Vancouver, BC V6T 1Z4, Canada.

Cultural Survival Quarterly. Cultural Survival, 11 Divinity Ave., Cambridge, MA 02138.

Educational Leadership. 125 N. West St, Alexandria, VA 22314-2798, (703) 549-9110.

Equity and Excellence. University of Massachusetts School of Education Quarterly, 130 Furcolo, University of Massachusetts, Amherst, 01003.

Journal of American Folklore. 1703 New Hampshire Ave. NW, Washington, DC 20009.

Journal of American Indian Education. Center for Indian Education, College of Education, Arizona State University, Tempe, AZ 85287-1311. *Journal of Ethnic Studies.* Western Washington University, Bellingham, WA 98225.

Journal of Navajo Education. Kayena Unified School District, P.O. Box 337, Kayents, AZ 86033.

Multicultural Education Journal. Barnett House, 11010 142nd St., Edmonton, Alberta T5N 2R1, Canada.

National Association for Bilingual Education News, Suite 605, 1220 L St. NW, Washington, DC 20005-1018.

Northeast Indian Quarterly. American Indian Program, 300 Caldwell Hall, Cornell University, Ithaca, NY 14853.

Studies in American Indian Literature. Department of English, University of Richmond, Richmond, VA 23173.

Teacher Magazine. Suite 250, 4301 Connecticut Ave. NW Washington, DC 20008, (202) 364-4114.

Tribal College: Journal of American Indian Higher Education. P.O. Box 898, Chestertown, MD 21620. (*http://tribalcollegejournal.org*)

Western American Literature. Department of English, UMC 32, Utah State University, Logan, UT 84322.

The Wicazo Sa Review. Indian Studies Journal, Route 8, Box 510, Dakota Meadows, Rapid City, SD 57702.

Winds of Change: A Magazine for American Indians. American Indian Science and Engineering Society, 1630 30th St., Suite 301, Boulder, CO 80301.

Language and Reading

Anders, P. L., and C. V. Lloyd. 1989. "The Significance of Prior Knowledge in the Learning of New Content-Specific Instruction." In D. Lapp, J. Flood, and N. Farnan, eds., *Content Area Reading and Learning Instruction Strategies.* Englewood Cliffs, NJ: Prentice Hall.

Au, K. Hu-Pei. 1980. "Participation Structures in a Reading Lesson with Hawaiian Children: Analysis of a Culturally Appropriate Instructional Event." *Anthropology Education Quarterly* 11, no. 2: 91–115.

Bauman, J. 1980. *A Guide to Issues in Indian Language Retention.* Washington, DC: Center for Applied Linguistics.

Hymes, D. 1981. *In Vain I Tried to Tell You: Essays in Native American Ethnopoetics.* Philadelphia: University of Pennsylvania Press.

Kroeber, K., ed. 1981. *Traditional Literatures of the American Indian.* Lincoln: University of Nebraska Press.

Leap, W. L. 1981. "American Indian Language Maintenance." In B. I. Siegel, ed., *Annual Review of Anthropology,* vol. 10. Palo Alto: Annual Reviews.

McCarty, T. L. 1980. "Language Use by Yavapai-Apache Students with Recommendation for Curriculum Design." *Journal of American Indian Education* 20, no. 1: 1–9.

McCarty, T. L., and O. Zepeda, eds. 1995. "Indigenous Language Education and Literacy." *Bilingual Research Journal* 19, no. 1.

Skinner, L. 1999. "Teaching through Traditions: Incorporating Languages and Culture into Curricula." In Karen G. Swisher and John W. Tippeconnic III, eds., *Next Steps: Research and Practice to Advance Indian Education.* Charleston, WV: ERIC Clearinghouse on Rural Education and Small Schools.

Soto, L. D. 1996. *Language, Culture and Power: Bilingual Families and the Struggle for Quality Education.* Albany: State University of New York Press.

Velie, A. R. 1982. *Four American Indian Literary Masters: N. Scott Momaday, James Welch, Leslie Marmon Silko, and Gerald Vizenor.* Norman: University of Oklahoma Press.

Watahomigie, L., and T. L. McCarty. 1998. "Language in Literacy in American Indian Alaska Native Communities." In Bertha Perez, ed., *Sociocultural Contexts of Language and Literacy.* Mahwah, NJ: Lawrence Erlbaum.

Mathematics and Science

Abruscat, J. 1996. *Teaching Children Science.* 4th ed. Boston, MA: Allyn and Bacon.

American Indian Science and Engineering Society. 1995. *Educating American Indian/Alaska Native Elementary and Secondary Students: Guidelines for Mathematics, Science, and Technology Programs.* Boulder, CO: American Indian Science and Engineering Society.

Anders, P. L., and C. V. Lloyd. 1989. "The Significance of Prior Knowledge in the Learning of New Content-Specific Instruction." In D. Lapp, J. Flood, and N. Farnan, eds. *Content Area Reading and Learning Instruction Strategies.* Englewood Cliffs, NJ: Prentice Hall.

Atwater, M. M. 1993. "Multicultural Science Education: Assumptions and Alternative Views." *Science Teacher* 60, no. 3: 32–37.

Aveni, A., ed. 1977. *Native American Astronomy.* Austin: University of Texas Press.
Aveni, A., and G. Urton, eds. 1982. *Ethnoastronomy and Archaeoastronomy in the American Tropics.* New York: New York Academy of Sciences.

Barba, R. H. 1995. *Science in the Multicultural Classroom: A Guide to Teaching and Learning.* Boston, MA: Allyn and Bacon.

Clarkson, P.C. 1991. *Bilingualism and Mathematics Learning.* Geelong, Victoria, Australia: Deakin University Press.

Kessler, C., and M. E. Quinn. 1980. "Bilingualism and Science Problem-Solving Ability." *Bilingual Education Paper Series* 4: 1–30.

Rodriguez, I., and L. Bethel. 1983. "An Inquiry Approach to Science/Language Teaching." *Journal of Research in Science Teaching* 20, no. 2: 291–296.

Schindler, D. E., and D. M. Davison. 1985. "Language, Culture, and the Mathematics Concepts of American Indian Learners." *Journal of American Indian Education* 24, no. 3: 27–34.

Williamson, R. A., ed. 1981. *Archaeoastronomy in the Americas.* Los Altos, CA: Ballena.

NONPRINT RESOURCES

Internet Resources

Bureau of Indian Affairs
http://www.doi.gov/bureau-indian-affairs.html

Web site includes recent press releases, ancestry information, and links to various offices relating to Native Americans.

Center for Information and Resources on Native American Topics
http://nav.webring.yahoo.com/hub?ring=nativeamring&list

This site provides access to resources that help to further the education of the young and promote a better understanding of Native American education.

Codetalk
http://www.codetalk.fed.us/

Information network sponsored by federal agencies with Native American programs. The "Topics of Interest" section provides links to sites dealing with a wide variety of topics such as tribal justice, law enforcement, freedom of religion, and environmental issues. The "Resources and Contacts" section provides links to various tribes and Native American organizations.

FindLaw: American Indian Law
http://www.findlaw.com/01topics/21indian/gov_laws.html

This site has links to primary sources such as the U.S. Constitution, U.S. Code, case law, and treaties relating to Native Americans.

The First Nations Education Centre
http://www.cmsd.bc.ca/Schools/FNEC/PROGRAMS.HTML

This site provides details of its programs, which are "over and above the existing school programs" and are planned and offered in cooperation with schools and communities. The program aims to promote understanding of and respect for the traditions, values, and beliefs of First Nations people from a past, present, and future perspective. There is a special emphasis on First Nations languages, and information is integrated into subject areas. There are three major programs: (1) First Nations Language and Culture Program; (2) First Nations Support Services Program; (3) Other Approved Programs.

Fourth World Documentation Project
http://www.halcyon.com/FWDP/fwdp.html

This site is an on-line "library of texts which record and preserve our peoples' struggles to regain their rightful place in the international community." Includes links to tribal and intertribal resolutions and papers which has links to, among other sites, tribal governments.

Index of Native American Resources on the Internet
http://hanksville.phast.umass.edu/misc/NAresources.html

This comprehensive site includes links to Native American resources for a variety of topics (e.g., culture, language, art, music, legal, activist sites, etc.). It also has links to the full text of selected books, articles, and speeches by and about Native Americans.

Legal Information Institute
http://www.law.cornell.edu

This site provides links to, among other sites, the U.S. Code, U.S. appellate court decisions, and federal and state statutes and codes. A useful starting point for finding statutory, regulatory, and case law.

Native American Home Pages
http://info.pitt.edu/~lmitten/indians.html

This award-winning (including the "Native American Who's Hot Award") site connects to numerous homepages of Native American individuals and tribes as well as organizations and businesses.

Native American Legal Resources
http://hanksville.phast.umass.edu/misc/indices/NAlegal.html

Links to web sites of legal sources related to indigenous issues in the United States, Canada, and Latin America.

Native American Rights Fund
http://www.narf.org

Provides links to the National Indian Law Library, laws and treaties, and a guide to Indian-related web sites (including links to numerous tribal web sites such as the Minnesota Chippewa Tribal Executive Committee).

NativeWeb
http://www.nativeweb.org

The Resource Center section of this site provides numerous links relating to Native American topics.

U.S. House of Representatives Internet Law Library: Indian Nations and Tribes
http://law.house.gov/31.htm

Links to treaties, tribal constitutions, tribal and intertribal resolutions, and various acts relating to Native Americans.

WWW Virtual Library—American Indians
http://www.handsville.org/Naresources/indices/Naetext.html

This site provides access to online magazines and journals, books, and articles with full online texts; online contemporary Native American writing; speeches and interviews; newspaper articles and journalism.

Other General Web Sites

http://nav.webring.yahoo.com/hub?ring=winddrea,&list

This site provides information about different cultural and heritage issues. Exploration of different Native American topics is available.

http://www.hist.unt.edu/09w-na

This site has many links to Native American general sites, tribal pages, Native American professionals, and Canada's First Nations.

http://www.curtis-collection.com/tribalindex.html

This site provides a link to information about eighty western Native American tribes visited by Edward Sheriff Curtis from 1890 to 1930. Curtis's work consists of twenty volumes of text describing all aspects of each Native American tribe's life and customs.

Videotapes

Hidden Nation (1994; 60 min.)
Keepsake Productions

This is the story of the United Houma Nations of Louisiana fight to gain tribal status and recognition.

In the White Man's Image (1990; 59 min)
PBS

This video is part of the American Experience series. It is the story of the attempt to "civilize" Native American students by making them attend the Carlisle Indian School.

Incident at Oglaga (1992; feature length)
Rent

Story of Leonard Peltier and the murders on the Pine Ridge Reservation in South Dakota.

Indian Country (1990; 60 min.)
PBS

Part of a *Frontline* series that explores life on the Quinault Indian Reservation in Washington State. Explores why strong federal leadership and support have failed to improve quality of life on the Indian reservations.

River People: Behind the Case of David Sohappy (1990; 50min).
Filmmakers Library

This video features David Sohappy, a Native American spiritual leader who was sentenced to five years in prison for selling salmon out of season. The video explores the conflict over the resources of the Columbia

River, fishing rights, and rights of religious freedom. Individuals are caught in the conflict between two cultures.

The Spirit of Crazy Horse (1990; 60 min.)
Pacific Arts

The video, part of the American Indian Collection, traces the Sioux as they are forced from their sacred land. It outlines the struggle of Crazy Horse and the tragedy of Wounded Knee as well as a number of other violent clashes with federal forces.

To Protect Mother Earth (1989; 60 min)
Cinema Prod., Inc.

Sequel to *Broken Treaty at Battle Mountain*. The theme of this video is the continuing battle between Native Americans and the U.S. government. The story focuses on the Dann sisters, two western Shoshone sisters, who try to prevent the government from seizing their ancestral land for use in nuclear testing.

Tribal Wisdom and the Modern World: The Tightrope of Power (1992; 60min)
Biniman Prod.

Millennium series no. 9. Describes the struggle of Obijibwa-Cree and Mohawk tribes against the Canadian federal government. This video explores the definitions of pluralism, democracy, and the state.

Where the Spirit Lives (1989; 97min)
Amazing Spirit Prod., Ltd.

The story of two Native American children who are kidnapped by the government and placed where they are emotionally and sometimes sexually abused. The children are forced to give up language, heritage, and their spirit.

Appendix

⚫⟶ Selected Laws

INDIAN CHILD WELFARE ACT, 25 U.S.C. 1901 (1978)

Sec. 1901.—Congressional findings

Recognizing the special relationship between the United States and the Indian tribes and their members and the Federal responsibility to Indian people, the Congress finds

(1) that clause 3, section 8, article I of the United States Constitution provides that "The Congress shall have power to regulate commerce with Indian tribes and, through this and other constitutional authority, Congress has plenary power over Indian affairs;

(2) that Congress, through statutes, treaties, and the general course of dealing with Indian tribes, has assumed the responsibility for the protection and preservation of Indian tribes and their resources;

(3) that there is no resource that is more vital to the continued existence and integrity of Indian tribes than their children and that the United States has a direct interest, as trustee, in protecting Indian children who are members of or are eligible for membership in an Indian tribe;

(4) that an alarmingly high percentage of Indian families are broken up by the removal, often unwarranted, of their children from them by nontribal public and private agencies and that an alarmingly high percentage of such children are placed in non-Indian foster and adoptive homes and institutions; and

(5) that the States, exercising their recognized jurisdiction over Indian child custody proceedings through administrative and judicial bodies, have often failed to recognize the essential tribal relations of Indian people and the cultural and social standards prevailing in Indian communities and families.

Sec. 1902.—Congressional declaration of policy

The Congress hereby declares that it is the policy of this Nation to protect the best interests of Indian children and to promote the stability and security of Indian tribes and families by the establishment of minimum Federal standards for the removal of Indian children from their families and the placement of such children in foster or adoptive homes which will reflect the unique values of Indian culture, and by providing for assistance to Indian tribes in the operation of child and family service programs.

Sec. 1903.—Definitions

For the purposes of this chapter, except as may be specifically provided otherwise, the term

(1) "child custody proceeding" shall mean and include

(i) "foster care placement" which shall mean any action removing an Indian child from its parent or Indian custodian for temporary placement in a foster home or institution or the home of a guardian or conservator where the parent or Indian custodian cannot have the child returned upon demand, but where parental rights have not been terminated;

(ii) "termination of parental rights" which shall mean any action resulting in the termination of the parent-child relationship;

(iii) "preadoptive placement" which shall mean the temporary placement of an Indian child in a foster home or institution after the termination of parental rights, but prior to or in lieu of adoptive placement; and

(iv) "adoptive placement" which shall mean the permanent placement of an Indian child for adoption, including any action resulting in a final decree of adoption.

Such term or terms shall not include a placement based upon an act which, if committed by an adult, would be deemed a crime or upon an award, in a divorce proceeding, of custody to one of the parents.

(2) "extended family member" shall be as defined by the law or custom of the Indian child's tribe or, in the absence of such law or custom, shall be a person who has reached the age of eighteen and who is the Indian child's grandparent, aunt or uncle, brother or sister, brother-in-law or sister-in-law, niece or nephew, first or second cousin, or stepparent;

(3) "Indian" means any person who is a member of an Indian tribe, or who is an Alaska Native and a member of a Regional Corporation as defined in 1606 of title 43;

(4) "Indian child" means any unmarried person who is under age eighteen and is either

(a) a member of an Indian tribe or

(b) is eligible for membership in an Indian tribe and is the biological child of a member of an Indian tribe;

(5) "Indian child's tribe" means

(a) the Indian tribe in which an Indian child is a member or eligible for membership or (b), in the case of an Indian child who is a member of or eligible for membership in more than one tribe, the Indian tribe with which the Indian child has the more significant contacts;

(6) "Indian custodian" means any Indian person who has legal custody of an Indian child under tribal law or custom or under State law or to whom temporary physical care, custody, and control has been transferred by the parent of such child;

(7) "Indian organization" means any group, association, partnership, corporation, or other legal entity owned or controlled by Indians, or a majority of whose members are Indians;

(8) "Indian tribe" means any Indian tribe, band, nation, or other organized group or community of Indians recognized as eligible for the services provided to Indians by the Secretary because of their status as Indians, including any Alaska Native village as defined in section 1602(c) of title 43;

(9) "parent" means any biological parent or parents of an Indian child or any Indian person who has lawfully adopted an Indian child, including adoptions under tribal law or custom. It does not include the unwed father where paternity has not been acknowledged or established;

(10) "reservation" means Indian country as defined in section 1151 of title 18 and any lands, not covered under such section, title to which is either held by the United States in trust for the benefit of any Indian tribe or individual or held by any Indian tribe or individual subject to a restriction by the United States against alienation;

(11) "Secretary" means the Secretary of the Interior; and

(12) "tribal court" means a court with jurisdiction over child custody proceedings and which is either a Court of Indian Offenses, a court established and operated under the code or custom of an Indian tribe, or any other administrative body of a tribe which is vested with authority over child custody proceedings. . . .

Sec. 1911.—Indian tribe jurisdiction over Indian child custody proceedings

(a) Exclusive jurisdiction

An Indian tribe shall have jurisdiction exclusive as to any State over any child custody proceeding involving an Indian child who resides or is domiciled within the reservation of such tribe, except where such jurisdiction is otherwise vested in the State by existing Federal law. Where an Indian child is a ward of a tribal court, the Indian tribe shall retain exclusive jurisdiction, notwithstanding the residence or domicile of the child.

(b) Transfer of proceedings; declination by tribal court

In any State court proceeding for the foster care placement of, or termination of parental rights to, an Indian child not domiciled or residing within the reservation of the Indian child's tribe, the court, in the absence of good cause to the contrary, shall transfer such proceeding to the jurisdiction of the tribe, absent objection by either parent, upon the petition of either parent or the Indian custodian or the Indian child's tribe: Provided, That such transfer shall be subject to declination by the tribal court of such tribe.

(c) State court proceedings; intervention

In any State court proceeding for the foster care placement of, or termination of parental rights to, an Indian child, the Indian custodian of the child and the Indian child's tribe shall have a right to intervene at any point in the proceeding.

(d) Full faith and credit to public acts, records, and judicial proceedings of Indian tribes

The United States, every State, every territory or possession of the United States, and every Indian tribe shall give full faith and credit to the public acts, records, and judicial proceedings of any Indian tribe applicable to Indian child custody proceedings to the same extent that such entities give full faith and credit to the public acts, records, and judicial proceedings of any other entity.

Sec. 1912.—Pending court proceedings

(a) Notice; time for commencement of proceedings; additional time for preparation

In any involuntary proceeding in a State court, where the court knows or has reason to know that an Indian child is involved, the party seeking the foster care placement of, or termination of parental rights to, an Indian child shall notify the parent or Indian custodian and the Indian child's tribe, by registered mail with return receipt requested, of the pending proceedings and of their right of intervention. If the identity or location of the parent or Indian custodian and the tribe cannot be determined, such notice shall be given to the Secretary in like manner, who shall have fifteen days after receipt to provide the requisite notice to the parent or Indian custodian and the tribe. No foster care placement or termination of parental rights proceeding shall be held until at least ten days after receipt of notice by the parent or Indian custodian and the tribe or the Secretary: Provided, That the parent or Indian custodian or the tribe shall, upon request, be granted up to twenty additional days to prepare for such proceeding.

(b) Appointment of counsel

In any case in which the court determines indigency, the parent or Indian custodian shall have the right to court-appointed counsel in any removal, placement, or termination proceeding. The court may, in its discretion, appoint counsel for the child upon a finding that such appointment is in the best interest of the child. Where State law makes no provision for appointment of counsel in such proceedings, the court shall promptly notify the Secretary upon appointment of counsel, and the Secretary, upon certification of the presiding judge, shall pay reasonable fees and expenses out of funds which may be appropriated pursuant to section *13* of this title.

(c) Examination of reports or other documents

Each party to a foster care placement or termination of parental rights proceeding under State law involving an Indian child shall have the right to examine all reports or other documents filed with the court upon which any decision with respect to such action may be based.

(d) Remedial services and rehabilitative programs; preventive measures

Any party seeking to effect a foster care placement of, or termination of parental rights to, an Indian child under State law shall satisfy the court that active efforts have been made to provide remedial services and rehabilitative programs designed to prevent the breakup of the Indian family and that these efforts have proved unsuccessful.

(e) Foster care placement orders; evidence; determination of damage to child

No foster care placement may be ordered in such proceeding in the absence of a determination, supported by clear and convincing evidence, including testimony of qualified expert witnesses, that the continued custody of the child by the parent or Indian custodian is likely to result in serious emotional or physical damage to the child.

(f) Parental rights termination orders; evidence; determination of damage to child

No termination of parental rights may be ordered in such proceeding in the absence of a determination, supported by evidence beyond a reasonable doubt, including testimony of qualified expert witnesses, that the continued custody of the child by the parent or Indian custodian is likely to result in serious emotional or physical damage to the child.

Sec. 1913.—Parental rights; voluntary termination

(a) Consent; record; certification matters; invalid consents

Where any parent or Indian custodian voluntarily consents to a foster care placement or to termination of parental rights, such consent shall not be valid unless executed in writing and recorded before a judge of a court of competent jurisdiction and accompanied by the presiding judge's certificate that the terms and consequences of the consent were fully explained in detail and were fully understood by the parent or Indian custodian. The court shall also certify that either the parent or Indian custodian fully understood the explanation in English or that it was interpreted into a language that the parent or Indian custodian understood. Any consent given prior to, or within ten days after, birth of the Indian child shall not be valid.

(b) Foster care placement; withdrawal of consent

Any parent or Indian custodian may withdraw consent to a foster care placement under State law at any time and, upon such withdrawal, the child shall be returned to the parent or Indian custodian.

(c) Voluntary termination of parental rights or adoptive placement; withdrawal of consent; return of custody

In any voluntary proceeding for termination of parental rights to, or adoptive placement of, an Indian child, the consent of the parent may be withdrawn for any reason at any time prior to the entry of a final decree of termination or adoption, as the case may be, and the child shall be returned to the parent.

(d) Collateral attack; vacation of decree and return of custody; limitations

After the entry of a final decree of adoption of an Indian child in any State court, the parent may withdraw consent thereto upon the grounds that consent was obtained through fraud or duress and may petition the court to vacate such decree. Upon a finding that such consent was obtained through fraud or duress, the court shall vacate such decree and return the child to the parent. No adoption which has been effective for at least two years may be invalidated under the provisions of this subsection unless otherwise permitted under State law.

Sec. 1914.—Petition to court of competent jurisdiction to invalidate action upon showing of certain violations

Any Indian child who is the subject of any action for foster care placement or termination of parental rights under State law, any parent or Indian custodian from whose custody such child was removed, and the Indian child's tribe may petition any court of competent jurisdiction to invalidate such action upon a showing that such action violated any provision of sections *1911, 1912,* and *1913* of this title.

Sec. 1915.—Placement of Indian children

(a) Adoptive placements; preferences

In any adoptive placement of an Indian child under State law, a preference shall be given, in the absence of good cause to the contrary, to a placement with

(1) a member of the child's extended family;

(2) other members of the Indian child's tribe; or

(3) other Indian families.

(b) Foster care or preadoptive placements; criteria; preferences

Any child accepted for foster care or preadoptive placement shall be placed in the least restrictive setting which most approximates a family and in which his special needs, if any, may be met. The child shall also be placed within reasonable proximity to his or her home, taking into account any special needs of the child. In any foster care or preadoptive placement, a preference shall be given, in the absence of good cause to the contrary, to a placement with

(i) a member of the Indian child's extended family;

(ii) a foster home licensed, approved, or specified by the Indian child's tribe;

(iii) an Indian foster home licensed or approved by an authorized non-Indian licensing authority; or

(iv) an institution for children approved by an Indian tribe or operated by an Indian organization which has a program suitable to meet the Indian child's needs.

(c) Tribal resolution for different order of preference; personal preference considered; anonymity in application of preferences

In the case of a placement under subsection (a) or (b) of this section, if the Indian child's tribe shall establish a different order of preference by resolution, the agency or court effecting the placement shall follow such order so long as the placement is the least restrictive setting appropriate to the particular needs of the child, as provided in subsection (b) of this section. Where appropriate, the preference of the Indian child or parent shall be considered: Provided, That where a consenting parent evidences a desire for anonymity, the court or agency shall give weight to such desire in applying the preferences.

(d) Social and cultural standards applicable

The standards to be applied in meeting the preference requirements of this section shall be the prevailing social and cultural standards of the Indian community in which the parent or extended family resides or with which the parent or extended family members maintain social and cultural ties.

(e) Record of placement; availability

A record of each such placement, under State law, of an Indian child shall be maintained by the State in which the placement was made, evidencing the efforts to comply with the order of preference specified in this section. Such record shall be made available at any time upon the request of the Secretary or the Indian child's tribe.

Sec. 1916.—Return of custody

(a) Petition; best interests of child

Notwithstanding State law to the contrary, whenever a final decree of adoption of an Indian child has been vacated or set aside or the adoptive parents voluntarily consent to the termination of their parental rights to the child, a biological parent or prior Indian custodian may petition for return of custody and the court shall grant such petition unless there is a showing, in a proceeding subject to the provisions of section *1912* of this title, that such return of custody is not in the best interests of the child.

(b) Removal from foster care home; placement procedure

Whenever an Indian child is removed from a foster care home or institution for the purpose of further foster care, preadoptive, or adoptive placement, such placement shall be in accordance with the provisions of this chapter, except in the case where an Indian child is being returned to the parent or Indian custodian from whose custody the child was originally removed.

Sec. 1917.—Tribal affiliation information and other information for protection of rights from tribal relationship; application of subject of adoptive placement; disclosure by court

Upon application by an Indian individual who has reached the age of eighteen and who was the subject of an adoptive placement, the court which entered the final decree shall inform such individual of the tribal affiliation, if any, of the individual's biological parents and provide such other information as may be necessary to protect any rights flowing from the individual's tribal relationship.

Sec. 1918.—Reassumption of jurisdiction over child custody proceedings

(a) Petition; suitable plan; approval by Secretary

Any Indian tribe which became subject to State jurisdiction pursuant to the provisions of the Act of August 15, 1953 (67 Stat. 588), as amended by title IV of the Act of April 11, 1968 (82 Stat. 73, 78), or pursuant to any other Federal law, may reassume jurisdiction over child custody proceedings. Before any Indian tribe may reassume jurisdiction over Indian child custody proceedings, such tribe shall present to the Secretary for approval a petition to reassume such jurisdiction which includes a suitable plan to exercise such jurisdiction.

(b) Criteria applicable to consideration by Secretary; partial retrocession

(1) In considering the petition and feasibility of the plan of a tribe under subsection (a) of this section, the Secretary may consider, among other things:

(i) whether or not the tribe maintains a membership roll or alternative provision for clearly identifying the persons who will be affected by the reassumption of jurisdiction by the tribe;

(ii) the size of the reservation or former reservation area which will be affected by retrocession and reassumption of jurisdiction by the tribe;

(iii) the population base of the tribe, or distribution of the population in homogeneous communities or geographic areas; and

(iv) the feasibility of the plan in cases of multitribal occupation of a single reservation or geographic area.

(2) In those cases where the Secretary determines that the jurisdictional provisions of section *1911*(a) of this title are not feasible, he is authorized to accept partial retrocession which will enable tribes to exercise referral jurisdiction as provided in section *1911*(b) of this title, or, where appropriate, will allow them to exercise exclusive jurisdiction as provided in section *1911*(a) of this title over limited community or geographic areas without regard for the reservation status of the area affected.

(c) Approval of petition; publication in Federal Register; notice; reassumption period; correction of causes for disapproval

If the Secretary approves any petition under subsection (a) of this section, the Secretary shall publish notice of such approval in the Federal Register and shall notify the affected State or States of such approval. The Indian tribe concerned shall reassume jurisdiction sixty days after publication in the Federal Register of notice of approval. If the Secretary disapproves any petition under subsection (a) of this section, the Secretary shall provide such technical assistance as may be necessary to enable the tribe to correct any deficiency which the Secretary identified as a cause for disapproval.

(d) Pending actions or proceedings unaffected

Assumption of jurisdiction under this section shall not affect any action or proceeding over which a court has already assumed jurisdiction, except as may be provided pursuant to any agreement under section *1919* of this title.

Sec. 1919.—Agreements between States and Indian tribes

(a) Subject coverage

States and Indian tribes are authorized to enter into agreements with each other respecting care and custody of Indian children and jurisdiction over child custody proceedings, including agreements which may provide for orderly transfer of jurisdiction on a case-by-case basis and agreements which provide for concurrent jurisdiction between States and Indian tribes.

(b) Revocation; notice; actions or proceedings unaffected

Such agreements may be revoked by either party upon one hundred and eighty days' written notice to the other party. Such revocation shall not affect any action or proceeding over which a court has already assumed jurisdiction, unless the agreement provides otherwise.

Sec. 1920.—Improper removal of child from custody; declination of jurisdiction; forthwith return of child: danger exception

Where any petitioner in an Indian child custody proceeding before a State court has improperly removed the child from custody of the parent or Indian custodian or has improperly retained custody after a visit or other temporary relinquishment of custody, the court shall decline jurisdiction over such petition and shall forthwith return the child to his parent or Indian custodian unless returning the child to his parent or custodian would subject the child to a substantial and immediate danger or threat of such danger.

Sec. 1921.—Higher State or Federal standard applicable to protect rights of parent or Indian custodian of Indian child

In any case where State or Federal law applicable to a child custody proceeding under State or Federal law provides a higher standard of protection to the rights of the parent or Indian custodian of an Indian child than the rights provided under this subchapter, the State or Federal court shall apply the State or Federal standard.

Sec. 1922.—Emergency removal or placement of child; termination; appropriate action

Nothing in this subchapter shall be construed to prevent the emergency removal of an Indian child who is a resident of or is domiciled on a reservation, but temporarily located off the reservation, from his parent or Indian custodian or the emergency placement of such child in a foster home or institution, under applicable State law, in order to prevent imminent physical damage or harm to the child. The State authority, official, or agency involved shall insure that the emergency removal or placement terminates immediately when such removal or placement is no longer necessary to prevent imminent physical damage or harm to the child and shall expeditiously initiate a child custody proceeding subject to the provisions of this subchapter, transfer the child to the jurisdiction of the appropriate Indian tribe, or restore the child to the parent or Indian custodian, as may be appropriate.

Sec. 1923.—Effective date

None of the provisions of this subchapter, except sections *1911*(a), *1918,* and *1919* of this title, shall affect a proceeding under State law for foster care placement, termination of parental rights, preadoptive placement, or adoptive placement which was initiated or completed prior to one hundred and eighty days after November 8, 1978, but shall apply to any subsequent proceeding in the same matter or subsequent proceedings affecting the custody or placement of the same child. . . .

Sec. 1931.—Grants for on or near reservation programs and child welfare codes

(a) Statement of purpose; scope of programs

The Secretary is authorized to make grants to Indian tribes and organizations in the establishment and operation of Indian child and family service programs on or near reservations and in the preparation and implementation of child welfare codes. The objective of every Indian child and family service program shall be to prevent the breakup of Indian families and, in particular, to insure that the permanent removal of an Indian child from the custody of his parent or Indian custodian shall be a last resort. Such child and family service programs may include, but are not limited to

(1) a system for licensing or otherwise regulating Indian foster and adoptive homes;

(2) the operation and maintenance of facilities for the counseling and treatment of Indian families and for the temporary custody of Indian children;

(3) family assistance, including homemaker and home counselors, day care, afterschool care, and employment, recreational activities, and respite care;

(4) home improvement programs;

(5) the employment of professional and other trained personnel to assist the tribal court in the disposition of domestic relations and child welfare matters;

(6) education and training of Indians, including tribal court judges and staff, in skills relating to child and family assistance and service programs;

(7) a subsidy program under which Indian adoptive children may be provided support comparable to that for which they would be eligible as foster children, taking into account the appropriate State standards of support for maintenance and medical needs; and

(8) guidance, legal representation, and advice to Indian families involved in tribal, State, or Federal child custody proceedings.

(b) Non-Federal matching funds for related Social Security or other Federal financial assistance programs; assistance for such programs unaffected; State licensing or approval for qualification for assistance under federally assisted program

Funds appropriated for use by the Secretary in accordance with this section may be utilized as non-Federal matching share in connection with funds provided under titles IV-B and XX of the Social Security Act (*42* U.S.C. *620* et seq., 1397 et seq.) or under any other Federal financial assistance programs which contribute to the purpose for which such funds are authorized to be appropriated for use under this chapter. The provision or possibility of assistance under this chapter shall not be a basis for the denial or reduction of any assistance otherwise author ized under titles IV-B and XX of the Social Security Act or any other federally assisted program. For purposes of qualifying for assistance under a federally assisted program, licensing or approval of foster or adoptive homes or institutions by an Indian tribe shall be deemed equivalent to licensing or approval by a State.

Sec. 1932.—Grants for off-reservation programs for additional services

The Secretary is also authorized to make grants to Indian organizations to establish and operate off-reservation Indian child and family service programs which may include, but are not limited to

(1) a system for regulating, maintaining, and supporting Indian foster and adoptive homes, including a subsidy program under which Indian adoptive children may be provided support comparable to that for which they would be eligible as Indian foster children, taking into account the appropriate State standards of support for maintenance and medical needs;

(2) the operation and maintenance of facilities and services for counseling and treatment of Indian families and Indian foster and adoptive children;

(3) family assistance, including homemaker and home counselors, day care, afterschool care, and employment, recreational activities, and respite care; and

(4) guidance, legal representation, and advice to Indian families involved in child custody proceedings.

Sec. 1933.—Funds for on and off reservation programs

(a) Appropriated funds for similar programs of Department of Health and Human Services; appropriation in advance for payments

In the establishment, operation, and funding of Indian child and family service programs, both on and off reservation, the Secretary may enter into agreements with the Secretary of Health and Human Services, and the latter Secretary is hereby authorized for such purposes to use funds appropriated for similar programs of the Department of Health and Human Services: Provided, That authority to make payments pursuant to such agreements shall be effective only to the extent and in such amounts as may be provided in advance by appropriation Acts.

(b) Appropriation authorization under section 13 of this title

Funds for the purposes of this chapter may be appropriated pursuant to the provisions of section *13* of this title.

Sec. 1934.—"Indian" defined for certain purposes

For the purposes of sections *1932* and *1933* of this title, the term "Indian" shall include persons defined in section *1603*(c) of this title. . . .

Sec. 1951.—Information availability to and disclosure by Secretary

(a) Copy of final decree or order; other information; anonymity affidavit; exemption from Freedom of Information Act

Any State court entering a final decree or order in any Indian child adoptive placement after November 8, 1978, shall provide the Secretary with a copy of such decree or order together with such other information as may be necessary to show

(1) the name and tribal affiliation of the child;

(2) the names and addresses of the biological parents;

(3) the names and addresses of the adoptive parents; and

(4) the identity of any agency having files or information relating to such adoptive placement.

Where the court records contain an affidavit of the biological parent or parents that their identity remain confidential, the court shall include such affidavit with the other information. The Secretary shall insure that the confidentiality of such information is maintained and such information shall not be subject to the Freedom of Information Act (*5* U.S.C. *552*), as amended.

(b) Disclosure of information for enrollment of Indian child in tribe or for determination of member rights or benefits; certification of entitlement to enrollment

Upon the request of the adopted Indian child over the age of eighteen, the adoptive or foster parents of an Indian child, or an Indian tribe, the Secretary shall disclose such information as may be necessary for the enrollment of an Indian child in the tribe in which the child may be eligible for enrollment or for determining any rights or benefits associated with that membership. Where the documents relating to such child contain an affidavit from the biological parent or parents requesting anonymity, the Secretary shall certify to the Indian child's tribe, where the information warrants, that the child's parentage and other circumstances of birth entitle the child to enrollment under the criteria established by such tribe.

Sec. 1952.—Rules and regulations

Within one hundred and eighty days after November 8, 1978, the Secretary shall promulgate such rules and regulations as may be necessary to carry out the provisions of this chapter. . . .

Sec. 1961.—Locally convenient day schools

(a) Sense of Congress

It is the sense of Congress that the absence of locally convenient day schools may contribute to the breakup of Indian families.

(b) Report to Congress; contents, etc.

The Secretary is authorized and directed to prepare, in consultation with appropriate agencies in the Department of Health and Human Services, a report on the feasibility of providing Indian children with schools located near their homes, and to submit such report to the Select Committee on Indian Affairs of the United States Senate and the Committee on Interior and Insular Affairs of the United States House of Representatives within two years from November 8, 1978. In developing this report the Secretary shall give particular consideration to the provision of educational facilities for children in the elementary grades.

Sec. 1962.—Copies to the States

Within sixty days after November 8, 1978, the Secretary shall send to the Governor, chief justice of the highest court of appeal, and the attorney general of each State a copy of this chapter, together with committee reports and an explanation of the provisions of this chapter.

Sec. 1963.—Severability

If any provision of this chapter or the applicability thereof is held invalid, the remaining provisions of this chapter shall not be affected thereby.

INDIAN EDUCATION ASSISTANCE ACT (AMENDS INDIAN EDUCATION ACT THROUGH 1994) 25 U.S.C. 455 (1975)

Sec. 455.—Contracts for education in public schools; submission of education plan by contractor as prerequisite; criteria for approval of plan by Secretary of the Interior; participation by non-Indian students

The Secretary of the Interior shall not enter into any contract for the education of Indians unless the prospective contractor has submitted to, and has had approved by the Secretary of the Interior, an education plan, which plan, in the determination of the Secretary, contains educational objectives which adequately address the educational needs of the Indian students who are to be beneficiaries of the contract and assures that the contract is capable of meeting such objectives: Provided, That where students other than Indian students participate in such programs, money expended under such contract shall be prorated to cover the participation of only the Indian students.

Sec. 456.—Local committee of Indian parents in school districts having school boards composed of non-Indian majority

(a) Election; functions

Whenever a school district affected by a contract or contracts for the education of Indians pursuant to sections *452* to *457* of this title has a local school board not composed of a majority of Indians, the parents of the Indian children enrolled in the school or schools affected by such contract or contracts shall elect a local committee from among their number. Such committee shall fully participate in the development of, and shall have the authority to approve or disapprove programs to be conducted under such contract or contracts, and shall carry out such other duties, and be so structured, as the Secretary of the Interior shall by regulation provide: Provided, however, That, whenever a local Indian committee or committees established pursuant to section 7814(c)(4) of title *20* or an Indian advisory school board or boards established pursuant to sections *452* to *457* of this title prior to January 4, 1975, exists in such school district, such committee or board may, in the discretion of the affected tribal governing body or bodies, be utilized for the purposes of this section.

(b) Revocation of contracts

The Secretary of the Interior may, in his discretion, revoke any contract if the contractor fails to permit a local committee to perform its duties pursuant to subsection (a) of this section.

Sec. 457.—Reimbursement to school districts for educating non-resident students

Any school district educating Indian students who are members of recognized Indian tribes, who do not normally reside in the State in which such school district is located, and who are residing in Federal boarding facilities for the purposes of attending public schools within such district may, in the discretion of the Secretary of the Interior, be reimbursed by him for the full per capita costs of educating such Indian students.

Sec. 458.—School construction, acquisition, or renovation contracts

(a) Authorization; prerequisites

The Secretary is authorized to enter into a contract or contracts with any State education agency or school district for the purpose of assisting such agency or district in the acquisition of sites for, or the construction, acquisition, or renovation of facilities (including all necessary equipment) in school districts on or adjacent to or in close proximity to any Indian reservation or other lands held in trust by the United States for Indians, if such facilities are necessary for the education of Indians residing on any such reservation or lands.

(b) Eligibility requirements for assistance in federally-affected areas; applicability to projects in determining maximum amount, allocation, of funds, etc.

The Secretary may expend not less than 75 per centum of such funds as are authorized and appropriated pursuant to this section on those projects which meet the eligibility requirements under subsections (a) and (b) of section 644 of title *20*. Such funds shall be allocated on the basis of existing funding priorities, if any, established by the Secretary of Education under subsections (a) and (b) of section 644 of title *20*. The Secretary of Education is directed to submit to the Secretary, at the beginning of each fiscal year, commencing with the first full fiscal year after January 4, 1975, a list of those projects eligible for funding under subsections (a) and (b) of section 644 of title *20*.

(c) Eligibility of private schools to receive funds; maximum amount

The Secretary may expend not more than 25 per centum of such funds as may be authorized and appropriated pursuant to this section on any school eligible to receive funds under section *458d* of this title.

(d) Duties of State education agencies pursuant to contracts

Any contract entered into by the Secretary pursuant to this section shall contain provisions requiring the relevant State educational agency to

(1) provide Indian students attending any such facilities constructed, acquired, or renovated, in whole or in part, from funds made available pursuant to this section with standards of education not less than those provided non-Indian students in the school district in which the facilities are situated; and

(2) meet, with respect to such facilities, the requirements of the State and local building codes, and other building standards set by the State educational agency or school district for other public school facilities under its jurisdiction or control or by the local government in the jurisdiction within which the facilities are situated.

(e) Advisory consultations by Secretary with affected entities and governing bodies prior to contracts; applicability

The Secretary shall consult with the entity designated pursuant to section *456* of this title, and with the governing body of any Indian tribe or tribes the educational opportunity for the members of which will be significantly affected by any contract entered into pursuant to this section. Such consultation shall be advisory only, but shall occur prior to the entering into of any such contract. The foregoing provisions of this subsection shall not be applicable where the application for a contract pursuant to this section is submitted by an elected school board of which a majority of its members are Indians.

(f) Evaluation and report to Congress of effectiveness of construction, etc., programs; scope and content of report

Within ninety days following the expiration of the three year period following January 4, 1975, the Secretary shall evaluate the effectiveness of the program pursuant to this section and transmit a report of such evaluation to the Congress. Such report shall include

(1) an analysis of construction costs and the impact on such costs of the provisions of subsection (f) of this section and the Act of March 3, 1921 (46 Stat. 1491), as amended (*40* U.S.C. *276a* et seq);

(2) a description of the working relationship between the Department of the Interior and the Department of Education including any memorandum of understanding in connection with the acquisition of data pursuant to subsection (b) of this section;

(3) projections of the Secretary of future construction needs of the public schools serving Indian children residing on or adjacent to Indian reservations;

(4) a description of the working relationship of the Department of the Interior with local or State educational agencies in connection with the contracting for construction, acquisition, or renovation of school facilities pursuant to this section; and

(5) the recommendations of the Secretary with respect to the transfer of the responsibility for administering subsections (a) and (b) of section 644 of title *20* from the Department of Education to the Department of the Interior.

(g) Authorization of appropriations

For the purpose of carrying out the provisions of this section, there is authorized to be appropriated the sum of $35,000,000 for the fiscal year ending June 30, 1974; $35,000,000 for each of the four succeeding fiscal years; and thereafter, such sums as may be necessary, all of such sums to remain available until expended.

Sec. 458a.—General education contract and grant provisions and requirements; school district quality and standards of excellence

No funds from any grant or contract pursuant to this part shall be made available to any school district unless the Secretary is satisfied that the quality and standard of education, including facilities and auxiliary services, for Indian students enrolled in the schools of such district are at least equal to that provided all other students from resources, other than resources provided in this part, available to the local school district.

Sec. 458b.—Availability of funds to agencies, institutions, and organizations

No funds from any contract or grant pursuant to this part shall be made available by any Federal agency directly to other than public agencies and Indian tribes, institutions, and organizations: Provided, That school districts, State education agencies, and Indian tribes, institutions, and organizations assisted by this part may use funds provided herein to contract for necessary services with any appropriate individual, organization, or corporation.

Sec. 458c.—Rules and regulations

(a) Prerequisites for promulgation

(1) Within six months from January 4, 1975, the Secretary shall, to the extent practicable, consult with national and regional Indian organizations with experiences in Indian education to consider and formulate appropriate rules and regulations to implement the provisions of this part.

(2) Within seven months from January 4, 1975, the Secretary shall present the proposed rules and regulations to the Committees on Interior and Insular Affairs of the United States Senate and House of Representatives.

(3) Within eight months from January 4, 1975, the Secretary shall publish proposed rules and regulations in the Federal Register for the purpose of receiving comments from interested parties.

(4) Within ten months from January 4, 1975, the Secretary shall promulgate rules and regulations to implement the provisions of this part.

(b) Revision and amendment

The Secretary is authorized to revise and amend any rules or regulations promulgated pursuant to subsection (a) of this section: Provided, That prior to any revision or amendment to such rules or regulations the Secretary shall, to the extent practicable, consult with appropriate national and regional Indian organizations, and shall publish any proposed revisions in the Federal Register not less than sixty days prior to the effective date of such rules and regulations in order to provide adequate notice to, and receive comments from, other interested parties.

Sec. 458d.—Eligibility for funds of tribe or tribal organization controlling or managing private schools

The Secretary is authorized and directed to provide funds, pursuant to this subchapter; the Act of April 16, 1934 (48 Stat. 596), as amended (25 U.S.C. 452 et seq.); or any other authority granted to him to any tribe or tribal organization which controls and manages any previously private school.

Sec. 458e.—Supplemental assistance to funds provided to local educational agencies

The assistance provided in this subchapter for the education of Indians in the public schools of any State is in addition and supplemental to assistance provided under Title IX of the Elementary and Secondary Education Act of 1965 (20 U.S.C. 7801 et seq.).

Sec. 458aa.—Establishment

The Secretary of the Interior (hereinafter in this part referred to as the "Secretary") shall establish and carry out a program within the Department of the Interior to be known as Tribal Self-Governance (hereinafter in this part referred to as "Self-Governance") in accordance with this part.

Sec. 458bb.—Selection of participating Indian tribes

(a) Continuing participation

Each Indian tribe that is participating in the Tribal Self-Governance Demonstration Project at the Department of the Interior under Title III on October 25, 1994, shall thereafter participate in Self-Governance under this part and cease participation in the Tribal Self-Governance Demonstration Project under Title III with respect to the Department of the Interior.

(b) Additional participants

(1) In addition to those Indian tribes participating in self-governance under subsection (a) of this section, the Secretary, acting through the Director of the Office of Self-Governance, may select up to 50 new tribes per year from the applicant pool described in subsection (c) of this section to participate in self-governance.

(2) If each tribe requests, two or more otherwise eligible Indian tribes may be treated as a single Indian tribe for the purpose of participating in Self-Governance as a consortium.

(c) Applicant pool

The qualified applicant pool for Self-Governance shall consist of each tribe that

(1) successfully completes the planning phase described in subsection (d) of this section;

(2) has requested participation in Self-Governance by resolution or other official action by the tribal governing body; and

(3) has demonstrated, for the previous three fiscal years, financial stability and financial management capability as evidenced by the tribe having no material audit exceptions in the required annual audit of the self-determination contracts of the tribe.

(d) Planning phase

Each Indian tribe seeking to begin participation in Self-Governance shall complete a planning phase in accordance with this subsection. The tribe shall be eligible for a grant to plan and negotiate participation in Self-Governance. The planning phase shall include

(1) legal and budgetary research; and

(2) internal tribal government planning and organizational preparation

Sec. 458cc.—Funding agreements

(a) Authorization

The Secretary shall negotiate and enter into an annual written funding agreement with the governing body of each participating tribal government in a manner consistent with the Federal Government's laws and trust relationship to and responsibility for the Indian people.

(b) Contents

Each funding agreement shall

(1) authorize the tribe to plan, conduct, consolidate, and administer programs, services, functions, and activities, or portions thereof, administered by the Department of the Interior through the Bureau of Indian Affairs, without regard to the agency or office of the Bureau of Indian Affairs within which the program, service, function, and activity, or portion thereof, is performed, including funding for agency, area, and central office functions in accordance with subsection (g)(3) of this section, and including any program, service, function, and activity, or portion thereof, administered under the authority of

(A) the Act of April 16, 1934 (*25* U.S.C. *452* et seq.);

(B) section *13* of this title; and

(C) programs, services, functions, and activities or portions thereof administered by the Secretary of the Interior that are otherwise available to Indian tribes or Indians for which appropriations are made to agencies other than the Department of the Interior;

(2) subject to such terms as may be negotiated, authorize the tribe to plan, conduct, consolidate, and administer programs, services, functions, and activities, or portions thereof, administered by the Department of the Interior, other than through the Bureau of Indian Affairs, that are otherwise available to Indian tribes or Indians, as identified in section *458ee*(c) of this title, except that nothing in this subsection may be construed to provide any tribe with a preference with respect to the opportunity of the tribe to administer programs, services, functions, and activities, or portions thereof, unless such preference is otherwise provided for by law;

(3) subject to the terms of the agreement, authorize the tribe to redesign or consolidate programs, services, functions, and activities, or portions thereof, and reallocate funds for such programs, services, functions, and activities, or portions thereof, except that, with respect to the reallocation, consolidation, and redesign of programs described in paragraph (2), a joint agreement between the Secretary and the tribe shall be required;

(4) prohibit the inclusion of funds provided

(A) pursuant to the Tribally Controlled College or University Assistance Act of 1978 (*25* U.S.C. *1801* et seq.);

(B) for elementary and secondary schools under the formula developed pursuant to section *2008* of this title; and

(C) the Flathead Agency Irrigation Division or the Flathead Agency Power Division, except that nothing in this section shall affect the contract authority of such divisions under section *450f* of this title;

(5) specify the services to be provided, the functions to be performed, and the responsibilities of the tribe and the Secretary pursuant to the agreement;

(6) authorize the tribe and the Secretary to reallocate funds or modify budget allocations within any year, and specify the procedures to be used;

(7) allow for retrocession of programs or portions of programs pursuant to section *450j*(e) of this title;

(8) provide that, for the year for which, and to the extent to which, funding is provided to a tribe under this section, the tribe

(A) shall not be entitled to contract with the Secretary for such funds under section *450f* of this title, except that such tribe shall be eligible for new programs on the same basis as other tribes; and

(B) shall be responsible for the administration of programs, services, functions, and activities pursuant to agreements entered into under this section; and

(9) prohibit the Secretary from waiving, modifying, or diminishing in any way the trust responsibility of the United States with respect to Indian tribes and individual Indians that exists under treaties, Executive orders, and other laws.

(c) Additional activities

Each funding agreement negotiated pursuant to subsections (a) and (b) of this section may, in accordance to such additional terms as the parties deem appropriate, also include other programs, services, functions, and activities, or portions thereof, administered by the Secretary of the Interior which are of special geographic, historical, or cultural significance to the participating Indian tribe requesting a compact.

(d) Provisions relating to Secretary

Funding agreements negotiated between the Secretary and an Indian tribe shall include provisions

(1) to monitor the performance of trust functions by the tribe through the annual trust evaluation, and

(2) for the Secretary to reassume a program, service, function, or activity, or portions thereof, if there is a finding of imminent jeopardy to a physical trust asset, natural resources, or public health and safety.

(e) Construction projects

(1) Regarding construction programs or projects, the Secretary

and Indian tribes may negotiate for the inclusion of specific provisions of the Office of Federal Procurement and Policy Act (*41* U.S.C. *401* et seq.) and Federal acquisition regulations in any funding agreement entered into under this subchapter. Absent a negotiated agreement, such provisions and regulatory requirements shall not apply.

(2) In all construction projects performed pursuant to this part, the Secretary shall ensure that proper health and safety standards are provided for in the funding agreements.

(f) Submission for review

Not later than 90 days before the proposed effective date of an agreement entered into under this section, the Secretary shall submit a copy of such agreement to

(1) each Indian tribe that is served by the Agency that is serving the tribe that is a party to the funding agreement;

(2) the Committee on Indian Affairs of the Senate; and

(3) the Subcommittee on Native American Affairs of the Committee on Natural Resources of the House of Representatives.

(g) Payment

(1) At the request of the governing body of the tribe and under the terms of an agreement entered into under this section, the Secretary shall provide funding to the tribe to carry out the agreement.

(2) The funding agreements authorized by this part and title III of this Act shall provide for advance payments to the tribes in the form of annual or semi-annual installments at the discretion of the tribes.

(3) Subject to paragraph (4) of this subsection and paragraphs (1) through (3) of subsection (b) of this section, the Secretary shall provide funds to the tribe under an agreement under this part for programs, services, functions, and activities, or portions thereof, in an amount equal to the amount that the tribe would have been eligible to receive under contracts and grants under this subchapter, including amounts for direct program and contract support costs and, in addition, any funds that are specifically or functionally related to the provision by the Secretary of services and benefits to the tribe or its members, without regard to the organization level within the Department where such functions are carried out.

(4) Funds for trust services to individual Indians shall be available under an agreement entered into under this section only to the extent that the same services that would have been provided by the Secretary are provided to individual Indians by the tribe.

(h) Civil actions

(1) Except as provided in paragraph (2), for the purposes of section *450m–1* of this title, the term "contract" shall include agreements entered into under this part.

(2) For the period that an agreement entered into under this part is in effect, the provisions of section *81* of this title, section *476* of this title, and the Act of July 3, 1952 (*25* U.S.C. *82a*), shall not apply to attorney and other professional contracts by Indian tribal governments participating in Self-Governance under this part.

(i) Facilitation

(1) Except as otherwise provided by law, the Secretary shall interpret each Federal law and regulation in a manner that will facilitate

(A) the inclusion of programs, services, functions, and activities in the agreements entered into under this section; and

(B) the implementation of agreements entered into under this section.

(2)

(A) A tribe may submit a written request for a waiver to the Secretary identifying the regulation sought to be waived and the basis for the request.

(B) Not later than 60 days after receipt by the Secretary of a written request by a tribe to waive application of a Federal regulation for an agreement entered into under this section, the Secretary shall either approve or deny the requested waiver in writing to the tribe. A denial may be made only upon a specific finding by the Secretary that identified language in the regulation may not be waived because such waiver is prohibited by Federal law. The Secretary's decision shall be final for the Department.

(j) Funds

All funds provided under funding agreements entered into pursuant to this subchapter, and all funds provided under contracts or grants made pursuant to this subchapter, shall be treated as non-Federal funds for purposes of meeting matching requirements under any other Federal law.

(k) Disclaimer

Nothing in this section is intended or shall be construed to expand or alter existing statutory authorities in the Secretary so as to authorize the Secretary to enter into any agreement under subsection (b)(2) of this section and section *458ee*(c)(1) of this title with respect to functions that are inherently Federal or where the statute establishing the existing program does not authorize the type of participation sought by the tribe: Provided, however an Indian tribe or tribes need not be identified in the authorizing statute in order for a program or element of a program to be included in a compact under subsection (b)(2) of this section.

(l) Incorporate self-determination provisions

At the option of a participating tribe or tribes, any or all provisions of part A of this subchapter shall be made part of an agreement entered into under title III of this Act or this part. The Secretary is obligated to include such provisions at the option of the participating tribe or tribes. If such provision is incorporated it shall have the same force and effect as if set out in full in title III or this part.

Sec. 458dd.—Budget request

The Secretary shall identify, in the annual budget request of the President to the Congress under section *1105* of title *31* any funds proposed to be included in agreements authorized under this part.

Sec. 458ee.—Reports

(a) Requirement

The Secretary shall submit to Congress a written report on January 1 of each year following October 25, 1994, regarding the administration of this part.

(b) Contents

The report shall

(1) identify the relative costs and benefits of Self-Governance;

(2) identify, with particularity, all funds that are specifically or functionally related to the provision by the Secretary of services and benefits to Self-Governance tribes and their members;

(3) identify the funds transferred to each Self-Governance tribe and the corresponding reduction in the Federal bureaucracy;

(4) include the separate views of the tribes; and

(5) include the funding formula for individual tribal shares of Central Office funds, together with the comments of affected Indian tribes, developed under subsection (d) of this section.

(c) Report on non-BIA programs

(1) In order to optimize opportunities for including non-Bureau of Indian Affairs programs, services, functions, and activities, or portions thereof, in agreements with tribes participating in Self-Governance under this part, the Secretary shall

(A) review all programs, services, functions, and activities, or portions thereof, administered by the Department of the Interior, other than through the Bureau of Indian Affairs, without regard to the agency or office concerned; and

(B) not later than 90 days after October 25, 1994, provide to the appropriate committees of Congress a listing of all such programs, services, functions, and activities, or portions thereof, that the Secretary determines, with the concurrence of tribes participating in Self-Governance under this part, are eligible for inclusion in such agreements at the request of a participating Indian tribe.

(2) The Secretary shall establish programmatic targets, after con-

sultation with tribes participating in Self-Governance under this part, to encourage bureaus of the Department to assure that a significant portion of such programs, services, functions, and activities are actually included in the agreements negotiated under section *458cc* of this title.

(3) The listing and targets under paragraphs (1) and (2) shall be published in the Federal Register and be made available to any Indian tribe participating in Self-Governance under this part. The list shall be published before January 1, 1995, and annually thereafter by January 1 preceding the fiscal year in which the targets are to be met.

(4) Thereafter, the Secretary shall annually review and publish in the Federal Register, after consultation with tribes participating in Self-Governance under this part, a revised listing and programmatic targets.

(d) Report on Central Office funds

Within 90 days after October 25, 1994, the Secretary shall, in consultation with Indian tribes, develop a funding formula to determine the individual tribal share of funds controlled by the Central Office of the Bureau of Indian Affairs for inclusion in the Self-Governance compacts. The Secretary shall include such formula in the annual report submitted to the Congress under subsection (b) of this section, together with the views of the affected Indian tribes.

Sec. 458ff.—Disclaimers

(a) Other services, contracts, and funds

Nothing in this part shall be construed to limit or reduce in any way the services, contracts, or funds that any other Indian tribe or tribal organization is eligible to receive under section *450f* of this title or any other applicable Federal law.

(b) Federal trust responsibilities

Nothing in this subchapter shall be construed to diminish the Federal trust responsibility to Indian tribes, individual Indians, or Indians with trust allotments.

(c) Application of other sections of subchapter

All provisions of sections *450c*(d), *450d, 450f*(c), *450i, 450j*(f), *450m–1,* and *450n* of this title shall apply to agreements provided under this part.

Sec. 458gg.—Regulations

(a) In general

Not later than 90 days after October 25, 1994, at the request of a majority of the Indian tribes with agreements under this part, the Secretary shall initiate procedures under subchapter III of chapter 5 of title 5 to negotiate and promulgate such regulations as are necessary to carry out this part.

(b) Committee

A negotiated rulemaking committee established pursuant to section 565 of title 5 to carry out this section shall have as its members only Federal and tribal government representatives, a majority of whom shall be representatives of Indian tribes with agreements under this part.

(c) Adaptation of procedures

The Secretary shall adapt the negotiated rulemaking procedures to the unique context of Self-Governance and the government-to-government relationship between the United States and the Indian tribes.

(d) Effect

The lack of promulgated regulations shall not limit the effect of this part.

Sec. 458hh.—Authorization of appropriations

There are authorized to be appropriated such sums as may be necessary to carry out this part.

INDIAN SELF-DETERMINATION AND EDUCATION ASSISTANCE ACT, 25 U.S.C. 450 (1975)

Sec. 450.—Congressional statement of findings

(a) Findings respecting historical and special legal relationship, and resultant responsibilities

The Congress, after careful review of the Federal Government's historical and special legal relationship with, and resulting responsibilities to, American Indian people, finds that

(1) the prolonged Federal domination of Indian service programs has served to retard rather than enhance the progress of Indian people and their communities by depriving Indians of the full opportunity to develop leadership skills crucial to the realization of self-government, and has denied to the Indian people an effective voice in the planning and implementation of programs for the benefit of Indians which are responsive to the true needs of Indian communities; and

(2) the Indian people will never surrender their desire to control their relationships both among themselves and with non-Indian governments, organizations, and persons.

(b) Further findings

The Congress further finds that

(1) true self-determination in any society of people is dependent upon an educational process which will insure the development of qualified people to fulfill meaningful leadership roles;

(2) the Federal responsibility for and assistance to education of Indian children has not effected the desired level of educational

achievement or created the diverse opportunities and personal satisfaction which education can and should provide; and

(3) parental and community control of the educational process is of crucial importance to the Indian people.

Sec. 450a.—Congressional declaration of policy

(a) Recognition of obligation of United States

The Congress hereby recognizes the obligation of the United States to respond to the strong expression of the Indian people for self-determination by assuring maximum Indian participation in the direction of educational as well as other Federal services to Indian communities so as to render such services more responsive to the needs and desires of those communities.

(b) Declaration of commitment

The Congress declares its commitment to the maintenance of the Federal Government's unique and continuing relationship with, and responsibility to, individual Indian tribes and to the Indian people as a whole through the establishment of a meaningful Indian self-determination policy which will permit an orderly transition from the Federal domination of programs for, and services to, Indians to effective and meaningful participation by the Indian people in the planning, conduct, and administration of those programs and services. In accordance with this policy, the United States is committed to supporting and assisting Indian tribes in the development of strong and stable tribal governments, capable of administering quality programs and developing the economies of their respective communities.

(c) Declaration of national goal

The Congress declares that a major national goal of the United States is to provide the quantity and quality of educational services and opportunities which will permit Indian children to compete and excel in the life areas of their choice, and to achieve the measure of self-determination essential to their social and economic well-being.

Sec. 450a–1.—Tribal and Federal advisory committees

Notwithstanding any other provision of law (including any regulation), the Secretary of the Interior and the Secretary of Health and Human Services are authorized to jointly establish and fund advisory committees or other advisory bodies composed of members of Indian tribes or members of Indian tribes and representatives of the Federal Government to ensure tribal participation in the implementation of the Indian Self-Determination and Education Assistance Act (*Public Law 93–638*) (*25* U.S.C. *450* et seq.)

Sec. 450b.—Definitions

For purposes of this subchapter, the term

(a) "construction programs" means programs for the planning, design, construction, repair, improvement, and expansion of buildings or facilities, including, but not limited to, housing, law enforcement and detention facilities, sanitation and water systems, roads, schools, administration and health facilities, irrigation and agricultural work, and water conservation, flood control, or port facilities;

(b) "contract funding base" means the base level from which contract funding needs are determined, including all contract costs;

(c) "direct program costs" means costs that can be identified specifically with a particular contract objective;

(d) "Indian" means a person who is a member of an Indian tribe;

(e) "Indian tribe" means any Indian tribe, band, nation, or other organized group or community, including any Alaska Native village or regional or village corporation as defined in or established pursuant to the Alaska Native Claims Settlement Act (85 Stat. 688) (*43* U.S.C. *1601* et seq.), which is recognized as eligible for the special programs and services provided by the United States to Indians because of their status as Indians;

(f) "indirect costs" means costs incurred for a common or joint purpose benefiting more than one contract objective, or which are not readily assignable to the contract objectives specifically benefited without effort disproportionate to the results achieved;

(g) "indirect cost rate" means the rate arrived at through negotiation between an Indian tribe or tribal organization and the appropriate Federal agency;

(h) "mature contract" means a self-determination contract that has been continuously operated by a tribal organization for three or more years, and for which there are no significant and material audit exceptions in the annual financial audit of the tribal organization: Provided, That upon the request of a tribal organization or the tribal organization's Indian tribe for purposes of section *450f*(a) of this title, a contract of the tribal organization which meets this definition shall be considered to be a mature contract;

(i) "Secretary," unless otherwise designated, means either the Secretary of Health and Human Services or the Secretary of the Interior or both;

(j) "self-determination contract" means a contract (or grant or cooperative agreement utilized under section *450e–1* of this title) entered into under part A of this subchapter between a tribal organization and the appropriate Secretary for the planning, conduct and administration of programs or services which are otherwise provided to Indian tribes and their members pursuant to Federal law: Provided, That except as provided the last proviso in section 450j(a) of this title, no contract (or grant or cooperative agreement utilized under section *450e–1* of this title) entered into under part A of this subchapter shall be construed to be a procurement contract;

(k) "State education agency" means the State board of education or other agency or officer primarily responsible for supervision by the State of public elementary and secondary schools, or, if there is no such officer or agency, an officer or agency designated by the Governor or by State law;

(l) "tribal organization" means the recognized governing body of any Indian tribe; any legally established organization of Indians which is controlled, sanctioned, or chartered by such governing body or which is democratically elected by the adult members of the Indian community to be served by such organization and which includes the maximum participation of Indians in all phases of its activities: Provided, That in any case where a contract is let or grant made to an organization to perform services benefiting more than one Indian tribe, the approval of each such Indian tribe shall be a prerequisite to the letting or making of such contract or grant; and

(m) "construction contract" means a fixed-price or cost-reimbursement self-determination contract for a construction project, except that such term does not include any contract

(1) that is limited to providing planning services and construction management services (or a combination of such services);

(2) for the Housing Improvement Program or roads maintenance program of the Bureau of Indian Affairs administered by the Secretary of the Interior; or

(3) for the health facility maintenance and improvement program administered by the Secretary of Health and Human Services.

Sec. 450c.—Reporting and audit requirements for recipients of Federal financial assistance

(a) Maintenance of records

(1) Each recipient of Federal financial assistance under this subchapter shall keep such records as the appropriate Secretary shall prescribe by regulation promulgated under sections *552* and *553* of title *5,* including records which fully disclose

(A) the amount and disposition by such recipient of the proceeds of such assistance,

(B) the cost of the project or undertaking in connection with which such assistance is given or used,

(C) the amount of that portion of the cost of the project or undertaking supplied by other sources, and

(D) such other information as will facilitate an effective audit.

(2) For the purposes of this subsection, such records for a mature contract shall consist of quarterly financial statements for the purpose of accounting for Federal funds, the annual single-agency audit required by chapter 75 of title 31 and a brief annual program report.

(b) Access to books, documents, papers, and records for audit and examination by Comptroller General, etc.

The Comptroller General and the appropriate Secretary, or any of their duly authorized representatives, shall, until the expiration of three years after completion of the project or undertaking referred to in the preceding subsection of this section, have access (for the purpose of audit and examination) to any books, documents, papers, and records of such recipients which in the opinion of the Comptroller General or the appropriate Secretary may be related or pertinent to the grants, contracts, subcontracts, subgrants, or other arrangements referred to in the preceding subsection.

(c) Availability by recipient of required reports and information to Indian people served or represented

Each recipient of Federal financial assistance referred to in subsection (a) of this section shall make such reports and information available to the Indian people served or represented by such recipient as and in a manner determined to be adequate by the appropriate Secretary.

(d) Repayment to Treasury by recipient of unexpended or unused funds

Except as provided in section 13a or 450j–1(a)(3) of this title, funds paid to a financial assistance recipient referred to in subsection (a) of this section and not expended or used for the purposes for which paid shall be repaid to the Treasury of the United States through the respective Secretary.

(e) Annual report to tribes

The Secretary shall report annually in writing to each tribe regarding projected and actual staffing levels, funding obligations, and expenditures for programs operated directly by the Secretary serving that tribe.

(f) Single-agency audit report; additional information; declination criteria and procedures

(1) For each fiscal year during which an Indian tribal organization receives or expends funds pursuant to a contract entered into, or grant made, under this subchapter, the tribal organization that requested such contract or grant shall submit to the appropriate Secretary a single-agency audit report required by chapter 75 of title 31.

(2) In addition to submitting a single-agency audit report pur-

suant to paragraph (1), a tribal organization referred to in such paragraph shall submit such additional information concerning the conduct of the program, function, service, or activity carried out pursuant to the contract or grant that is the subject of the report as the tribal organization may negotiate with the Secretary.

(3) Any disagreement over reporting requirements shall be subject to the declination criteria and procedures set forth in section *450f* of this title.

Sec. 450d.—Criminal activities involving grants, contracts, etc.; penalties

Whoever, being an officer, director, agent, or employee of, or connected in any capacity with, any recipient of a contract, subcontract, grant, or subgrant pursuant to this subchapter or the Act of April 16, 1934 (48 Stat. 596), as amended (*25* U.S.C. *452* et seq.), embezzles, willfully misapplies, steals, or obtains by fraud any of the money, funds assets, or property which are the subject of such a grant, subgrant, contract, or subcontract, shall be fined not more than $10,000 or imprisoned for not more than two years, or both, but if the amount so embezzled, misapplied, stolen, or obtained by fraud does not exceed $100, he shall be fined not more than $1,000 or imprisoned not more than one year, or both.

Sec. 450e.—Wage and labor standards

(a) Similar construction in locality

All laborers and mechanics employed by contractors or subcontractors (excluding tribes and tribal organizations) in the construction, alteration, or repair, including painting or decorating of buildings or other facilities in connection with contracts or grants entered into pursuant to this subchapter, shall be paid wages at not less than those prevailing on similar construction in the locality, as determined by the Secretary of Labor in accordance with the Davis-Bacon Act of March 3, 1931 (46 Stat. 1494), as amended (*40* U.S.C. *276a* et seq.). With respect to construction, alteration, or repair work to which the Act of March 3, 1921 is applicable under the terms of this section, the Secretary of Labor shall have the authority and functions set forth in Reorganization Plan Numbered 14, of 1950, and section *276c* of title *40*.

(b) Preference requirements for wages and grants

Any contract, subcontract, grant, or subgrant pursuant to this subchapter, the Act of April 16, 1934 (48 Stat. 596), as amended (*25* U.S.C. *452* et seq.), or any other Act authorizing Federal contracts with or grants to Indian organizations or for the benefit of Indians, shall require that to the greatest extent feasible

(1) preferences and opportunities for training and employment

in connection with the administration of such contracts or grants shall be given to Indians; and

(2) preference in the award of subcontracts and subgrants in connection with the administration of such contracts or grants shall be given to Indian organizations and to Indian-owned economic enterprises as defined in section 1452 of this title.

(c) Self-determination contracts

Notwithstanding subsections (a) and (b) of this section, with respect to any self-determination contract, or portion of a self-determination contract, that is intended to benefit one tribe, the tribal employment or contract preference laws adopted by such tribe shall govern with respect to the administration of the contract or portion of the contract.

Sec. 450e–1.—Grant and cooperative agreements

The provisions of this subchapter shall not be subject to the requirements of chapter 63 of title 31: Provided, That a grant agreement or a cooperative agreement may be utilized in lieu of a contract under sections 450f and 450g of this title when mutually agreed to by the appropriate Secretary and the tribal organization involved.

Sec. 450e–2.—Use of excess funds

Beginning in fiscal year 1998 and thereafter, where the actual costs of construction projects under self-determination contracts, compacts, or grants, pursuant to Public Laws 93–638, 103–413, or 100–297, are less than the estimated costs thereof, use of the resulting excess funds shall be determined by the appropriate Secretary after consultation with the tribes.

Sec. 450f.—Self-determination contracts

(a) Request by tribe; authorized programs

(1) The Secretary is directed, upon the request of any Indian tribe by tribal resolution, to enter into a self-determination contract or contracts with a tribal organization to plan, conduct, and administer programs or portions thereof, including construction programs

(A) provided for in the Act of April 16, 1934 (48 Stat. 596), as amended (25 U.S.C. 452 et seq.);

(B) which the Secretary is authorized to administer for the benefit of Indians under the Act of November 2, 1921 (42 Stat. 208) (25 U.S.C. 13), and any Act subsequent thereto;

(C) provided by the Secretary of Health and Human Services under the Act of August 5, 1954 (68 Stat. 674), as amended (42 U.S.C. 2001 et seq.);

(D) administered by the Secretary for the benefit of Indians for which appropriations are made to agencies other than the Department of Health and Human Services or the Department of the Interior; and

(E) for the benefit of Indians because of their status as Indians without regard to the agency or office of the Department of Health and Human Services or the Department of the Interior within which it is performed.

The programs, functions, services, or activities that are contracted under this paragraph shall include administrative functions of the Department of the Interior and the Department of Health and Human Services (whichever is applicable) that support the delivery of services to Indians, including those administrative activities supportive of, but not included as part of, the service delivery programs described in this paragraph that are otherwise contractable. The administrative functions referred to in the preceding sentence shall be contractable without regard to the organizational level within the Department that carries out such functions.

(2) If so authorized by an Indian tribe under paragraph (1) of this subsection, a tribal organization may submit a proposal for a self-determination contract, or a proposal to amend or renew a self-determination contract, to the Secretary for review. Subject to the provisions of paragraph (4), the Secretary shall, within ninety days after receipt of the proposal, approve the proposal and award the contract unless the Secretary provides written notification to the applicant that contains a specific finding that clearly demonstrates that, or that is supported by a controlling legal authority that

(A) the service to be rendered to the Indian beneficiaries of the particular program or function to be contracted will not be satisfactory;

(B) adequate protection of trust resources is not assured;

(C) the proposed project or function to be contracted for cannot be properly completed or maintained by the proposed contract;

(D) the amount of funds proposed under the contract is in excess of the applicable funding level for the contract, as determined under section 450j-1(a) of this title; or

(E) the program, function, service, or activity (or portion thereof) that is the subject of the proposal is beyond the scope of programs, functions, services, or activities covered under paragraph (1) because the proposal includes activities that cannot lawfully be carried out by the contractor.

Notwithstanding any other provision of law, the Secretary may extend or otherwise alter the 90-day period specified in the second sentence of this subsection, if before the expiration of such period, the Secretary obtains the voluntary and express written consent of the tribe or tribal organization to extend or otherwise alter such period. The contractor shall include in the proposal of the contractor the standards under which the tribal organization will operate the contracted program, service, function, or activity, including in the area of construction, provisions regarding the use of licensed and qualified architects, applicable health and safety standards, adherence to applicable Federal, State, local, or tribal building codes and engineering standards. The standards referred to in the preceding sentence shall ensure structural integrity, accountability of funds, adequate competition for subcontracting under tribal or other applicable law, the commencement, performance, and completion of the contract, adherence to project plans and specifications (including any applicable Federal construction guidelines and manuals), the use of proper materials and workmanship, necessary inspection and testing, and changes, modifications, stop work, and termination of the work when warranted.

(3) Upon the request of a tribal organization that operates two or more mature self-determination contracts, those contracts may be consolidated into one single contract.

(4) The Secretary shall approve any severable portion of a contract proposal that does not support a declination finding described in paragraph (2). If the Secretary determines under such paragraph that a contract proposal

(A) proposes in part to plan, conduct, or administer a program, function, service, or activity that is beyond the scope of programs covered under paragraph (1), or

(B) proposes a level of funding that is in excess of the applicable level determined under section 450j-*1*(a) of this title, subject to any alteration in the scope of the proposal that the Secretary and the tribal organization agree to, the Secretary shall, as appropriate, approve such portion of the program, function, service, or activity as is authorized under paragraph (1) or approve a level of funding authorized under section 450j-*1*(a) of this title. If a tribal organization elects to carry out a severable portion of a contract proposal pursuant to this paragraph, subsection (b) of this section shall only apply to the portion of the contract that is declined by the Secretary pursuant to this subsection.

(b) Procedure upon refusal of request to contract

Whenever the Secretary declines to enter into a self-determination contract or contracts pursuant to subsection (a) of this section, the Secretary shall

(1) state any objections in writing to the tribal organization,

(2) provide assistance to the tribal organization to overcome the stated objections, and

(3) provide the tribal organization with a hearing on the record with the right to engage in full discovery relevant to any issue raised in the matter and the opportunity for appeal on the objections raised,

under such rules and regulations as the Secretary may promulgate, except that the tribe or tribal organization may, in lieu of filing such appeal, exercise the option to initiate an action in a Federal district court and proceed directly to such court pursuant to section 450m–1(a) of this title.

(c) Liability insurance; waiver of defense

(1) Beginning in 1990, the Secretary shall be responsible for obtaining or providing liability insurance or equivalent coverage, on the most cost-effective basis, for Indian tribes, tribal organizations, and tribal contractors carrying out contracts, grant agreements and cooperative agreements pursuant to this subchapter. In obtaining or providing such coverage, the Secretary shall take into consideration the extent to which liability under such contracts or agreements are covered by the Federal Tort Claims Act.

(2) In obtaining or providing such coverage, the Secretary shall, to the greatest extent practicable, give a preference to coverage underwritten by Indian-owned economic enterprises as defined in section 1452 of this title, except that, for the purposes of this subsection, such enterprises may include non-profit corporations.

(3)

(A) Any policy of insurance obtained or provided by the Secretary pursuant to this subsection shall contain a provision that the insurance carrier shall waive any right it may have to raise as a defense the sovereign immunity of an Indian tribe from suit, but that such waiver shall extend only to claims the amount and nature of which are within the coverage and limits of the policy and shall not authorize or empower such insurance carrier to waive or otherwise limit the tribe's sovereign immunity outside or beyond the coverage or limits of the policy of insurance.

(B) No waiver of the sovereign immunity of an Indian tribe pursuant to this paragraph shall include a waiver to the extent of any potential liability for interest prior to judgment or for punitive damages or for any other limitation on liability imposed by the law of the State in which the alleged injury occurs.

(d) Tribal organizations and Indian contractors deemed part of Public Health Service

For purposes of section 233 of title 42, with respect to claims by any person, initially filed on or after December 22, 1987, whether or not such person is an Indian or Alaska Native or is served on a fee basis or under other circumstances as permitted by Federal law or regulations for personal injury, including death, resulting from the performance prior to, including, or after December 22, 1987, of medical, surgical, dental, or related functions, including the conduct of clinical studies or investigations, or for purposes of section *2679*, title *28*, with respect to claims by any such person, on or after November 29, 1990, for personal injury, including death, resulting from the operation of an emergency motor vehicle, an Indian tribe, a tribal organization or Indian contractor carrying out a contract, grant agreement, or cooperative agreement under sections 450f or 450h of this title is deemed to be part of the Public Health Service in the Department of Health and Human Services while carrying out any such contract or agreement and its employees (including those acting on behalf of the organization or contractor as provided in section *2671* of title *28* and including an individual who provides health care services pursuant to a personal services contract with a tribal organization for the provision of services in any facility owned, operated, or constructed under the jurisdiction of the Indian Health Service) are deemed employees of the Service while acting within the scope of their employment in carrying out the contract or agreement: Provided, That such employees shall be deemed to be acting within the scope of their employment in carrying out such contract or agreement when they are required, by reason of such employment, to perform medical, surgical, dental or related functions at a facility other than the facility operated pursuant to such contract or agreement, but only if such employees are not compensated for the performance of such functions by a person or entity other than such Indian tribe, tribal organization or Indian contractor.

(e) Burden of proof at hearing or appeal declining contract; final agency action

(1) With respect to any hearing or appeal conducted pursuant to subsection (b)(3) of this section or any civil action conducted pursuant to section 450m-*1*(a) of this title, the Secretary shall have the burden of proof to establish by clearly demonstrating the validity of the grounds for declining the contract proposal (or portion thereof).

(2) Notwithstanding any other provision of law, a decision by an official of the Department of the Interior or the Department of Health and Human Services, as appropriate (referred to in this paragraph as the "Department") that constitutes final agency action and that relates to an appeal within the Department that is conducted under subsection (b)(3) of this section shall be made either

(A) by an official of the Department who holds a position at a higher organizational level within the Department than the level of the departmental agency (such as the Indian Health Service or the Bureau of Indian Affairs) in which the decision that is the subject of the appeal was made; or

(B) by an administrative judge

Notes on Sec. 450g.

Section, *Pub. L. 93–638,* title I, Sec. 103, Jan. 4, 1975, 88 Stat. 2206; *Pub. L. 96–88,* title V, Sec. 509(b), Oct. 17, 1979, 93 Stat. 695; *Pub. L. 100–202,* Sec. 101(g) (title II), Dec. 22, 1987, 101 Stat. 1329–213, 1329–246; *Pub. L. 100–446,* title II, Sept. 27, 1988, 102 Stat. 1817, which related to contracts by Secretary of Health and Human Services with tribal organizations, was repealed except for the last sentence of subsec. (c), providing that tribal organizations and Indian contractors be deemed part of Public Health Service, which was redesignated subsec. (d) of section *450f* of this title.

NATIVE AMERICAN EDUCATIONAL ASSISTANCE ACT (AMENDS INDIAN SELF-DETERMINATION AND EDUCATION ASSISTANCE ACT THROUGH 1996), 25 U.S.C. 2001 (1988)

Sec. 2001. Standards for basic education of Indian children in Bureau of Indian Affairs schools

(a) Purpose

(1) The purpose of the standards developed under this section shall be to afford Indian students being served by a Bureau funded school with the same opportunities as all other students to achieve the National Education Goals embodied in the Goals 2000: Educate America Act (*20* U.S.C. *5801* et seq.). Consistent with the provisions of this section and section *2011* of this title, the Secretary shall take such actions as are necessary to coordinate standards developed and implemented under this section with those in the State improvement plans developed and implemented pursuant to the Goals 2000: Educate America Act for the States in which each Bureau funded school operates. In developing and reviewing such standards and coordination, the Secretary shall utilize the findings and recommendations of the panel established in section 315(b)(4) of such Act.

(2) The Secretary shall take immediate steps to encourage school boards of Bureau funded schools to engage their communities in adopting declarations of purposes of education in their communities, analyzing the implications of such purposes for their schools, and determining how such purposes may be made to motivate students and faculties and otherwise animate their schools by May 1, 1995. Such declarations shall represent the aspirations of a community for the kinds of persons such community wants its children to increasingly become, and shall include such purposes as assuring that all learners are becoming accomplished in ways important to themselves and respected by their parents and

communities, shaping worthwhile and satisfying lives for themselves, exemplifying the best values of the community and humankind, and becoming increasingly effective in shaping the character and quality of the world all learners share.

(b) Studies and surveys

Within 18 months of the publication of the voluntary national content standards described in section 203(a)(2) of the Goals 2000: Educate America Act (*20* U.S.C. *5823*(a)(2)), the Secretary, in consultation with the Secretary of Education and Indian organizations and tribes, shall carry out or cause to be carried out by contract with an Indian organization such studies and surveys, making the fullest use possible of other existing studies, surveys, and plans, as are necessary to establish and revise standards for the basic education of Indian children attending Bureau funded schools. Such studies and surveys shall take into account factors such as academic needs, local cultural differences, type and level of language skills, geographic isolation, and appropriate teacher-student ratios for such children, and shall be directed toward the attainment of equal educational opportunity for such children.

(c) Revision of minimum academic standards

(1) The Secretary shall revise the minimum academic standards published in the Federal Register of September 9, 1985 (50 Fed. Reg. 174) for the basic education of Indian children in accordance with the purpose described in subsection (a) of this section and the findings of the studies and surveys described in subsection (b) of this section, and shall publish such revised standards in the Federal Register for the purpose of receiving comments from the tribes and other interested parties. Within 21 months of October 20, 1994, the Secretary shall establish final standards, distribute such standards to all the tribes and publish such final standards in the Federal Register. The Secretary shall revise such final standards periodically as necessary. Prior to any revision of such final standards, the Secretary shall distribute such proposed revision to all the tribes, and publish such proposed revision in the Federal Register, for the purpose of receiving comments from the tribes and other interested parties.

(2) The standards described in paragraph (1) shall apply to Bureau schools, and subject to subsection (f) of this section, to contract or grant schools, and may also serve as a model for educational programs for Indian children in public schools. In establishing and revising such standards, the Secretary shall take into account the special needs of Indian students and the support and reinforcement of the specific cultural heritage of each tribe.

(d) Alternative or modified standards

The Secretary shall provide alternative or modified standards in lieu of the standards established under subsection (c) of this section, where necessary, so that the programs of each school shall be in compliance with the minimum standards required for accreditation of schools in the State where the school is located.

(e) Waiver of standards

A tribal governing body, or the local school board so designated by the tribal governing body, shall have the local authority to waive, in part or in whole, the standards established under subsection (c) and (d) of this section, where such standards are deemed by such body to be inappropriate. The tribal governing body or designated school board shall, within 60 days thereafter, submit to the Secretary a proposal for alternative standards that take into account the specific needs of the tribe's children. Such revised standards shall be established by the Secretary unless specifically rejected by the Secretary for good cause and in writing to the affected tribes or local school board, which rejection shall be final and unreviewable "subsections."

(f) Implementation of standards

(1) The Secretary, through contracting and grant-making procedures, shall assist school boards of contract or grant schools in the implementation of the standards established under subsections (c) and (d) of this section, if the school boards request that such standards, in part or in whole, be implemented. At the request of a contract or grant school board, the Secretary shall provide alternative or modified standards for the standards established under subsections (c) and (d) of this section to take into account the needs of the Indian children and the contract or grant school.

(2) Within 1 year of August 15, 1985, the Bureau shall, either directly or through contract with an Indian organization, establish a consistent system of reporting standards for fiscal control and fund accounting for all contract or grant schools. Such standards shall yield data results comparable to those used by Bureau schools.

(g) Annual plan for meeting of standards

Subject to subsections (e) and (f) of this section, the Secretary shall begin to implement the standards established under this section immediately upon the date of their establishment. Not later than January 1, 1995, and at each time thereafter that the annual budget request for Bureau educational services is presented, the Secretary shall submit to the appropriate committees of Congress a detailed plan to bring all Bureau schools and contract or grant schools up to the level required by the applicable standards established under this section. Such plan shall include detailed information on the status of each school's educational program in relation to the applicable standards established under this section, specific cost estimates for meeting such standards at each school, and specific time lines for bringing each school up to the level required by such standards.

(h) Closure or consolidation of schools

(1) Except as specifically required by statute, no school or peripheral dormitory operated by the Bureau on or after January 1, 1992, may be closed or consolidated or have its program substantially curtailed unless done according to the requirements of this subsection, except that, in those cases where the tribal governing body, or the local school board concerned (if so designated by the tribal governing body), requests closure or consolidation, the requirements of this subsection shall not apply. The requirements of this subsection shall not apply when a temporary closure, consolidation, or substantial curtailment is required by plant conditions which constitute an immediate hazard to health and safety.

(2) The Secretary shall, by regulation, promulgate standards and procedures for the closing, consolidation, or substantial curtailment of Bureau schools in accordance with the requirements of this subsection.

(3) Whenever closure, transfer to any other authority, consolidation, or substantial curtailment of a school is under active consideration or review by any division of the Bureau or the Department of the Interior, the affected tribe, tribal governing body, and designated local school board, will be notified as soon as such consideration or review begins, kept fully and currently informed, and afforded an opportunity to comment with respect to such consideration or review. When a formal decision is made to close, transfer to any other authority, consolidate, or substantially curtail a school, the affected tribe, tribal governing body, and designated local school board shall be notified at least 6 months prior to the end of the school year preceding the proposed closure date. Copies of any such notices and information shall be transmitted promptly to the Congress and published in the Federal Register.

(4) The Secretary may terminate, contract, transfer to any other authority, or consolidate or substantially curtail the operation or facilities of

(A) any Bureau funded school that is operated on or after April 1, 1987,

(B) any program of such a school that is operated on or after April 1, 1987, or

(C) any school board of a school operated under a grant under the Tribally Controlled Schools Act of 1988 (*25* U.S.C. *2501* et seq.), only if the tribal governing body approves such action.

(i) Authorization of appropriations

There are authorized to be appropriated such sums as may be necessary, for academic program costs, in order to bring all Bureau schools and contract or grant schools up to the level required by the applicable standards established under this section.

(j) Alcohol and substance abuse prevention and treatment

(1) All Bureau funded schools shall include within their curriculum a program of instruction relating to alcohol and substance abuse prevention and treatment. The Assistant Secretary shall provide the technical assistance necessary to develop and implement such a program for students in kindergarten and grades 1 through 12, at the request of

(A) any Bureau school (subject to the approval of the school board of such school);

(B) any school board of a school operating under a contract entered into under the Indian Self-Determination and Education Assistance Act (25 U.S.C. 450 et seq.); or

(C) any school board of a school operating under a grant under the Tribally Controlled Schools Act of 1988 (25 U.S.C. 2501 et seq.).

(2) In schools operated directly by the Bureau, the Secretary shall provide for

(A) accurate reporting of all incidents relating to alcohol and substance abuse; and

(B) individual student crisis intervention.

(3) The programs requested under paragraph (1) shall be developed in consultation with the Indian tribe that is to be served by such program and health personnel in the local community of such tribe.

(4) Schools requesting program assistance under this subsection are encouraged to involve family units and, where appropriate, tribal elders and Native healers in such instructions.

(k) "Tribal governing body" defined

For purposes of this section, the term "tribal governing body" means, with respect to any school, the tribal governing body, or tribal governing bodies, that represent at least 90 percent of the students served by such school.

(l) Application for contracts or grants for non-Bureau funded schools or expansion of Bureau funded schools

(1)

(A)

(i) The Secretary shall only consider the factors described in subparagraphs (B) and (C) in reviewing

(I) applications from any tribe for the awarding of a contract or grant for a school that is not a Bureau funded school; and

(II) applications from any tribe or school board of any Bureau funded school for

(aa) a school which is not a Bureau funded school; or

(bb) the expansion of a Bureau funded school which would increase the amount of funds received by the Indian tribe or school board under section 2007 of this title.

(ii) The Secretary shall give consideration to all of the factors under clause (i), but none of the applications under clause (i) may be denied based primarily upon the geographic proximity of public education.

(B) The Secretary shall consider the following factors relating to the program that is the subject of an application described in subparagraph (A):

(i) The adequacy of facilities or the potential to obtain or provide adequate facilities.

(ii) Geographic and demographic factors in the affected areas.

(iii) Adequacy of the applicant's program plans or, in the case of a Bureau funded school, of projected needs analysis done either by a tribe or by Bureau personnel.

(iv) Geographic proximity of comparable public education.

(v) The stated needs of all affected parties, including students, families, tribal governments at both the central and local levels, and school organizations.

(C) The Secretary shall consider with respect to applications described in subparagraph (A) the following factors relating to all the educational services available at the time the application is considered:

(i) Geographic and demographic factors in the affected areas.

(ii) Adequacy and comparability of programs already available.

(iii) Consistency of available programs with tribal educational codes or tribal legislation on education.

(iv) The history and success of these services for the proposed population to be served, as determined from all factors and not just standardized examination performance.

(2)

(A) The Secretary shall make a determination of whether to approve any application described in paragraph (1)(A) by not later than the date that is 180 days after the day on which such application is submitted to the Secretary.

(B) If the Secretary fails to make the determination described in subparagraph (A) with respect to an application by the date described in subparagraph (A), the application shall be treated as having been approved by the Secretary.

(3)

(A) Any application described in paragraph (1)(A) may be submitted to the Secretary only if

(i) the application has been approved by the tribal governing body of the students served by (or to be served by) the school or program that is the subject of the application, and

(ii) written evidence of such approval is submitted with the application.

(B) Each application described in paragraph (1)(A)

(i) shall provide information concerning each of the factors described in paragraph (1)(B), and

(ii) may provide information concerning the factors described in paragraph (1)(C).

(4) Whenever the Secretary makes a determination to deny approval of any application described in paragraph (1)(A), the Secretary shall

(A) state the objections in writing to the applicant by not later than the date that is 180 days after the day on which the application is submitted to the Secretary,

(B) provide assistance to the applicant to overcome stated objections, and

(C) provide the applicant a hearing, under the same rules and regulations pertaining to the Indian Self-Determination and Education Assistance Act (*25* U.S.C. *450* et seq.), and an opportunity to appeal the objections raised by the Secretary.

(5)

(A) Except as otherwise provided in this paragraph, the action which is the subject of any application described in paragraph (1)(A) that is approved by the Secretary shall become effective with the commencement of the academic year succeeding the fiscal year in which the application is approved, or at an earlier date determined by the Secretary.

(B) If an application is treated as having been approved by the Secretary by reason of paragraph (2)(B), the action that is the subject of the application shall become effective on the date that is 18 months after the date on which the application is submitted to the Secretary, or at an earlier date determined by the Secretary.

Sec. 2002.—National criteria for dormitory situations

(a) Study of costs

The Secretary, in consultation with the Secretary of the Department of Education, and in consultation with Indian organizations and tribes, shall conduct or cause to be conducted by contract with an Indian organization, a study of the costs applicable to boarding arrangements for Indian students provided in Bureau schools, and contract or grant schools, for the purpose of establishing national criteria for such dormitory situations. Such criteria shall include adult-child ratios, needs for counselors (including special needs related to off-reservation boarding arrangements), space, and privacy.

(b) Distribution and publication of criteria

Not later than January 1, 1996, the Secretary shall propose such criteria, and shall distribute such proposed criteria to the tribes and publish such proposed criteria in the Federal Register for the purpose of receiving comments from the tribes and other interested parties. Within 18 months of October 20, 1994, the Secretary shall establish final criteria, distribute such final criteria to all the tribes, and publish such final criteria in the Federal Register. The Secretary shall revise such final criteria periodically as necessary. Any revisions to the criteria established under this section shall be developed subject to requirements established under section *2011* of this title.

(c) Implementation

The Secretary shall begin to implement the criteria established under this section immediately upon the date of the establishment of such criteria. Not later than January 1, 1997, and at each time thereafter that the annual budget request for Bureau educational services is presented, the Secretary shall submit to the appropriate committees of Congress a detailed plan to bring all Bureau contract boarding schools up to the criteria established under this section. Such plan shall include predictions for the relative need for each boarding school in the future, detailed information on the status of each school in relation to the criteria established under this section, specific cost estimates for meeting such criteria at each school, and specific time lines for bringing each school up to the level required by such criteria.

(d) Waiver

(1) The criteria established under this section may be waived in the same manner as the standards provided under section *2001*(c) of this title may be waived under section *2001*(e) of this title.

(2) No school in operation on or before January 1, 1987 (regardless of compliance or noncompliance with the criteria established under this section) may be closed, transferred to another authority, consolidated or have its program substantially curtailed for failure to meet the criteria.

(e) Authorization of appropriations

There are authorized to be appropriated such sums as may be necessary in order to bring each school up to the level required by the criteria established under this section.

Sec. 2003.—Regulations

(a) Incorporation of part 32 of title 25 of Code of Federal Regulations

The provisions of part 32 of title 25 of the Code of Federal Regulations, as in effect on January 1, 1987, are incorporated into this Act and shall be treated as though such provisions are set forth in this subsection. Accordingly, such provisions may be altered only by means of an amendment to this subsection that is contained in an Act or joint resolution which is enacted into law. To the extent that such provisions of part 32 do not conform with this Act or any statutory provision of law enacted before November 1, 1978, the provisions of this Act and the provisions of such other statutory law shall govern.

(b) Application of parts 31, 33, 36, 39, 42, and 43 of title 25 of Code of Federal Regulations

The provisions of parts 31, 33, 36, 39, 42, and 43 of title 25 of the Code of Federal Regulations, as in effect on January 1, 1987, shall be applied by the Federal Government and shall not, before July 1, 1989, be amended, revoked, or altered in any manner. No officer or employee of the executive branch shall have the authority to issue any other regulations, prior to July 1, 1989, that supersede, supplement, or otherwise affect the provisions of such parts. To the extent that the provisions of such parts do not conform with this Act or any statutory provision of law enacted before November 1, 1978, the provisions of this Act and the provisions of such other statutory law shall govern.

(c) Regulations prescribed after June 30, 1989

After June 30, 1989, no regulation prescribed for the application of any program provided under this chapter shall become effective unless

(1) the regulation has been published as a proposed regulation in the Federal Register,

(2) an opportunity of not less than 90 days has been afforded the public to comment on the published proposed regulation, and

(3) the regulation has, after such period for public comment, been published in the Federal Register as a final regulation.

(d) "Regulation" defined

For purposes of this section, the term "regulation" means any rules, regulations, guidelines, interpretations, orders, or requirements of general applicability prescribed by any officer or employee of the executive branch.

Sec. 2004.—School boundaries

(a) Establishment

The Secretary shall, in accordance with this section, establish separate geographical attendance areas for each Bureau school.

(b) Alternative or revised boundaries

(1) Except as provided in paragraph (2), on or after July 1, 1985, no attendance area shall be changed or established with respect to any Bureau funded school unless the tribal governing body or the local school board concerned (if so designated by the tribal governing body) has been

(i) afforded at least six months notice of the intention of the Bureau to change or establish such attendance area, and

(ii) given the opportunity to propose alternative boundaries. Any tribe may petition the Secretary for revision of existing attendance area boundaries. The Secretary shall accept such proposed alternative or revised boundaries unless the Secretary finds, after consultation with the affected tribe or tribes, that such revised boundaries do not reflect the needs of the Indian students to be served or do not provide adequate stability to all of the affected programs.

(2) In any case where there is more than 1 Bureau funded school located on an Indian reservation, at the direction of the tribal governing body, the relevant school boards of the Bureau funded schools on the reservation may, by mutual consent, establish the relevant attendance areas for such schools, subject to the approval of the tribal governing body. Any such boundaries so established shall be accepted by the Secretary.

(c) Reservation as boundary

In any case where there is only 1 Bureau operated program located on an Indian reservation, the attendance area for the program shall be the boundaries of the reservation served, and those students residing near the reservation shall also receive services from such program.

(d) Coordination and consultation with tribes and school boards

The Bureau shall include in the regulations the requirement that each appropriate education line officer coordinate and consult with the affected tribes and relevant school boards in the establishment of such geographic boundaries.

Sec. 2005.—Facilities construction

(a) Compliance with health and safety standards

The Secretary shall immediately begin to bring all schools, dormitories, and other facilities operated by the Bureau or under contract or grant with the Bureau in connection with the education of Indian children into compliance with all applicable Federal, tribal, or State health and safety standards, whichever provide greater protection (except that the tribal standards to be applied shall be no greater than any otherwise applicable Federal or State standards), with section 794 of title *29*, and with the Americans with Disabilities Act of 1990 (*42* U.S.C. *12101* et seq.), except that nothing in this section shall require termination of the operations of any facility which does not comply with such provisions and which is in use on October 20, 1994.

(b) Omitted

(c) Priorities

Within six months of November 1, 1978, the Secretary shall submit to the appropriate committees of Congress, and publish in the Federal Register, the system used to establish priorities for school construction projects. At the time any budget request for school construction is presented, the Secretary shall publish in the Federal Register and submit with the budget request the current list of all school construction priorities.

(d) Hazardous conditions at Bureau schools

(1) A Bureau school may be closed or consolidated, and the programs of a Bureau school may be substantially curtailed, by reason of plant conditions that constitute an immediate hazard to health and safety only if a health and safety officer of the Bureau determines that such conditions exist at the Bureau school.

(2)

(A) In making determinations described in paragraph (1) before July 1, 1989, health and safety officers of the Bureau shall use the health and safety guidelines of the Bureau that were in effect on January 1, 1988.

(B)

(i) If

(I) the Secretary fails to publish in the Federal Register in final form before July 1, 1989, and

(II) action described in paragraph (1) is taken after June 30, 1989, and before the date on which such regulations are published in final form in the Federal Register by reason of the condition of any plant, an inspection of the condition of such plant shall be conducted by an appropriate tribal, county, municipal, or State health and safety officer to determine whether conditions at such plant constitute an immediate hazard to health and safety. Such inspection shall be completed by not later than the date that is 30 days after the date on which the action described in paragraph (1) is taken.

(ii) The inspection required under clause (i) shall be conducted by a health and safety officer designated jointly by the Secretary and the tribes affected by the action described in paragraph (1). If the Secretary and such tribes are unable to agree on the designation of the health and safety officer, the Secretary shall designate the health and safety officer and shall provide notice of such designation to each of such tribes before the inspection is conducted by such officer.

(iii) If the health and safety officer conducting an inspection of a plant required under clause (i) determines that conditions at the plant do not constitute an immediate hazard to health and safety, any consolidation or curtailment that was made by reason of conditions at the plant shall immediately cease and any school closed by reason of conditions at the plant shall be reopened immediately.

(3) If

(A) a Bureau school is temporarily closed or consolidated, or the programs of a Bureau school are substantially curtailed, by reason of plant conditions that constitute an immediate hazard to health and safety, and

(B) the Secretary estimates that the closure, consolidation, or curtailment will be more than 1 year in duration, the Secretary shall submit to the Congress, by not later than the date that is 6 months after the date on which the closure, consolidation, or curtailment is initiated, a report which sets forth the reasons for such temporary actions and the actions the Secretary is taking to eliminate the conditions that constitute the hazard.

(e) Authorization of appropriations

There are authorized to be appropriated such sums as may be necessary to carry out subsection (a) of this section.

Sec. 2006.—Bureau of Indian Affairs education functions

(a) Formulation and establishment of policy and procedure; supervision of programs and expenditures

The Secretary shall vest in the Assistant Secretary for Indian Affairs all functions with respect to formulation and establishment of policy and procedure, and supervision of programs and expenditures of Federal funds for the purpose of Indian education administered by the Bureau. The Assistant Secretary shall carry out such functions through the Director of the Office of Indian Education.

(b) Direction and supervision of personnel operations

The Director of the Office shall direct and supervise the operations of all personnel directly and substantially involved with provision of education services by the Bureau, including school or institution custodial or maintenance personnel. The Assistant Secretary for Indian Affairs shall provide for the adequate coordination between the affected Bureau Offices and the Office to facilitate the consideration of all contract functions relating to education. Except as required by section *2009* of this title, nothing in this Act shall be construed to require the provision of separate support services for Indian education.

(c) Evaluation of programs; services and support functions; technical and coordinating assistance

Education personnel who are under the direction and supervision of the Director of the Office in accordance with the first sentence of subsection (b) of this section shall

(1) monitor and evaluate Bureau education programs,

(2) provide all services and support functions for education programs with respect to personnel matters involving staffing actions and functions, and

(3) provide technical and coordinating assistance in areas such as procurement, contracting, budgeting, personnel, and curriculum.

(d) Construction and improvement of facilities; operation and maintenance of facilities

(1) The Assistant Secretary shall submit in the annual Budget a plan

(A) for school facilities to be constructed under the system required by section 2005(c) of this title;

(B) for establishing priorities among projects and for the improvement and repair of education facilities, which together shall form the basis for the distribution of appropriated funds; and

(C) including a 5-year plan for capital improvements.

(2)

(A) The Assistant Secretary shall establish a program, including the distribution of appropriated funds, for the operation and maintenance of education facilities. Such program shall include

(i) a method of computing the amount necessary for each education facility;

(ii) similar treatment of all Bureau funded schools;

(iii) a notice of an allocation of appropriated funds from the Director of the Office directly to the appropriate education line officers; and

(iv) a system for the conduct of routine preventive maintenance.

(B) The appropriate education line officers shall make arrangements for the maintenance of education facilities with the local supervisors of the Bureau maintenance personnel who are under the authority of the agency superintendent or area directors, respectively. The local supervisors of Bureau maintenance personnel shall take appropriate action to implement the decisions made by the appropriate education line officers, except that no funds under this chapter may be authorized for expenditure unless such appropriate education line officer is assured that the necessary maintenance has been, or will be, provided in a reasonable manner. Subject to the requirements of subsection (b) of this section, nothing in this Act shall be construed to require the provision of separate operations and maintenance personnel for the Office.

(3) The requirements of this subsection shall be implemented not later than July 1, 1995.

(e) Acceptance of gifts and bequests

Notwithstanding any other provision of law, the Director shall promulgate guidelines for the establishment of mechanisms for the acceptance of gifts and bequests for the use of, and benefit of, particular schools or designated Bureau operated education programs, including, where appropriate, the establishment and administration of trust funds. When a Bureau operated program is the beneficiary of such a gift or bequest, the Director shall make provisions for monitoring its use, and shall report to the appropriate committees of Congress the amount and terms of such gift or bequest, the use to which such gift or bequest is put, and any positive results achieved by such action.

(f) "Functions" defined

For the purpose of this section the term "functions" includes powers and duties.

Sec. 2007.—Allotment formula

(a) Factors considered; revision to reflect standards

(1) The Secretary shall establish, by regulation adopted in accordance with section 2019 of this title, a formula for determining the minimum annual amount of funds necessary to sustain each Bureau funded school. In establishing such formula, the Secretary shall consider

(A) the number of eligible Indian students served and size of the school;

(B) special cost factors, such as

(i) the isolation of the school;

(ii) the need for special staffing, transportation, or educational programs;

(iii) food and housing costs;

(iv) maintenance and repair costs associated with the physical condition of the educational facilities;

(v) special transportation and other costs of isolated and small schools;

(vi) the costs of boarding arrangements, where determined necessary by a tribal governing body or designated local school board;

(vii) costs associated with greater lengths of service by educational personnel; and

(viii) special programs for gifted and talented students;

(C) the cost of providing academic services which are at least equivalent to those provided by public schools in the State in which the school is located; and

(D) such other relevant factors as the Secretary determines are appropriate.

(2) Upon the establishment of the standards required by sections *2001* and *2002* of this title, the Secretary shall revise the formula established under this subsection to reflect the cost and funding standards so established. Prior to January 1, 1996, the Secretary shall review the formula established under this section and shall take such steps as may be necessary to increase the availability of counseling services for students in off-reservation boarding schools and other Bureau operated residential facilities. Concurrent with such action, the Secretary shall review the standards established under section *2001* of this title to be certain that adequate provision is made for parental notification regarding, and consent for, such counseling services.

(b) Pro rata allotment

Notwithstanding any other provisions of law, Federal funds appropriated for the general local operation of Bureau funded schools shall be allotted pro rata in accordance with the formula established under subsection (a) of this section.

(c) Annual adjustment; reservation of amount for training

(1) For fiscal year 1990, and for each subsequent fiscal year, the Secretary shall adjust the formula established under subsection (a) of this section to

(A) use a weighted unit of 1.2 for each eligible Indian student enrolled in the seventh and eighth grades of the school in considering the number of eligible Indian students served by the school;

(B) consider a school with an enrollment of less than 50 eligible Indian students as having an average daily attendance of 50 eligible Indian students for purposes of implementing the adjustment factor for small schools; and

(C) take into account the provision of residential services on a less than 9-month basis at a school when the school board and supervisor of the school determine that a less than 9-month basis will be implemented for the school year involved.

(2)

(A) The Secretary shall reserve for national school board training 0.2 percent of the funds appropriated for each fiscal year for distribution under this section. Such training shall be conducted through the same organizations through which, and in the same manner in which, the training was conducted in fiscal year 1992, except that the contracts for distribution of such funds shall require that such funds be distributed by the recipient organizations in a manner that assures the same pro rata share is made available for training for each school board in the system. If the contract for such training is not awarded before May 1 of each fiscal year, the contract under which such training was provided for the fiscal year preceding such fiscal year shall be renewed by the Secretary for such fiscal year. The agenda for the training sessions shall be established by the school boards through their regional or national organizations.

(B) For each year in which the Secretary uses a weighted unit formula established under subsection (a) of this section to fund Bureau schools, a Bureau school which generates less than 168 weighted units shall receive an additional 2 weighted units to defray school board activities.

(C) From the funds allotted in accordance with the formula established under subsection (a) of this section for each Bureau school, the local school board of such school may reserve an amount which does not exceed the greater of

(i) $5,000, or

(ii) the lesser of

(I) $15,000, or

(II) 1 percent of such allotted funds, for school board activities for such school, including and notwithstanding any other provision of law, meeting expenses and the cost of membership in, and support of, organizations engaged in activities on behalf of Indian education.

(3) The Secretary shall adjust the formula established under subsection (a) of this section to use a weighted unit of 2.0 for each eligible Indian student that

(A) is gifted and talented, and

(B) is enrolled in the school on a full-time basis,

in considering the number of eligible Indian students served by the school.

(4)

(A) The Secretary shall adjust the formula established under subsection (a) of this section to use a weighted unit of 0.25 for each eligible Indian student who is enrolled in a year-long credit course in an Indian or Native language as part of the regular curriculum of a school, in considering the number of eligible Indian students served by such school.

(B) The adjustment required under subparagraph (A) shall be used for such school after

(i) the certification of the Indian or Native language curriculum by the school board of such school to the Secretary, together with an estimate of the number of full-time students expected to be enrolled in the curriculum in the second school year following the school year for which the certification is made; and

(ii) the funds appropriated for allotment under this section are designated by the appropriations Act appropriating such funds as the amount necessary to implement such adjustment at such school without reducing allotments made under this section to any school by virtue of such adjustment.

(d) Reservation of amount for emergencies

The Secretary shall reserve from the funds available for distribution for each fiscal year under this section an amount which, in the aggregate, shall equal 1 percent of the funds available for such purpose for that fiscal year. Such funds shall be used, at the discretion of the Director of the Office, to meet emergencies and unforeseen contingencies affecting the education programs funded under this section. Funds reserved under this subsection may only be expended for education services or programs at a schoolsite (as defined in section 2503(c)(2) of this title). Funds reserved under this subsection shall remain available without fiscal year limitation until expended. However, the aggregate amount available from all fiscal years may not exceed 1 percent of the current year funds. Whenever the Secretary makes funds available under this subsection, the Secretary shall report such action to the appropriate committees of Congress within the annual budget submission.

(e) Supplemental appropriations

Supplemental appropriations enacted to meet increased pay costs attributable to school level personnel shall be distributed under this section.

(f) "Eligible Indian student" defined

For the purpose of this section, the term "eligible Indian student" means a student who

(1) is a member of or is at least a 1/4 degree Indian blood descendant of a member of an Indian tribe which is eligible for the special programs and services provided by the United States through the Bureau to Indians because of their status as Indians, and

(2) resides on or near an Indian reservation or meets the criteria for attendance at a Bureau off-reservation boarding school.

(g) Tuition

(1) An eligible Indian student may not be charged tuition for attendance at a Bureau school or contract or grant school. A student attending a Bureau school under paragraph (2)(C) may not be charged tuition.

(2) The Secretary may permit the attendance at a Bureau school of a student who is not an eligible Indian student if

(A) the Secretary determines that the student's attendance will not adversely affect the school's program for eligible Indian students because of cost, overcrowding, or violation of standards,

(B) the school board consents,

(C) the student is a dependent of a Bureau, Indian Health Service, or tribal government, employee who lives on or near the school site, or

(D) a tuition is paid for the student that is not more than that charged by the nearest public school district for out-of-district students, is in addition to the school's allocation under this section.

(3) The school board of a contract or grant school may permit students who are not eligible Indian students under this subsection to attend its contract school or grant school and any tuition collected for those students is in addition to funding under this section.

(h) Funds available without fiscal year limitation

Notwithstanding any other provision of law, at the election of the school board of a Bureau school made at any time during the fiscal year, a portion equal to not more than 15 percent of the funds allocated with respect to a school under this section for any fiscal year shall remain available to the school for expenditure without fiscal year limitation. The Assistant Secretary shall take steps as may be necessary to implement this provision immediately.

(i) Students boarding at Richfield Dormitory, Richfield, Utah

Beginning with academic year 1994–1995, tuition for the out-of-State students boarding at the Richfield Dormitory in Richfield, Utah, who attend Sevier County high schools in Richfield, Utah, shall be paid from the Indian school equalization program funds authorized in this section and section 2010 of this title at a rate not to exceed the amount per weighted student unit for that year for the instruction of such students. No additional administrative cost funds shall be added to the grant.

Sec. 2008.—Administrative cost grants

(a) Purpose; effect upon appropriated amounts

(1) The Secretary shall, subject to the availability of appropriated funds, provide grants to each tribe or tribal organization operating a contract school or grant school in the amount determined under this section with respect to the tribe or tribal organization for the purpose of paying the administrative and indirect costs incurred in operating contract or grant schools in order to

(A) enable tribes and tribal organizations operating such schools, without reducing direct program services to the beneficiaries of the program, to provide all related administrative overhead services and operations necessary to meet the requirements of law and prudent management practice, and

(B) carry out other necessary support functions which would otherwise be provided by the Secretary or other Federal officers or employees, from resources other than direct program funds, in support of comparable Bureau operated programs.

(2) Amounts appropriated to fund the grants provided under this section shall be in addition to, and shall not reduce, the amounts appropriated for the program being administered by the contract or grant school.

(b) Determination of amount; reduction for Federal education program payments; reimbursement by Federal departments or agencies

(1) The amount of the grant provided to each tribe or tribal organization under this section for each fiscal year shall be determined by applying the administrative cost percentage rate of the tribe or tribal organization to the aggregate of the Bureau elementary and secondary functions operated by the tribe or tribal organization for which funds are received from or through the Bureau. The administrative cost percentage rate determined under subsection (c) of this section does not apply to other programs operated by the tribe or tribal organization.

(2) The Secretary shall

(A) reduce the amount of the grant determined under paragraph (1) to the extent that payments for administrative costs are actually received by an Indian tribe or tribal organization under any Federal education program included in the direct cost base of the tribe or tribal organization, and

(B) take such actions as may be necessary to be reimbursed by any other department or agency of the Federal Government for the portion of grants made under this section for the costs of administering any program for Indians that is funded by appropriations made to such other department or agency.

(c) Administrative cost percentage rate

(1) For purposes of this section, the administrative cost percentage rate for a contract or grant school for a fiscal year is equal to the percentage determined by dividing

(A) the sum of

(i) the amount equal to

(I) the direct cost base of the tribe or tribal organization for the fiscal year, multiplied by

(II) the minimum base rate, plus

(ii) the amount equal to

(I) the standard direct cost base, multiplied by

(II) the maximum base rate, by

(B) the sum of

(i) the direct cost base of the tribe or tribal organization for the fiscal year, plus

(ii) the standard direct cost base.

(2) The administrative cost percentage rate shall be determined to the 1/100 of a decimal point.

(d) Administrative cost account; availability of funds; effect upon indirect cost recovery determinations

(1)

(A) Funds received by a tribe or contract or grant school as grants under this section for tribal elementary or secondary educational programs may be combined by the tribe or contract or grant school into a single administrative cost account without the necessity of maintaining separate funding source accounting.

(B) Indirect cost funds for programs at the school which share common administrative services with tribal elementary or secondary educational programs may be included in the administrative cost account described in subparagraph (A).

(2) Funds received as grants under this section with respect to tribal elementary or secondary education programs shall remain available to the contract or grant school without fiscal year limitation and without diminishing the amount of any grants otherwise payable to the school under this section for any fiscal year beginning after the fiscal year for which the grant is provided.

(3) Funds received as grants under this section for Bureau funded programs operated by a tribe or tribal organization under a contract or agreement shall not be taken into consideration for purposes of indirect cost underrecovery and overrecovery determinations by any Federal agency for any other funds, from whatever source derived.

(4) In applying this section and section 105 of the Indian Self-Determination and Education Assistance Act (*25* U.S.C. *450j*) with respect to an Indian tribe or tribal organization that

(A) receives funds under this section for administrative costs incurred in operating a contract or grant school or a school operated under the Tribally Controlled Schools Act of 1988 (*25* U.S.C. *2501* et seq.), and

(B) operates 1 or more other programs under a contract or grant provided under the Indian Self-Determination and Education Assistance Act (*25* U.S.C. *450* et seq.), the Secretary shall ensure that the Indian tribe or tribal organization is provided with the full amount of the administrative costs, and of the indirect costs, that are associated with operating the contract or grant school, a school operated under the Tribally Controlled Schools Act of 1988, and all of such other programs, except that funds appropriated for implementation of this section shall be used only to supply the amount of the grant required to be provided by this section.

(e) Definitions

For purposes of this section:

(1)

(A) The term "administrative cost" means the costs of necessary administrative functions which

(i) the tribe or tribal organization incurs as a result of operating a tribal elementary or secondary educational program,

(ii) are not customarily paid by comparable Bureau operated programs out of direct program funds, and

(iii) are either

(I) normally provided for comparable Bureau programs by Federal officials using resources other than Bureau direct program funds, or

(II) are otherwise required of tribal self-determination program operators by law or prudent management practice.

(B) The term "administrative cost" may include

(i) contract or grant (or other agreement) administration;

(ii) executive, policy, and corporate leadership and decisionmaking;

(iii) program planning, development, and management;

(iv) fiscal, personnel, property, and procurement management;

(v) related office services and record keeping; and

(vi) costs of necessary insurance, auditing, legal, safety and security services.

(2) The term "Bureau elementary and secondary functions" means

(A) all functions funded at Bureau schools by the Office;

(B) all programs

(i) funds for which are appropriated to other agencies of the Federal Government, and

(ii) which are administered for the benefit of Indians through Bureau schools; and

(C) all operation, maintenance, and repair funds for facilities and government quarters used in the operation or support of elementary and secondary education functions for the benefit of Indians, from whatever source derived.

(3)

(A)

Except as otherwise provided in this subparagraph (B), the direct cost base of a tribe or tribal organization for the fiscal year is the aggregate direct cost program funding for all tribal elementary or secondary educational programs operated by the tribe or tribal organization during

(i) the second fiscal year preceding such fiscal year, or

(ii) if such programs have not been operated by the tribe or tribal organization during the 2 preceding fiscal years, the first fiscal year preceding such fiscal year.

(B) In the case of Bureau elementary or secondary education functions which have not previously been operated by a tribe or tribal organization under contract, grant, or agreement with the Bureau, the direct cost base for the initial year shall be the projected aggregate direct cost program funding for all Bureau elementary and secondary functions to be operated by the tribe or tribal organization during that fiscal year.

(4) The term "maximum base rate" means 50 percent.

(5) The term "minimum base rate" means 11 percent.

(6) The term "standard direct cost base" means $600,000.

(7) The term "tribal elementary or secondary educational programs" means all Bureau elementary and secondary functions, together with any other Bureau programs or portions of programs (excluding funds for social services that are appropriated to agencies other than the Bureau and are expended through the Bureau, funds for major subcontracts, construction, and other major capital expenditures, and unexpended funds carried over from prior years) which share common administrative cost functions, that are operated directly by a tribe or tribal organization under a contract, grant, or agreement with the Bureau.

(f) Studies for determination of factors affecting costs, minimum and maximum base rates, and standard direct cost base; report to Congress

(1) Upon April 28, 1988, the Secretary shall

(A) conduct such studies as may be needed to establish an empirical basis for determining relevant factors substantially affecting the required administrative costs of tribal elementary and secondary educational programs, using the formula set forth in subsection (c) of this section, and

(B) conduct a study to determine

(i) a maximum base rate which ensures that the amount of the grants provided under this section will provide adequate (but not excessive) funding of the administrative costs of the smallest tribal elementary or secondary educational programs,

(ii) a minimum base rate which ensures that the amount of the grants provided under this section will provide adequate (but not excessive) funding of the administrative costs of the largest tribal elementary or secondary educational programs, and

(iii) a standard direct cost base which is the aggregate direct cost funding level for which the percentage determined under subsection (c) of this section will

(I) be equal to the median between the maximum base rate and the minimum base rate, and

(II) ensure that the amount of the grants provided under this section will provide adequate (but not excessive) funding of the administrative costs of tribal elementary or secondary educational programs closest to the size of the program.

(2) The studies required under paragraph (1) shall

(A) be conducted in full consultation (in accordance with section *2011* of this title) with

(i) the tribes and tribal organizations that are affected by the application of the formula set forth in subsection (c) of this section, and

(ii) all national and regional Indian organizations of which such tribes and tribal organizations are typically members;

(B) be conducted onsite with a representative statistical sample of the tribal elementary or secondary educational programs under a contract entered into with a nationally reputable public accounting and business consulting firm;

(C) take into account the availability of skilled labor, commodities, business and automatic data processing services, related Indian preference and Indian control of education requirements, and any other market factors found substantially to affect the administrative costs and efficiency of each such tribal elementary or secondary educational program studied in order to assure that all required administrative activities can reasonably be delivered in a cost effective manner for each such program, given an administrative cost allowance generated by the values, percentages, or other factors found in the studies to be relevant in such formula;

(D) identify, and quantify in terms of percentages of direct program costs, any general factors arising from geographic isolation, or numbers of programs administered, independent of program size factors used to compute a base administrative cost percentage in such formula; and

(E) identify any other incremental cost factors substantially affecting the costs of required administrative cost functions at any of the tribal elementary or secondary educational programs studied and determine whether the factors are of general applicability to other such programs, and (if so) how the factors may effectively be incorporated into such formula.

(3) In carrying out the studies required under this subsection, the Secretary shall obtain the input of, and afford an opportunity to participate to, the Inspector General of the Department of the Interior.

(4) Determinations described in paragraph (2)(C) shall be based

on what is pragmatically possible to do at each location studied, given prudent management practice, irrespective of whether required administrative services were actually or fully delivered at these sites, or other services were delivered instead, during the period of the study.

(5) Upon completion of the studies conducted under paragraph (1), but in no case later than October 1, 1989, the Secretary shall submit to the Congress a report on the findings of the studies, together with determinations based upon such findings that would affect the definitions of terms used in the formula that is set forth in subsection (c) of this section.

(6) The Secretary shall include in the Bureau's justification for each appropriations request for each fiscal year beginning after fiscal year 1989, a projection of the overall costs associated with the formula set forth in subsection (c) of this section for all tribal elementary or secondary educational programs which the Secretary expects to be funded in the fiscal year for which the appropriations are sought.

(7) For purposes of this subsection, the size of tribal elementary or secondary educational programs is determined by the aggregate direct cost program funding level for all Bureau funded programs which share common administrative cost functions.

(g) Authorization of appropriations; procedure where amount of funds necessary exceeds appropriated amount

(1) There are authorized to be appropriated for each fiscal year such sums as may be necessary to carry out this section.

(2) If the total amount of funds necessary to provide grants to tribes and tribal organizations in the amounts determined under subsection (b) of this section for a fiscal year exceeds the amount of funds appropriated to carry out this section for such fiscal year, the Secretary shall reduce the amount of each grant determined under subsection (b) of this section for such fiscal year by an amount that bears the same relationship to such excess as the amount of such grant determined under subsection (b) of this section bears to the total of all grants determined under subsection (b) of this section for all tribes and tribal organizations for such fiscal year.

(h) Amounts for fiscal years 1989, 1990, and 1991

(1) Notwithstanding any other provision of this section, the amount of the grants provided under this section for fiscal year 1989 shall

(A) in lieu of being determined under subsection (b) of this section, be determined for each tribal elementary or secondary educational program on the same basis that indirect costs were determined for such programs for fiscal year 1988, and

(B) be subject to the provisions of subsection (d) of this section.

(2) Notwithstanding any other provision of this section, the

amount of the grant provided under this section for fiscal year 1990 with respect to each tribal elementary and secondary educational program that was operated by a tribe or tribal organization in fiscal year 1989 shall be equal to

(A) if the amount of the grant determined under subsection (b) of this section for fiscal year 1990 with respect to such program exceeds the amount received by the tribe or tribal organization with respect to such program for administrative costs for fiscal year 1988 (or fiscal year 1989 if such program was not operated by the tribe or tribal organization during fiscal year 1988), the sum of

(i) such amount received, plus

(ii) 1/3 of the excess of

(I) such amount determined under subsection (b) of this section, over

(II) such amount received, or

(B) if such amount received exceeds such amount determined under subsection (b) of this section, the excess of

(i) such amount received, over

(ii) an amount equal to 1/3 of the excess of

(I) such amount received, over

(II) such amount determined under subsection (b) of this section.

(3) Notwithstanding any other provision of this section, the amount of the grants provided under this section for fiscal year 1991 with respect to each tribal elementary and secondary educational program that was operated by a tribe or tribal organization in fiscal year 1989 shall be equal to

(A) if the amount of the grant determined under subsection (b) of this section for fiscal year 1991 with respect to such program exceeds the amount received by the tribe or tribal organization with respect to such program for administrative costs for fiscal year 1990, the sum of

(i) such amount received, plus

(ii) 1/2 of the excess of

(I) such amount determined under subsection (b) of this section, over

(II) such amount received, or

(B) if such amount received exceeds such amount determined under subsection (b) of this section, the excess of

(i) such amount received, over

(ii) an amount equal to 1/2 of the excess of

(I) such amount received over,

(II) such amount determined under subsection (b) of this section.

(i) Application of section to certain tribally controlled schools

The provisions of this section shall also apply to those schools operating under the Tribally Controlled Schools Act of 1988 (*25* U.S.C. *2501* et seq.).

Sec. 2009.—Division of Budget Analysis

(a) Establishment

Within 24 months of October 20, 1994, the Secretary shall establish within the Office a Division of Budget Analysis (hereinafter referred to as the "Division"). Such Division shall be under the direct supervision and control of the Director of the Office.

(b) Functions

The Division shall have the capacity to conduct such studies, surveys, or other activities as are necessary to gather demographic information on Bureau-funded schools (current and future) and project the amount necessary to provide Indian students in such schools the educational program set forth in this chapter.

(c) Annual reports

The Division shall prepare projections on such amounts, along with such other information as the Director of the Office shall require, for each fiscal year beginning after October 1, 1996. The Director of the Office and the Assistant Secretary for Indian Affairs shall use such reports when preparing their annual budget submissions.

Sec. 2010.—Uniform direct funding and support

(a) Establishment of system

(1) Within six months after October 20, 1994, the Secretary shall establish, by regulation adopted in accordance with section 2019 of this title, a system for the direct funding and support of all Bureau funded schools. Such system shall allot funds, in accordance with section *2007* of this title. All amounts appropriated for distribution under this section may be made available under paragraph (2).

(2)

(A) For the purpose of affording adequate notice of funding available pursuant to the allotments made by section *2007* of this title, amounts appropriated in an appropriation Act for any fiscal year shall become available for obligation by the affected schools on July 1 of the fiscal year in which such amounts are appropriated without further action by the Secretary, and shall remain available for obligation through the succeeding fiscal year.

(B) The Secretary shall, on the basis of the amount appropriated in accordance with this paragraph

(i) publish, on July 1 of the fiscal year for which the funds are appropriated, allotments to each affected school made under section *2007* of this title of 85 percent of such appropriation; and

(ii) publish, not later than September 30 of such fiscal year, the allotments to be made under section *2007* of this title of the remaining 15 percent of such appropriation, adjusted to reflect actual student attendance.

(3)

(A) Notwithstanding any law or regulation, the supervisor of a Bureau school may expend an aggregate of not more than $35,000 of the amount allotted the school under section *2007* of this title to acquire supplies and equipment for the school without competitive bidding if

(i) the cost for any single item purchased does not exceed $10,000;

(ii) the school board approves the procurement;

(iii) the supervisor certifies that the cost is fair and reasonable;

(iv) the documents relating to the procurement executed by the supervisor or other school staff cite this paragraph as authority for the procurement; and

(v) the transaction is documented in a journal maintained at the school clearly identifying when the transaction occurred, what was acquired and from whom, the prices paid, the quantities acquired, and any other information the supervisor or school board considers relevant.

(B) The Director shall be responsible for determining the application of this paragraph, including the authorization of specific individuals to carry out this paragraph, and shall be responsible for the provision of guidelines on the use of this paragraph and adequate training on such guidelines.

(4) If a sequestration order issued under the Balanced Budget and Emergency Deficit Control Act of 1985 reduces the amount of funds available for allotment under section *2007* of this title for any fiscal year by more than 7 percent of the amount of funds available for allotment under such section during the preceding fiscal year

(A) the Secretary, notwithstanding any other law, may use

(i) funds appropriated for the operation of any Bureau school that is closed or consolidated, and

(ii) funds appropriated for any program that has been curtailed at any Bureau school, to fund allotments made under section *2007* of this title, and

(B) the Secretary may waive the application of the provisions of section *2001*(h) of this title with respect to the closure or consolidation of a school, or the curtailment of a program at a school, during such fiscal year if the funds described in clauses (i) and (ii) of subparagraph (A)

with respect to such school are used to fund allotments made under section *2007* of this title for such fiscal year.

(b) Local financial plans for expenditure of funds

In the case of all Bureau schools, allotted funds shall be expended on the basis of local financial plans which shall be prepared by the local school supervisor in active consultation with the local school board for each school, and the local school board for each school shall have the authority to ratify, reject, or amend such financial plan, and expenditures thereunder, and, on its own determination or in response to the supervisor of the school, to revise such financial plan to meet needs not foreseen at the time of preparation of the financial plan. The supervisor shall provide the appropriate union representative of the education employees with copies of proposed draft financial plans and all amendments or modifications thereto, at the same time such copies are submitted to the local school board. The supervisor of the school may appeal any such action of the local school board to the appropriate education line officer of the Bureau agency by filing a written statement describing the action and the reasons the supervisor believes such action should be overturned. A copy of such statement shall be submitted to the local school board and such board shall be afforded an opportunity to respond, in writing, to such appeal. After reviewing such written appeal and response, the appropriate education line officer may, for good cause, overturn the action of the local school board. The appropriate line education officer shall transmit the determination of such appeal in the form of a written opinion to such board and to such supervisor identifying the reasons for overturning such action.

(c) Use of self-determination grant funds

Funds for self-determination grants under section *450h*(a)(2) of this title shall not be used for providing technical assistance and training in the field of education by the Bureau unless such services are provided in accordance with a plan, agreed to by the tribe or tribes affected and the Bureau, under which control of education programs is intended to be transferred to such tribe or tribes within a specific period of time negotiated under such agreement. The Secretary may approve applications for funding tribal divisions of education and the development of tribal codes of education from funds appropriated pursuant to section 450h(a) of this title.

(d) Technical assistance and training

In the exercise of its authority under this section, a local school board may request technical assistance and training from the Secretary, and the Secretary shall, to the greatest extent possible, provide such services, and make appropriate provisions in the budget of the Office for such services.

(e) Summer program of academic and support services

(1) A financial plan under subsection (b) of this section for a school may include, at the discretion of the local administrator and the school board of such school, a provision for a summer program of academic and support services for students of the school. Any such program may include activities related to the prevention of alcohol and substance abuse. The Assistant Secretary of Indian Affairs shall provide for the utilization of any such school facility during any summer in which such utilization is requested.

(2) Notwithstanding any other provision of law, funds authorized under the Act of April 16, 1934 (*25* U.S.C. *452* et seq.) and this Act may be used to augment the services provided in each summer program at the option, and under the control, of the tribe or Indian controlled school receiving such funds.

(3) The Assistant Secretary of Indian Affairs, acting through the Director of the Office, shall provide technical assistance and coordination for any program described in paragraph (1) and shall, to the extent possible, encourage the coordination of such programs with any other summer programs that might benefit Indian youth, regardless of the funding source or administrative entity of any such program.

(f) Cooperative agreements

(1) From funds allotted to a Bureau school under section *2007* of this title, the Secretary shall, if specifically requested by the tribal governing body (within the meaning of section *2001*(k) of this title), implement any cooperative agreement entered into between the tribe, the Bureau school board, and the local public school district which meets the requirements of paragraph (2) and involves the school. The tribe, the Bureau school board, and the local public school district shall determine the terms of the agreement. Such agreement may encompass coordination of all or any part of the following:

(A) Academic program and curriculum, unless the Bureau school is currently accredited by a State or regional accrediting entity and would not continue to be so accredited.

(B) Support services, including procurement and facilities maintenance.

(C) Transportation.

(2) Each agreement entered into pursuant to the authority provided in paragraph (1) shall confer a benefit upon the Bureau school commensurate with the burden assumed, though this requirement shall not be construed so as to require equal expenditures or an exchange of similar services.

(g) Product or result of student projects

Notwithstanding any other provision of law, where there is agreement on action between the superintendent and the school board of a Bureau funded school, the product or result of a project conducted in whole or in major part by a student may be given to that student upon the completion of such project.

(h) Federal matching funds requirements

Notwithstanding any other provision of law, funds received by a Bureau funded school under this chapter shall not be considered Federal funds for purposes of meeting a matching funds requirement in any Federal program.

Sec. 2011.—Policy for Indian control of Indian education

(a) Facilitation of Indian control

It shall be the policy of the Secretary and the Bureau, in carrying out the functions of the Bureau, to facilitate Indian control of Indian affairs in all matters relating to education.

(b) Consultation with tribes

(1) All actions under this Act shall be done with active consultation with tribes.

(2) The consultation required under paragraph (1) means a process involving the open discussion and joint deliberation of all options with respect to potential issues or changes between the Bureau and all interested parties. During such discussions and joint deliberations, interested parties (including tribes and school officials) shall be given an opportunity to present issues including proposals regarding changes in current practices or programs which will be considered for future action by the Bureau. All interested parties shall be given an opportunity to participate and discuss the options presented or to present other alternatives, with the views and concerns of the interested parties given effect unless the Secretary determines, from information educed or presented by the interested parties during 1 or more of the discussions and deliberations, that there is a substantial reason for another course of action. The Secretary shall submit to any Member of Congress, within 18 days of the receipt of a written request by such Member, a written explanation of any decision made by the Secretary which is not consistent with the views of the interested parties.

Sec. 2012.—Education personnel

(a) In general

(1) Chapter 51, subchapter III of chapter 53, and chapter 63 of title 5, relating to classification, pay, and leave, respectively, and the sections of such title relating to the appointment, promotion, and removal of civil service employees, shall not apply to educators or to education positions (as defined in subsection (n) of this section).

(2) Paragraph (1) shall take effect 1 year after November 1, 1978.

(b) Regulations

Not later than the effective date of subsection (a)(2) of this section, the Secretary shall prescribe regulations to carry out this section. Such regulations shall govern

(1) the establishment of education positions,

(2) the establishment of qualifications for educators,

(3) the fixing of basic compensation for educators and education positions,

(4) the appointment of educators,

(5) the discharge of educators,

(6) the entitlement of educators to compensation,

(7) the payment of compensation to educators,

(8) the conditions of employment of educators,

(9) the length of the school year applicable to education positions described in subsection (n)(1)(A) of this section,

(10) the leave system for educators, and

(11) such other matters as may be appropriate.

(c) Qualifications of educators

(1) In prescribing regulations to govern the qualifications of educators, the Secretary shall require

(A)

(i) that lists of qualified and interviewed applicants for education positions be maintained in each agency and area office of the Bureau from among individuals who have applied at the agency or area level for an education position or who have applied at the national level and have indicated in such application an interest in working in certain areas or agencies; and

(ii) that a list of qualified and interviewed applicants for education positions be maintained in the Office from among individuals who have applied at the national level for an education position and who have expressed interest in working in an education position anywhere in the United States;

(B) that a local school board shall have the authority to waive on a case-by-case basis, any formal education or degree qualifications established by regulation pursuant to subsection (b)(2) of this section, in order for a tribal member to be hired in an education position to teach courses on tribal culture and language and that subject to subsection (d)(2)(A) of this section, a determination by a school board that such a person be hired shall be followed by the supervisor; and

(C) that it shall not be a prerequisite to the employment of an individual in an education position at the local level that such individual's name appear on the national list maintained pursuant to paragraph (1)(A)(ii) or that such individual has applied at the national level for an education position.

(2) The Secretary may authorize the temporary employment in an education position of an individual who has not met the certification standards established pursuant to regulations, if the Secretary determines that failure to do so would result in that position remaining vacant.

(d) Hiring of educators

(1) In prescribing regulations to govern the appointment of educators, the Secretary shall require

(A)

(i) that educators employed in a school (other than the supervisor of the school) shall be hired by the supervisor of the school unless there are no qualified applicants available, in which case the vacant position shall be filled at the national level from the list maintained pursuant to subsection (c)(1)(A)(ii) of this section;

(ii) each school supervisor shall be hired by the education line officer of the agency office of the Bureau in which the school is located; and

(iii) educators employed in an agency office of the Bureau shall be hired by the superintendent for education of the agency office;

(B) that before an individual is employed in an education position in a school by the supervisor of a school (or, with respect to the position of supervisor, by the appropriate agency education line officer), the local school board for the school shall be consulted, and that subject to paragraph (2), a determination by the school board that such individual should or should not be so employed shall be followed by the supervisor (or with respect to the position of supervisor, by the agency superintendent for education); and

(C) that before an individual may be employed in an education position at the agency level, the appropriate agency school board shall be consulted, and that, subject to paragraph (3), a determination by such school board that such individual should or should not be employed shall be followed by the agency superintendent for education.

(2)

(A) The supervisor of a school may appeal to the appropriate agency education line officer any determination by the local school board for the school that an individual be employed, or not be employed, in an education position in the school (other than that of supervisor) by filing a written statement describing the determination and the reasons the supervisor believes such determination should be overturned. A copy of such statement shall be submitted to the local school board and such board shall be afforded an opportunity to respond, in writing, to such appeal. After reviewing such written appeal and response, the education line officer may, for good cause, overturn the determination of the local school board. The education line officer shall transmit the determination of such appeal in the form of a written opinion to such board and to such supervisor identifying the reasons for overturning such determination.

(B) The education line officer of an agency office of the Bureau may appeal to the Director of the Office any determination by the local school board for the school that an individual be employed, or not be employed, as the supervisor of a school by filing a written statement describing the determination and the reasons the supervisor believes such determination should be overturned. A copy of such statement shall be submitted to the local school board and such board shall be afforded an opportunity to respond, in writing, to such appeal. After reviewing such written appeal and response, the Director may, for good cause, overturn the determination of the local school board. The Director shall transmit the determination of such appeal in the form of a written opinion to such board and to such education line officer identifying the reasons for overturning such determination.

(3) The education line officer of an agency office of the Bureau may appeal to the Director of the Office any determination by the agency school board that an individual be employed, or not be employed, in an education position in such agency office by filing a written statement describing the determination and the reasons the supervisor believes such determination should be overturned. A copy of such statement shall be submitted to the agency school board and such board shall be afforded an opportunity to respond, in writing, to such appeal. After reviewing such written appeal and response, the Director may, for good cause, overturn the determination of the agency school board. The Director shall transmit the determination of such appeal in the form of a written opinion to such board and to such education line officer identifying the reasons for overturning such determination.

(4) Any individual who applies at the local level for an education position shall state on such individual's application whether or not such individual has applied at the national level for an education position in the Bureau. If such individual is employed at the local level, such individual's name shall immediately be forwarded to the Secretary, who shall, as soon as possible but in no event in more than 30 days, ascertain the accuracy of the statement made by such individual pursuant to the first sentence of this paragraph. If the individual's statement is found to have been false, such individual, at the Secretary's discretion, may be

disciplined or discharged. If the individual had applied at the national level for an education position in the Bureau, the appointment of such individual at the local level shall be conditional for a period of 90 days, during which period the Secretary may appoint a more qualified individual (as determined by the Secretary) from the list maintained at the national level pursuant to subsection (c)(1)(A)(ii) of this section to the position to which such individual was appointed.

(5) Except as expressly provided, nothing in this section shall be construed as conferring upon local school boards, authority over, or control of, educators.

(e) Discharge and conditions of employment of educators

(1) In prescribing regulations to govern the discharge and conditions of employment of educators, the Secretary shall require

(A) that procedures be established for the rapid and equitable resolution of grievances of educators;

(B) that no educator may be discharged without notice of the reasons therefore and opportunity for a hearing under procedures that comport with the requirements of due process; and

(C) educators employed in Bureau schools shall be notified 60 days prior to the end of the school year whether their employment contract will be renewed for the following year.

(2) The supervisor of a Bureau school may discharge (subject to procedures established under paragraph (1)(B)) for cause (as determined under regulations prescribed by the Secretary) any educator employed in such school. Upon giving notice of proposed discharge to an educator, the supervisor involved shall immediately notify the local school board for the school of such action. A determination by the local school board that such educator shall not be discharged shall be followed by the supervisor. The supervisor shall have the right to appeal such action to the education line officer of the appropriate agency office of the Bureau. Upon such an appeal, the agency education line officer may, for good cause and in writing to the local school board, overturn the determination of the local school board with respect to the employment of such individual.

(3) Each local school board for a Bureau school shall have the right

(A) to recommend to the supervisor of such school that an educator employed in the school be discharged; and

(B) to recommend to the education line officer of the appropriate agency office of the Bureau and to the Director of the Office, that the supervisor of the school be discharged.

(f) Indian preferences

(1) Notwithstanding any provision of the Indian preference laws, such laws shall not apply in the case of any personnel action within the purview of this section respecting an applicant or employee not entitled to Indian preference if each tribal organization concerned grants, in writing, a waiver of the application of such laws with respect to such personnel action, if such a waiver is in writing deemed to be a necessity by the tribal organization, except that this paragraph shall in no way relieve the Bureau of the Bureau's responsibility to issue timely and adequate announcements and advertisements concerning any such personnel action if such action is intended to fill a vacancy (no matter how such vacancy is created).

(2) For purposes of this subsection, the term "tribal organization" means

(A) the recognized governing body of any Indian tribe, band, nation, pueblo, or other organized community, including a Native village (as defined in section 1602(c) of title 43); or

(B) in connection with any personnel action referred to in this subsection, any local school board as defined in section 2026 of this title, and which has been delegated by such governing body the authority to grant a waiver under such subsection with respect to such personnel action.

(3) The term "Indian preference laws" means section 472 of this title or any other provision of law granting a preference to Indians in promotions and other personnel actions, except that such term shall not be considered to include section 450e(b) of this title.

(g) Applicability of chapter 51 of title 5

Subject to the authority of the Office of Personnel Management to determine finally the applicability of chapter 51 of title 5 to specific positions and employees in the executive branch, the Secretary shall determine in accordance with subsection (a)(1) of this section the applicability or inapplicability of such chapter to positions and employees in the Bureau.

(h) Compensation or annual salary

(1)

(A) Except as otherwise provided in this section, the Secretary shall fix the basic compensation or annual salary rate for educators and education positions at rates comparable to the rates in effect under the General Schedule for individuals with comparable qualifications, and holding comparable positions, to whom chapter 51 of title 5 is applicable or on the basis of the Federal Wage System schedule in effect for the locality.

(B) By not later than October 28, 1988, the Secretary shall establish, for contracts for the 1991–1992 academic year, and thereafter, the rates of basic compensation, or annual salary rates, for the positions of teachers and counselors (including dormitory counselors and home-living counselors) at the rates of basic compensation applicable (on the date of enactment of such amendments and thereafter) to comparable positions in overseas schools under the Defense Department Overseas Teachers Pay and Personnel Practices Act (*20* U.S.C. *901* et seq.), unless the Secretary establishes such rates within such 6-month period through collective bargaining with the appropriate union representative of the education employees that is recognized by the Bureau.

(C) By not later than October 28, 1988, the Secretary shall establish the rates of basic compensation or annual salary rates for the positions of teachers and counselors (including dormitory and home-living counselors)

(i) for contracts for the 1989–1990 academic year, at rates which reflect 1/3 of the changes in the rates applicable to such positions on April 28, 1988, that must be made to conform the rates to the rates established under subparagraph (B) for such positions for contracts for the 1991–1992 academic year, and

(ii) for contracts for the 1990–1991 academic year, at rates which reflect 2/3 of such changes.

(D) The establishment of rates of basic compensation and annual salary rates by the Secretary under subparagraphs (B) and (C) shall not preclude the use of regulations and procedures used by the Bureau before April 28, 1988, in making determinations regarding promotions and advancements through levels of pay that are based on the merit, education, experience, or tenure of the educator.

(E)

(i) Except as provided in clause (ii), the establishment of rates of basic compensation and annual salary rates by the Secretary under subparagraphs (B) and (C) shall not affect the continued employment or compensation of an educator who was employed in an education position on October 31, 1979, and who did not make the election under paragraph (2) of subsection (o) of this section.

(ii) Any individual described in clause (i) may, during the 5-year period beginning on the date on which the Secretary establishes rates of basic compensation and annual salary rates under subparagraph (B), make an irrevocable election to have the basic compensation rate or annual salary rate of such individual determined in accordance with this paragraph.

(iii) If an individual makes the election described in clause (ii), such election shall not affect the application to the individual of the same retirement system and leave system that applies to the individual during the fiscal year preceding the fiscal year in which such election is made, except that the individual must use leave accrued during a contract period by the end of that contract period.

(F) The President shall include with the budget submitted under section *1105* of title *31* for each of the fiscal years 1990, 1991, and 1992 a written statement by the Secretary which specifies

(i) the amount of funds the Secretary needs to pay basic compensation and the annual salaries of educators for such fiscal year, and

(ii) the amount of funds the Secretary estimates would be needed to pay basic compensation and the annual salaries of educators for such fiscal year if the amendments made to this paragraph by the Indian Education Amendments of 1988 had not been enacted.

(2) Each educator employed in an education position in Alaska shall be paid a cost-of-living allowance equal to 25 percent of the rate of basic compensation to which such educator is entitled.

(3)

(A) The Secretary may pay a postdifferential not to exceed 25 percent of the rate of basic compensation, on the basis of conditions of environment or work which warrant additional pay as a recruitment and retention incentive.

(B)

(i) Upon the request of the supervisor and the local school board of a Bureau school, the Secretary shall grant the supervisor of the school authorization to provide 1 or more post differentials under subparagraph (A) unless the Secretary determines for clear and convincing reasons (and advises the board in writing of those reasons) that certain of the requested post differentials should be disapproved or decreased because there is no disparity of compensation for the involved employees or positions in the Bureau school, as compared with the nearest public school, that is either

(I) at least 5 percent, or

(II) less than 5 percent and affects the recruitment or retention of employees at the school.

(ii) The request under clause (i) shall be deemed granted as requested at the end of the 60th day after the request is received in the Central Office of the Bureau unless before that time the request is approved, approved with modification, or disapproved by the Secretary.

(iii) The Secretary or the supervisor of a Bureau school may discontinue or decrease a post differential authorized by reason of this subparagraph at the beginning of a school year after either

(I) the local school board requests that such differential be discontinued or decreased, or

(II) the Secretary or the supervisor determines for clear and convincing reasons (and advises the board in writing of those reasons) that there is no disparity of compensation that would affect the recruitment or retention of employees at the school after the differential is discontinued or decreased.

(i) Annual and sick leave

Any individual

(1) who on November 1, 1978, is holding a position which is determined under subsection (f) of this section to be an education position and who elects under subsection (o)(2) of this section to be covered under the provisions of this section, or

(2) who is an employee of the Federal Government or the municipal government of the District of Columbia and is transferred, promoted, or reappointed, without break in service, from a position under a different leave system to an education position, shall be credited for the purpose of the leave system provided under regulations prescribed pursuant to subsection (b)(10) of this section, with the annual and sick leave to such individual's credit immediately before the effective date of such election, transfer, promotion, or reappointment.

(j) Liquidation of remaining leave upon termination

Upon termination of employment with the Bureau, any annual leave remaining to the credit of an individual within the purview of this section shall be liquidated in accordance with sections 5551(a) and 6306 of title 5, except that leave earned or accrued under regulations prescribed pursuant to subsection (b)(10) of this section shall not be so liquidated.

(k) Transfer of remaining leave upon transfer, promotion, or reemployment

In the case of any educator who is transferred, promoted, or reappointed, without break in service, to a position in the Federal Government under a different leave system, any remaining leave to the credit of such person earned or credited under the regulations prescribed pursuant to subsection (b)(10) of this section shall be transferred to such person's credit in the employing agency on an adjusted basis in accordance with regulations which shall be prescribed by the Office of Personnel Management.

(l) Ineligibility for employment of voluntarily terminated educators

An educator who voluntarily terminates employment with the Bureau before the expiration of the existing employment contract between such educator and the Bureau shall not be eligible to be employed in another education position in the Bureau during the remainder of the term of such contract.

(m) Dual compensation

In the case of any educator employed in an education position described in subsection (n)(1)(A) of this section who

(1) is employed at the close of a school year,

(2) agrees in writing to serve in such a position for the next school year, and

(3) is employed in another position during the recess period immediately preceding such next school year, or during such recess period receives additional compensation referred to in section 5533 of title 5, relating to dual compensation, shall not apply to such educator by reason of any such employment during a recess period for any such receipt of additional compensation.

(n) Definitions

For the purpose of this section

(1) The term "education position" means a position in the Bureau the duties and responsibilities of which

(A) are performed on a school-year basis principally in a Bureau school and involve

(i) classroom or other instruction or the supervision or direction of classroom or other instruction;

(ii) any activity (other than teaching) which requires academic credits in educational theory and practice equal to the academic credits in educational theory and practice required for a bachelor's degree in education from an accredited institution of higher education;

(iii) any activity in or related to the field of education notwithstanding that academic credits in educational theory and practice are not a formal requirement for the conduct of such activity; or

(iv) support services at, or associated with, the site of the school; or

(B) are performed at the agency level of the Bureau and involve the implementation of education-related programs other than the position for agency superintendent for education.

(2) The term "educator" means an individual whose services are required, or who is employed, in an education position.

(o) Covered individuals; election

(1) Subsections (a) through (n) of this section apply to an educator hired after November 1, 1979 (and to an educator who elected application under paragraph (2)) and to the position in which such individual is employed. Subject to paragraph (2), the enactment of this Act shall not affect the continued employment of an individual employed on October 31, 1979 in an education position, or such individual's right to receive the compensation attached to such position.

(2) Any individual employed in an education position on October 31, 1979, may, not later than November 1, 1983, make an irrevocable election to be covered under the provisions of subsections (a) through (n) of this section.

(p) Furlough without consent

(1) An educator who was employed in an education position on October 31, 1979, who was eligible to make an election under paragraph (2) of subsection (o) at that time, and who did not make the election under paragraph (2) of subsection (o), may not be placed on furlough (within the meaning of section *7511*(a)(5) of title 5) without the consent of such educator for an aggregate of more than 4 weeks within the same calendar year, unless

(A) the supervisor, with the approval of the local school board (or of the education line officer upon appeal under paragraph (2)), of the Bureau school at which such educator provides services determines that a longer period of furlough is necessary due to an insufficient amount of funds available for personnel compensation at such school, as determined under the financial plan process as determined under section *2010*(b) of this title, and

(B) all educators (other than principals and clerical employees) providing services at such Bureau school are placed on furloughs of equal length, except that the supervisor, with the approval of the local school board (or of the agency education line officer upon appeal under paragraph (2)), may continue 1 or more educators in pay status if

(i) such educators are needed to operate summer programs, attend summer training sessions, or participate in special activities including curriculum development committees; and

(ii) such educators are selected based upon such educator's qualifications, after public notice of the minimum qualifications reasonably necessary and without discrimination as to supervisory, nonsupervisory, or other status of the educators who apply.

(2) The supervisor of a Bureau school may appeal to the appropriate agency education line officer any refusal by the local school board to approve any determination of the supervisor that is described in paragraph (1)(A) by filing a written statement describing the determination and the reasons the supervisor believes such determination should be approved. A copy of such statement shall be submitted to the local school board and such board shall be afforded an opportunity to respond, in writing, to such appeal. After reviewing such written appeal and response, the education line officer may, for good cause, approve the determination of the supervisor. The educational line officer shall transmit the determination of such appeal in the form of a written opin-

ion to such local school board and to the supervisor identifying the reasons for approving such determination.

Sec. 2013.—Management information system

The Secretary shall establish within the Office, within 1 year after October 19, 1984, a computerized management information system, which shall provide information to the Office. Such information shall include

(1) student enrollment;

(2) curriculum;

(3) staff;

(4) facilities;

(5) community demographics;

(6) student assessment information; and

(7) information on the administrative and program costs attributable to each Bureau program, divided into discreet elements.

Sec. 2014.—Bureau education policies

Within 180 days of November 1, 1978, the Secretary shall develop, publish in the Federal Register, and submit to all agency and area offices of the Bureau, all tribal governments, and the appropriate committees of the Congress, a draft set of education policies, procedures, and practices for education-related action of the Bureau. The Secretary shall, within 1 year of November 1, 1978, provide that such uniform policies, procedures, and practices shall be finalized and promulgated. Thereafter, such policies, procedures, and practices and their periodic revisions, shall serve as the foundation for future Bureau actions in education.

Sec. 2015.—Uniform education procedures and practices

The Secretary shall cause the various divisions of the Bureau to formulate uniform procedures and practices with respect to such concerns of those divisions as relate to education, and shall report such practices and procedures to the Congress.

Sec. 2016.—Recruitment of Indian educators

The Secretary shall institute a policy for the recruitment of qualified Indian educators and a detailed plan to promote employees from within the Bureau. Such plan shall include opportunities for acquiring work experience prior to actual work assignment.

Sec. 2017.—Biennial report

(a) The Secretary shall submit to each appropriate committee of the Congress a detailed biennial report on the state of education within the Bureau and any problems encountered in the field of education during the 2-year period covered by the report. Such report shall contain suggestions for improving the Bureau educational system and increasing local Indian control of such system. Such report shall also include the current status of tribally controlled community colleges. The annual budget submission for the Bureau's education programs shall, among other things, include

(1) information on the funds provided previously private schools under section *458d* of this title and recommendations with respect to the future use of such funds;

(2) the needs and costs of operation and maintenance of tribally controlled community colleges eligible for assistance under the Tribally Controlled College or University Assistance Act of 1978 (*25* U.S.C. *1801* et seq.) and recommendations with respect to meeting such needs and costs; and

(3) the plans required by sections 2001(g), 2002(c), and 2005(b), of this title.

(b) The Inspector General of the Department of the Interior shall establish a system to ensure that financial and compliance audits are conducted of each Bureau school at least once in every three years. Audits of Bureau schools shall be based upon the extent to which such school has complied with its local financial plan under section 2010 of this title.

Sec. 2018.—Rights of Indian students

Within six months of November 1, 1978, the Secretary shall prescribe such rules and regulations as are necessary to ensure the constitutional and civil rights of Indian students attending Bureau schools, including such students' right to privacy under the laws of the United States, such students' right to freedom of religion and expression and such students' right to due process in connection with disciplinary actions, suspensions, and expulsions.

Notes on Sec. 2019.

Section, *Pub. L. 95–561,* title XI, Sec. 1139, as added Pub. L. 103–382, title III, Sec. 381, Oct. 20, 1994, 108 Stat. 4011, related to promulgation of regulations.

A prior section 2019, *Pub. L. 95–561,* title XI, Sec. 1139, Nov. 1, 1978, 92 Stat. 2328; *Pub. L. 100–297,* title V, Sec. 5117, Apr. 28, 1988, 102 Stat. 382; *Pub. L. 100–427,* Sec. 1(c)(1), (2), Sept. 9, 1988, 102 Stat. 1603; *Pub. L. 101–301,* Sec. 5(a), May 24, 1990, 104 Stat. 207, defined terms used in this chapter, prior to the general amendment of this chapter by *Pub. L. 103–382.*

NATIVE AMERICAN LANGUAGES ACT, 25 U.S.C. 2901 (1990)

Sec. 2901.—Findings

The Congress finds that

(1) the status of the cultures and languages of Native Americans is unique and the United States has the responsibility to act together with Native Americans to ensure the survival of these unique cultures and languages;

(2) special status is accorded Native Americans in the United States, a status that recognizes distinct cultural and political rights, including the right to continue separate identities;

(3) the traditional languages of Native Americans are an integral part of their cultures and identities and form the basic medium for the transmission, and thus survival, of Native American cultures, literatures, histories, religions, political institutions, and values;

(4) there is a widespread practice of treating Native Americans

(5) there is a lack of clear, comprehensive, and consistent Federal policy on treatment of Native American languages which has often resulted in acts of suppression and extermination of Native American languages and cultures;

(6) there is convincing evidence that student achievement and performance, community and school pride, and educational opportunity is clearly and directly tied to respect for, and support of, the first language of the child or student;

(7) it is clearly in the interests of the United States, individual States, and territories to encourage the full academic and human potential achievements of all students and citizens and to take steps to realize these ends;

(8) acts of suppression and extermination directed against Native American languages and cultures are in conflict with the United States policy of self-determination for Native Americans;

(9) languages are the means of communication for the full range of human experiences and are critical to the survival of cultural and political integrity of any people; and

(10) language provides a direct and powerful means of promoting international communication by people who share languages.

Sec. 2902.—Definitions

For purposes of this chapter

(1) The term "Native American" means an Indian, Native Hawaiian, or Native American Pacific Islander.

(2) The term "Indian" has the meaning given to such term under section *7881*(4) of title *20*.

(3) The term "Native Hawaiian" has the meaning given to such term by section *7912*(1) of title *20*.

(4) The term "Native American Pacific Islander" means any descendent of the aboriginal people of any island in the Pacific Ocean that is a territory or possession of the United States.

(5) The terms "Indian tribe" and "tribal organization" have the respective meaning given to each of such terms under section *450b* of this title.

(6) The term "Native American language" means the historical, traditional languages spoken by Native Americans.

(7) The term "traditional leaders" includes Native Americans who have special expertise in Native American culture and Native American languages.

(8) The term "Indian reservation" has the same meaning given to the term "reservation" under section *1452* of this title.

Sec. 2903.—Declaration of policy

It is the policy of the United States to

(1) preserve, protect, and promote the rights and freedom of Native Americans to use, practice, and develop Native American languages;

(2) allow exceptions to teacher certification requirements for Federal programs, and programs funded in whole or in part by the Federal Government, for instruction in Native American languages when such teacher certification requirements hinder the employment of qualified teachers who teach in Native American languages, and to encourage State and territorial governments to make similar exceptions;

(3) encourage and support the use of Native American languages as a medium of instruction in order to encourage and support

(A) Native American language survival,

(B) educational opportunity,

(C) increased student success and performance,

(D) increased student awareness and knowledge of their culture and history, and

(E) increased student and community pride;

(4) encourage State and local education programs to work with Native American parents, educators, Indian tribes, and other Native American governing bodies in the implementation of programs to put this policy into effect;

(5) recognize the right of Indian tribes and other Native American governing bodies to use the Native American languages as a medium of instruction in all schools funded by the Secretary of the Interior;

(6) fully recognize the inherent right of Indian tribes and other Native American governing bodies, States, territories, and possessions of the United States to take action on, and give official status to, their Native American languages for the purpose of conducting their own business;

(7) support the granting of comparable proficiency achieved through course work in a Native American language the same academic credit as comparable proficiency achieved through course work in a foreign language, with recognition of such Native American language proficiency by institutions of higher education as fulfilling foreign language entrance or degree requirements; and

(8) encourage all institutions of elementary, secondary and higher education, where appropriate, to include Native American languages in the curriculum in the same manner as foreign languages and to grant proficiency in Native American languages the same full academic credit as proficiency in foreign languages.

Sec. 2904.—No restrictions

The right of Native Americans to express themselves through the use of Native American languages shall not be restricted in any public proceeding, including publicly supported education programs.

Sec. 2905.—Evaluations

(a) The President shall direct the heads of the various Federal departments, agencies, and instrumentalities to

(1) evaluate their policies and procedures in consultation with Indian tribes and other Native American governing bodies as well as traditional leaders and educators in order to determine and implement changes needed to bring the policies and procedures into compliance with the provisions of this chapter;

(2) give the greatest effect possible in making such evaluations, absent a clear specific Federal statutory requirement to the contrary, to the policies and procedures which will give the broadest effect to the provisions of this chapter; and

(3) evaluate the laws which they administer and make recommendations to the President on amendments needed to bring such laws into compliance with the provisions of this chapter.

(b) By no later than the date that is 1 year after October 30, 1990, the President shall submit to the Congress a report containing recommendations for amendments to Federal laws that are needed to bring such laws into compliance with the provisions of this chapter.

Sec. 2906.—Use of English

Nothing in this chapter shall be construed as precluding the use of Federal funds to teach English to Native Americans.

TRIBALLY CONTROLLED SCHOOLS ACT, 25 U.S.C. 2501 (1988)

Sec. 2501.—Findings

The Congress, after careful review of the Federal Government's historical and special legal relationship with, and resulting responsibilities to, Indians, finds that

(1) the Indian Self-Determination and Education Assistance Act (25 U.S.C. 450 et seq.), which was a product of the legitimate aspirations and a recognition of the inherent authority of Indian nations, was and is a crucial positive step towards tribal and community control;

(2) the Bureau of Indian Affairs' administration and domination of the contracting process under such Act (25 U.S.C. 450 et seq.) has not provided the full opportunity to develop leadership skills crucial to the realization of self-government, and has denied to the Indian people an effective voice in the planning and implementation of programs for the benefit of Indians which are responsive to the true needs of Indian communities;

(3) Indians will never surrender their desire to control their relationships both among themselves and with the non-Indian governments, organizations, and persons;

(4) true self-determination in any society of people is dependent upon an educational process which will ensure the development of qualified people to fulfill meaningful leadership roles;

(5) the Federal administration of education for Indian children has not effected the desired level of educational achievement nor created the diverse opportunities and personal satisfaction which education can and should provide;

(6) true local control requires the least possible Federal interference; and

(7) the time has come to enhance the concepts made manifest in the Indian Self-Determination and Education Assistance Act (25 U.S.C. 450 et seq.).

Sec. 2502.—Declaration of policy

(a) Recognition

The Congress recognizes the obligation of the United States to respond to the strong expression of the Indian people for self-determination by assuring maximum Indian participation in the direction of educational services so as to render such services more responsive to the needs and desires of those communities.

(b) Commitment

The Congress declares its commitment to the maintenance of the Federal Government's unique and continuing trust relationship with and responsibility to the Indian people through the establishment of a meaningful Indian self-determination policy for education which will deter further perpetuation of Federal bureaucratic domination of programs.

(c) National goal

The Congress declares that a major national goal of the United States is to provide the resources, processes, and structures which will enable tribes and local communities to effect the quantity and quality of educational services and opportunities which will permit Indian children to compete and excel in the life areas of their choice, and to achieve the measure of self-determination essential to their social and economic well-being.

(d) Educational needs

The Congress affirms the reality of the special and unique educational needs of Indian peoples, including the need for programs to meet the linguistic and cultural aspirations of Indian tribes and communities. These may best be met through a grant process.

(e) Federal relations

The Congress declares its commitment to these policies and its support, to the full extent of its responsibility, for Federal relations with the Indian Nations.

(f) Termination

The Congress hereby repudiates and rejects House Concurrent Resolution 108 of the 83rd Congress and any policy of unilateral termination of Federal relations with any Indian Nation.

Sec. 2503.—Grants authorized

(a) In general

(1) The Secretary shall provide grants to Indian tribes, and tribal organizations, that

(A) operate contract schools under title XI of the Education Amendments of 1978 (25 U.S.C. 2001 et seq.) and notify the Secretary of their election to operate the schools with assistance under this chapter rather than continuing as contract schools;

(B) operate other tribally controlled schools eligible for assistance under this chapter and submit applications (which are approved by their tribal governing bodies) to the Secretary for such grants; or

(C) elect to assume operation of Bureau schools with assistance under this chapter and submit applications (which are approved by their tribal governing bodies) to the Secretary for such grants.

(2) Grants provided under this chapter shall be deposited into the general operating fund of the tribally controlled school with respect to which the grant is provided.

(3)

(A) Except as otherwise provided in this paragraph, grants provided under this chapter shall be used to defray, at the discretion of the school board of the tribally controlled school with respect to which the grant is provided, any expenditures for education-related activities for which any funds that compose the grant may be used under the laws described in section *2504*(a) of this title, including but not limited to, expenditures for

(i) school operations, academic, educational, residential, guidance and counseling, and administrative purposes, and

(ii) support services for the school, including transportation.

(B) Grants provided under this chapter may, at the discretion of the school board of the tribally controlled school with respect to which such grant is provided, be used to defray operation and maintenance expenditures for the school if any funds for the operation and maintenance of the school are allocated to the school under the provisions of any of the laws described in section *2504*(a) of this title.

(C) If funds allocated to a tribally controlled school under title I of the Elementary and Secondary Education Act of 1965 (*20* U.S.C. *6301* et seq.), the Individuals with Disabilities Education Act (*20* U.S.C. *1400* et seq.), or any Federal education law other than title XI of the Education Amendments of 1978 (*25* U.S.C. *2001* et seq.) are included in a grant provided under this chapter, a portion of the grant equal to the amount of the funds allocated under such law shall be expended only for those activities for which funds provided under such law may be expended under the terms of such law.

(b) Limitations

(1) No more than one grant may be provided under this chapter with respect to any Indian tribe or tribal organization for any fiscal year.

(2) Funds provided under any grant made under this chapter may not be used in connection with religious worship or sectarian instruction.

(3) Funds provided under any grant made under this chapter may not be expended for administrative costs (as defined under section 1128A(e)(1) of the Education Amendments of 1978) in excess of the amount generated for such costs under section 1128A of such Act.

(c) Limitation on transfer of funds among schoolsites

(1) In the case of a grantee which operates schools at more than one schoolsite, the grantee may expend no more than the lesser of

(A) 10 percent of the funds allocated for a schoolsite under section 1128 of the Education Amendments of 1978, or

(B) $400,000 of such funds, at any other schoolsite.

(2) For purposes of this subsection, the term "schoolsite" means the physical location and the facilities of an elementary or secondary educational or residential program operated by, or under contract with, the Bureau for which a discreet student count is identified under the funding formula established under section 1128 of the Education Amendments of 1978.

(d) No requirement to accept grants

Nothing in this chapter may be construed

(1) to require a tribe or tribal organization to apply for or accept, or

(2) to allow any person to coerce any tribe or tribal organization into applying for, or accepting, a grant under this chapter to plan, conduct, and administer all of, or any portion of, any Bureau program. Such applications, and the timing of such applications, shall be strictly voluntary. Nothing in this chapter may be construed as allowing or requiring any grant with any entity other than the entity to which the grant is provided.

(e) No effect on Federal responsibility

Grants provided under this chapter shall not terminate, modify, suspend, or reduce the responsibility of the Federal Government to provide a program.

(f) Retrocession

Whenever a tribal governing body requests retrocession of any program for which assistance is provided under this chapter, such retrocession shall become effective upon a date specified by the Secretary not more than 120 days after the date on which the tribal governing body requests the retrocession, or such later date as may be mutually agreed upon by the Secretary and the tribal governing body. If such a program is retroceded, the Secretary shall provide to any Indian tribe served by such program at least the same quantity and quality of services that would have been provided under such program at the level of funding provided under this chapter prior to the retrocession. The tribe requesting retrocession shall specify whether the retrocession is to status as a Bureau school or as a contract school under title XI of the Education Amendments of 1978 (*25 U.S.C. 2001* et seq.). Except as otherwise determined by the Secretary, the tribe or tribal organization operating the program to be retroceded must transfer to the Secretary (or to the tribe or tribal organization which will operate the program as a contract school) the existing equipment and materials which were acquired

(1) with assistance under this chapter, or

(2) upon assumption of operation of the program under this

chapter if it was a Bureau funded school under title XI of the Education Amendments of 1978 before receiving assistance under this chapter.

(g) No termination for administrative convenience

Grants provided under this Act may not be terminated, modified, suspended, or reduced only for the convenience of the administering agency.

Sec. 2504.—Composition of grants

(a) In general

The grant provided under this chapter to an Indian tribe or tribal organization for any fiscal year shall consist of

(1) the total amount of funds allocated for such fiscal year under sections 1128 and 1128a of the Education Amendments of 1978 with respect to the tribally controlled schools eligible for assistance under this chapter that are operated by such Indian tribe or tribal organization, including, but not limited to, funds provided under such sections, or under any other provision of law, for transportation costs,

(2) to the extent requested by such Indian tribe or tribal organization, the total amount of funds provided from operations and maintenance accounts and, notwithstanding section *450j* of this title, or any other provision of law, other facilities accounts for such schools for such fiscal year (including but not limited to all those referenced under section 1126(d) of the Education Amendments of 1978 (*25* U.S.C. *2006*(d)), or any other law), and

(3) the total amount of funds provided under

(A) title I of the Elementary and Secondary Education Act of 1965 (*20* U.S.C. *6301* et seq.),

(B) the Individuals with Disabilities Education Act (*20* U.S.C. *1400* et seq.), and

(C) any other Federal education law, that are allocated to such schools for such fiscal year.

(b) Special rules

(1) In the allocation of funds under sections 1128, 1128A, and 1126(d) (*25* U.S.C. *2006*(d)) of the Education Amendments of 1978, tribally controlled schools for which grants are provided under this chapter shall be treated as contract schools.

(2) In the allocation of funds provided under

(A) title I of the Elementary and Secondary Education Act of 1965 (*20* U.S.C. *6301* et seq.),

(B) the Individuals with Disabilities Education Act (*20* U.S.C. *1400* et seq.), and

(C) any other Federal education law, that are distributed through the Bureau, tribally controlled schools for which grants are provided under this chapter shall be treated as Bureau schools.

(3)

(A) Funds allocated to a tribally controlled school by reason of paragraph (1) or (2) shall be subject to the provisions of this chapter and shall not be subject to any additional restriction, priority, or limitation that is imposed by the Bureau with respect to funds provided under

(i) title I of the Elementary and Secondary Education Act of 1965 (*20* U.S.C. *6301* et seq.),

(ii) the Individuals with Disabilities Education Act (*20* U.S.C. *1400* et seq.), or

(iii) any Federal education law other than title XI of the Education Amendments of 1978 (*25* U.S.C. *2001* et seq.).

(B) Indian tribes and tribal organizations to which grants are provided under this chapter, and tribally controlled schools for which such grants are provided, shall not be subject to any requirements, obligations, restrictions, or limitations imposed by the Bureau that would otherwise apply solely by reason of the receipt of funds provided under any law referred to in clause (i), (ii), or (iii) of subparagraph (A).

(4) Notwithstanding the provision of paragraph 2503(a)(2) of this title, with respect to funds from facilities improvement and repair, alteration and renovation (major or minor), health and safety, or new construction accounts included in the grant under such paragraph (a)(2), the grantee shall maintain a separate account for such funds and shall, at the end of the period designated for the work covered by the funds received, render a separate accounting of the work done and the funds used to the Secretary. Funds received from these accounts may only be used for the purposes for which they were appropriated and for the work encompassed by the application or submission under which they were received, except that a school receiving a grant under this chapter for facilities improvement and repair may use such grant funds for new construction if the tribal government or other organization provides funding for the new construction equal to at least one-fourth of the total cost of such new construction. Where the appropriations measure or the application submission does not stipulate a period for the work covered by the funds so designated, the Secretary and the grantee shall consult and determine such a period prior to the transfer of funds: Provided, That such period may be extended upon mutual agreement.

(5) If the Secretary fails to make a determination within 180 days of a request filed by an Indian tribe or tribal organization to include in such tribe or organization's grant the funds described in subsection (a)(2) of this section, the Secretary shall be deemed to have approved

such request and the Secretary shall immediately amend the grant accordingly. Such tribe or organization may enforce its rights under subsection (a)(2) of this section and this paragraph, including any denial of or failure to act on such tribe or organization's request, pursuant to the disputes authority described in section 2508(e) of this title.

Sec. 2505.—Eligibility for grants

(a) In general

(1) A tribally controlled school is eligible for assistance under this chapter if the school

(A) was, on April 28, 1988, a contract school under title XI of the Education Amendments of 1978 (25 U.S.C. 2001 et seq.) and the tribe or tribal organization operating the school submits to the Secretary a written notice of election to receive a grant under this chapter,

(B) was a Bureau school under title XI of the Education Amendments of 1978 and has met the requirements of subsection (b) of this section,

(C) is a school for which the Bureau has not provided funds, but which has met the requirements of subsection (c) of this section, or

(D) is a school with respect to which an election has been made under paragraph (2) and which has met the requirements of subsection (b) of this section.

(2) Any application which has been submitted under the Indian Self-Determination and Education Assistance Act (25 U.S.C. 450 et seq.) by an Indian tribe for a school which is not in operation on April 28, 1988, shall be reviewed under the guidelines and regulations for applications submitted under the Indian Self-Determination and Education Assistance Act that were in effect at the time the application was submitted, unless the Indian tribe or tribal organization elects to have the application reviewed under the provisions of subsection (b) of this section.

(b) Additional requirements for Bureau schools and certain electing schools

(1) A school that was a Bureau funded school under title XI of the Education Amendments of 1978 (25 U.S.C. 2001 et seq.) on April 28, 1988, and any school with respect to which an election is made under subsection (a)(2) of this section, meets the requirements of this subsection if

(A) the Indian tribe or tribal organization that operates, or desires to operate, the school submits to the Secretary an application requesting that the Secretary

(i) transfer operation of the school to the Indian tribe or tribal organization, if the Indian tribe or tribal organization is not already operating the school, and

(ii) make a determination of whether the school is eligible for assistance under this chapter, and

(B) the Secretary makes a determination that the school is eligible for assistance under this chapter.

(2)

(A) By no later than the date that is 120 days after the date on which an application is submitted to the Secretary under paragraph (1)(A), the Secretary shall determine

(i) if the school is not being operated by the Indian tribe or tribal organization, whether to transfer operation of the school to the Indian tribe or tribal organization, and

(ii) whether the school is eligible for assistance under this chapter.

(B) In considering applications submitted under paragraph (1)(A), the Secretary

(i) shall transfer operation of the school to the Indian tribe or tribal organization, if the Indian tribe or tribal organization is not already operating the school, and

(ii) shall determine that the school is eligible for assistance under this chapter, unless the Secretary finds by clear and convincing evidence that the services to be provided by the Indian tribe or tribal organization will be deleterious to the welfare of the Indians served by the school.

(C) In considering applications submitted under paragraph (1)(A), the Secretary shall consider whether the Indian tribe or tribal organization would be deficient in operating the school with respect to

(i) equipment,

(ii) bookkeeping and accounting procedures,

(iii) substantive knowledge of operating the school,

(iv) adequately trained personnel, or

(v) any other necessary components in the operation of the school.

(c) Additional requirements for school which is not a Bureau funded school

(1) A school which is not a Bureau funded school under title XI of the Education Amendments of 1978 (*25 U.S.C. 2001* et seq.) meets the requirements of this subsection if

(A) the Indian tribe or tribal organization that operates, or desires to operate, the school submits to the Secretary an application requesting a determination by the Secretary of whether the school is eligible for assistance under this chapter, and

(B) the Secretary makes a determination that the school is eligible for assistance under this chapter.

(2)

(A) By no later than the date that is 180 days after the date on which an application is submitted to the Secretary under paragraph (1)(A), the Secretary shall determine whether the school is eligible for assistance under this chapter.

(B) In making the determination under subparagraph (A), the Secretary shall give equal consideration to each of the following factors:

(i) with respect to the applicant's proposal

(I) the adequacy of facilities or the potential to obtain or provide adequate facilities;

(II) geographic and demographic factors in the affected areas;

(III) adequacy of applicant's program plans;

(IV) geographic proximity of comparable public education; and

(V) the needs as expressed by all affected parties, including but not limited to students, families, tribal governments at both the central and local levels, and school organizations; and

(ii) with respect to all education services already available

(I) geographic and demographic factors in the affected areas;

(II) adequacy and comparability of programs already available;

(III) consistency of available programs with tribal education codes or tribal legislation to education; and

(IV) the history and success of these services for the proposed population to be served, as determined from all factors and not just standardized examination performance.

(C) The Secretary may not make a determination under this paragraph that is primarily based upon the geographic proximity of comparable public education.

(D) Applications submitted under paragraph (1)(A) shall include information on the factors described in subparagraph (B)(i), but the applicant may also provide the Secretary such information relative to the factors described in subparagraph (B)(ii) as the applicant considers appropriate.

(E) If the Secretary fails to make a determination under subparagraph (A) with respect to an application within 180 days after the date on which the Secretary received the application, the Secretary shall be treated as having made a determination that the tribally controlled school is eligible for assistance under the title and the grant shall become effective 18 months after the date on which the Secretary received the application, or an earlier date, at the Secretary's discretion.

(d) Applications and reports

(1) All applications and reports submitted to the Secretary under this chapter, and any amendments to such applications or reports, shall

be filed with the agency or area education officer designated by the Director of the Office of Indian Education of the Bureau of Indian Affairs. The date on which such filing occurs shall, for purposes of this chapter, be treated as the date on which the application or amendment is submitted to the Secretary.

(2) Any application that is submitted under this chapter shall be accompanied by a document indicating the action taken by the tribal governing body in authorizing such application.

(e) Effective date for approved applications

Except as provided in subsection (c)(2)(E) of this section, a grant provided under this chapter, and any transfer of the operation of a Bureau school made under subsection (b) of this section, shall become effective beginning with the academic year succeeding the fiscal year in which the application for the grant or transfer is made, or at an earlier date determined by the Secretary.

(f) Denial of applications

(1) Whenever the Secretary declines to provide a grant under this chapter, to transfer operation of a Bureau school under subsection (b) of this section, or determines that a school is not eligible for assistance under this chapter, the Secretary shall

(A) state the objections in writing to the tribe or tribal organization within the allotted time,

(B) provide assistance to the tribe or tribal organization to overcome all stated objections,

(C) provide the tribe or tribal organization a hearing on the record, under the same rules and regulations that apply under the Indian Self-Determination and Education Assistance Act (25 U.S.C. 450 et seq.), and

(D) provide an opportunity to appeal the objection raised.

(2) The Secretary shall reconsider any amended application submitted under this chapter within 60 days after the amended application is submitted to the Secretary.

Sec. 2506.—Duration of eligibility determination

(a) In general

If the Secretary determines that a tribally controlled school is eligible for assistance under this chapter, the eligibility determination shall remain in effect until the determination is revoked by the Secretary, and the requirements of subsection (b) or (c) of section 2505 of this title, if applicable, shall be considered to have been met with respect to such school until the eligibility determination is revoked by the Secretary.

(b) Annual reports

Each recipient of a grant provided under this chapter shall submit to the Secretary and to the tribal governing body (within the meaning of section 1121(j) of the Education Amendments of 1978) of the tribally controlled school an annual report that shall be limited to

(1) an annual financial statement reporting revenue and expenditures as defined by the cost accounting established by the grantee;

(2) a biannual financial audit conducted pursuant to the standards of the Single Audit Act of 1984 (*31* U.S.C. *7501* et seq.);

(3) an annual submission to the Secretary of the number of students served and a brief description of programs offered under the grant; and

(4) a program evaluation conducted by an impartial entity, to be based on the standards established for purposes of subsection (c)(1)(A)(ii) of this section.

(c) Revocation of eligibility

(1)

(A) The Secretary shall not revoke a determination that a school is eligible for assistance under this chapter if

(i) the Indian tribe or tribal organization submits the reports required under subsection (b) of this section with respect to the school, and

(ii) at least one of the following subclauses applies with respect to the school:

(I) The school is certified or accredited by a State or regional accrediting association as recognized by the Secretary of Education, or is a candidate in good standing for such accreditation under the rules of the State or regional accrediting association, showing that credits achieved by students within the education programs are, or will be, accepted at grade level by a State certified or regionally accredited institution.

(II) A determination made by the Secretary that there is a reasonable expectation that the accreditation described in subclause (I), or the candidacy in good standing for such accreditation, will be reached by the school within 3 years and that the program offered by the school is beneficial to the Indian students.

(III) The school is accredited by a tribal department of education if such accreditation is accepted by a generally recognized regional or State accreditation agency.

(IV) The school accepts the standards promulgated under section 1121 of the Education Amendments of 1978 (*25* U.S.C. *2001*) and an evaluation of performance is conducted under this section in conformance with the regulations pertaining to Bureau operated schools by an impartial evaluator chosen by the grantee, but no grantee shall be required to comply with these standards to a higher degree than a comparable Bureau operated school.

(V) A positive evaluation of the school is conducted once every 3 years under standards adopted by the contractor under a contract for a school entered into under the Indian Self-Determination and Education Assistance Act (25 U.S.C. 450 et seq.) (or revisions of such standards agreed to by the Secretary and the grantee) prior to April 28, 1988, such evaluation to be conducted by an impartial evaluator agreed to by the Secretary and the grantee. If the Secretary and a grantee other than the tribal governing body fail to agree on such an evaluator, the tribal governing body shall choose the evaluator or perform the evaluation. If the Secretary and a grantee which is the tribal governing body fail to agree on such an evaluator, this subclause shall not apply.

(B) The choice of standards employed for purposes of subparagraph (A)(ii) shall be consistent with section 1121(e) of the Education Amendments of 1978.

(2) The Secretary shall not revoke a determination that a school is eligible for assistance under this chapter, or reassume control of a school that was a Bureau school prior to approval of an application submitted under section 2505(b)(1)(A) of this title, until the Secretary

(A) provides notice to the tribally controlled school and the tribal governing body (within the meaning of section 1121(j) of the Education Amendments of 1978) of the tribally controlled school which states

(i) the specific deficiencies that led to the revocation or resumption determination, and

(ii) the actions that are needed to remedy such deficiencies, and

(B) affords such authority an opportunity to effect any remedial actions.

The Secretary shall provide such technical assistance as is necessary to effect such remedial actions. Such notice and technical assistance shall be in addition to a hearing and appeal to be conducted pursuant to the regulations described in section 2505(f)(1)(C) of this title.

(d) Applicability of section pursuant to election under section 2508(b)

With respect to a tribally controlled school which receives assistance under this chapter pursuant to an election made under section 2508(b) of this title

(1) subsection (b) of this section shall apply; and

(2) the Secretary may not revoke eligibility for assistance under this chapter except in conformance with subsection (c) of this section.

Sec. 2507.—Payment of grants; investment of funds

(a) Payments

(1) Except as otherwise provided in this subsection, the Secretary shall make payments to grantees under this chapter in 2 payments, of which

(A) the first payment shall be made not later than July 15 of each year in an amount equal to one-half of the amount which the grantee was entitled to receive during the preceding academic year; and

(B) the second payment, consisting of the remainder to which the grantee is entitled for the academic year, shall be made not later than December 1 of each year.

(2) For any school for which no payment under this chapter was made from Bureau funds in the preceding academic year, full payment of the amount computed for the first academic year of eligibility under this chapter shall be made not later than December 1 of the academic year.

(3) With regard to funds for grantees that become available for obligation on October 1 of the fiscal year for which such funds are appropriated, the Secretary shall make payments to grantees not later than December 1 of the fiscal year.

(4) The provisions of chapter *39* of title *31* shall apply to the payments required to be made by paragraphs (1), (2), and (3).

(5) Paragraphs (1), (2), and (3) shall be subject to any restriction on amounts of payments under this chapter that are imposed by a continuing resolution or other Act appropriating the funds involved.

(b) Investment of funds

(1) Notwithstanding any other provision of law, any interest or investment income that accrues on any funds provided under this chapter after such funds are paid to the Indian tribe or tribal organization and before such funds are expended for the purpose for which such funds were provided under this chapter shall be the property of the Indian tribe or tribal organization and shall not be taken into account by any officer or employee of the Federal Government in determining whether to provide assistance, or the amount of assistance, under any provision of Federal law.

(2) Funds provided under this chapter may be

(A) invested by the Indian tribe or tribal organization only in obligations of the United States or in obligations or securities that are guaranteed or insured by the United States, or

(B) deposited only into accounts that are insured by an agency or instrumentality of the United States.

(c) Recoveries

For the purposes of underrecovery and overrecovery determinations by any Federal agency for any other funds, from whatever source derived, funds received under this chapter shall not be taken into consideration.

Sec. 2508.—Application with respect to Indian Self-Determination and Education Assistance Act

(a) Certain provisions to apply to grants

All provisions of sections 5, 6, 7, 104, 105(f), 106(f), 109, and 111 of the Indian Self-Determination and Education Assistance Act (*25* U.S.C. *450c, 450d, 450e, 450i, 450j*(f), *450j–1*(f), *450m, 450n*), except those provisions relating to indirect costs and length of contract, shall apply to grants provided under this chapter.

(b) Election for grant in lieu of contract

(1) Contractors for activities to which this chapter applies who have entered into a contract under the Indian Self-Determination and Education Assistance Act (*25* U.S.C. *450* et seq.) that is in effect on April 28, 1988, may, by giving notice to the Secretary, elect to have the provisions of this chapter apply to such activity in lieu of such contract.

(2) Any election made under paragraph (1) shall take effect on the later of

(A) October 1 of the fiscal year succeeding the fiscal year in which such election is made, or

(B) the date that is 60 days after the date of such election.

(3) In any case in which the 60-day period referred to in paragraph (2)(B) is less than 60 days before the beginning of the succeeding fiscal year, such election shall not take effect until the fiscal year after the fiscal year succeeding the election. For fiscal year 1989, the Secretary may waive this paragraph for elections received prior to September 30, 1988.

(c) No duplication

No funds may be provided under any contract entered into under the Indian Self-Determination and Education Assistance Act (*25* U.S.C. *450* et seq.) to pay any expenses incurred in providing any program or service if a grant has been made under this chapter to pay such expenses.

(d) Transfers and carryovers

(1) A tribe or tribal organization assuming the operation of a Bureau school with assistance under this chapter shall be entitled to the transfer or use of buildings, equipment, supplies, and materials to the same extent as if it were contracting under the Indian Self-Determination and Education Assistance Act (*25* U.S.C. *450* et seq.).

(2) A tribe or tribal organization assuming the operation of a contract school with assistance under this chapter shall be entitled to the transfer or use of the buildings, equipment, supplies, and materials that were used in the operation of the contract school to the same extent as

if it were contracting under the Indian Self-Determination and Education Assistance Act (25 U.S.C. 450 et seq.).

(3) Any tribe or tribal organization which assumes operation of a Bureau school with assistance under this chapter and any tribe or tribal organization which elects to operate a school with assistance under this chapter rather than to continue as a contract school shall be entitled to any funds which would carryover from the previous fiscal year as if such school were operated as a contract school.

(e) Exceptions, problems, and disputes

Any exception or problem cited in an audit conducted pursuant to section 2506(b)(2) of this title, any dispute regarding a grant authorized to be made pursuant to this chapter or any amendment to such grant, and any dispute involving an administrative cost grant under section 1128a of the Education Amendments of 1978 shall be handled under the provisions governing such exceptions, problems, or disputes in the case of contracts under the Indian Self-Determination and Education Assistance Act of 1975 (*Public Law 93–658; 25* U.S.C. *450* et seq.). The Equal Access to Justice Act shall apply to administrative appeals filed after September 8, 1988, by grantees regarding a grant under this chapter, including an administrative cost grant.

Sec. 2509.—Role of Director

Applications for grants under this chapter, and all application modifications, shall be reviewed and approved by personnel under the direction and control of the Director of the Office of Indian Education Programs. Required reports shall be submitted to education personnel under the direction and control of the Director of such Office.

Sec. 2510.—Regulations

The Secretary is authorized to issue regulations relating to the discharge of duties specifically assigned to the Secretary by this chapter. In all other matters relating to the details of planning, development, implementing, and evaluating grants under this chapter, the Secretary shall not issue regulations. Regulations issued pursuant to this chapter shall not have the standing of a Federal statute for the purposes of judicial review.

Sec. 2511.—Definitions

For purposes of this chapter

(1) The term "eligible Indian student" has the meaning of such term in section 1128(f) of the Education Amendments of 1978.

(2) The term "Indian tribe" means any Indian tribe, band, nation, or other organized group or community, including any Alaska Native Village or regional or village corporation (as defined in or established pursuant to the Alaskan Native Claims Settlement Act (43 U.S.C. 1601 et

seq.)), which is recognized as eligible for the special programs and services provided by the United States to Indians because of their status as Indians.

(3)

(A) The term "tribal organization" means

(i) the recognized governing body of any Indian tribe, or

(ii) any legally established organization of Indians which

(I) is controlled, sanctioned, or chartered by such governing body or is democratically elected by the adult members of the Indian community to be served by such organization, and

(II) includes the maximum participation of Indians in all phases of its activities.

(B) In any case in which a grant is provided under this chapter to an organization to perform services benefiting more than one Indian tribe, the approval of the governing bodies of Indian tribes representing 80 percent of those students attending the tribally controlled school shall be considered a sufficient tribal authorization for such grant.

(4) The term "Secretary" means the Secretary of the Interior.

(5) The term "tribally controlled school" means a school, operated by a tribe or a tribal organization, enrolling students in kindergarten through grade 12, including preschools, which is not a local educational agency and which is not directly administered by the Bureau of Indian Affairs.

(6) The term "a local educational agency" means a public board of education or other public authority legally constituted within a State for either administrative control or direction of, or to perform a service function for, public elementary or secondary schools in a city, county, township, school district, or other political subdivision of a State, or such combination of school districts or counties as are recognized in a State as an administrative agency for its public elementary or secondary schools. Such term includes any other public institution or agency having administrative control and direction of a public elementary or secondary school.

(7) The term "Bureau" means the Bureau of Indian Affairs of the Department of the Interior.

•❖ Index

AACTE. *See* American Association for Colleges for Teacher Education

AAIA. *See* Association on American Indian Affairs

AAIP. *See* Association of American Indian Physicians

ABCFM. *See* American Board for Commissioners for Foreign Missions

Academic failure, 95–106
crossover effect and remedial programs, 104–106
grade repetition, 102
inappropriate curricula and, 101–102
inappropriate testing and, 102–103
lack of parental involvement and, 106
large schools and, 96–97
low expectations and tracking and, 103–104
passive teaching methods and, 100–101
teacher training and, 99–100
uncaring teachers and, 97–99
See also Dropping out

ACTS. *See* Association of Community Tribal Schools

Administrators, 30–31, 81–82. *See also* Schools

Adoption, 47, 72

Adult education, BIA funding for, 146

AERA. *See* American Education Research Association

Agriculture, 6, 21, 44. *See also* Allotment system

AIAI. *See* American Indian Archaeological Institute

AICAE. *See* American Indian Council of Architects and Engineers

AICF. *See* American Indian College Fund

AICRC. *See* American Indian Culture Research Center

AIGC. *See* American Indian Graduate Center

AIGTAM. *See* American Indian Gifted and Talented Assessment Model

AIHCA. *See* American Indian Health Care Association

AIHEC. *See* American Indian Higher Education Consortium

AIHF. *See* American Indian Heritage Foundation

AIHS. *See* American Indian Historical Society

AILA. *See* American Indian Library Association

AIM. *See* American Indian Movement

AIO. *See* Americans for Indian Opportunity

AIPRC. *See* American Indian Policy Review Commission

AIRD. *See* American Indian Research and Development

AIRPA. *See* American Indian Registry for the Performing Arts

AISES. *See* American Indian Science and Engineering Society

Alabama, tribal contacts and recognized tribes, 154

Alcohol, 5, 36
Allotment system, 16, 26–27, 44–45, 59–60
American Association for Colleges for Teacher Education (AACTE), 33
American Board for Commissioners for Foreign Missions (ABCFM), 10–11
American Education Research Association (AERA), 149
American Indian Archaeological Institute (AIAI), 139
American Indian College Fund (AICF), 139
American Indian Council of Architects and Engineers (AICAE), 139
American Indian Culture Research Center (AICRC), 139–140
American Indian Curricula Development Program, 140
American Indian Gifted and Talented Assessment Model (AIGTAM), 94
American Indian Graduate Center (AIGC), 140
American Indian Health Care Association (AIHCA), 140
American Indian Heritage Foundation (AIHF), 140
American Indian Higher Education Consortium (AIHEC), 36, 140
American Indian Historical Society (AIHS), 141
American Indian Library Association (AILA), 141
American Indian Movement (AIM), 32
American Indian organizations, 139–145
American Indian Policy Review Commission (AIPRC), 71
American Indian Registry for the Performing Arts (AIRPA), 141

American Indian Research and Development (AIRD), 141
American Indian Science and Education Center, 141
American Indian Science and Engineering Society (AISES), 141
Americans for Indian Opportunity (AIO), 142
Americans for Restitution and Rightings of Old Wrongs (ARROW, Inc.), 142
Arizona, tribal colleges in, 151
ARROW, Inc. *See* Americans for Restitution and Rightings of Old Wrongs
ASAIL. *See* Association for the Study of American Indian Literatures
Assimilation (acculturalization)
  of eastern tribes, 2–3, 18
  as goal of education, 10–11, 13–16, 17, 18, 22–23, 41, 44, 82–83, 85–86 (*See also* Indian Schools system)
  vs. multiculturalism, 82–84
  placement of native children in nonnative homes, 47, 72
  policy criticized in Meriam Report, 26–27
  termination policy, 46, 62–68
Association for the Study of American Indian Literatures (ASAIL), 149
Association of American Indian Physicians (AAIP), 142
Association of Community Tribal Schools (ACTS), 142
Association on American Indian Affairs (AAIA), 142
Attendance
  enforcement and accounting methods, 25
  mandatory attendance, 16–17
  See also Dropping out

Augustus F. Hawkins–Robert T. Stafford Elementary and Secondary School Improvement Amendments (1988), 75. *See also* Indian Education Act (1972)

Bay Mills Community College, 150
BIA. *See* Bureau of Indian Affairs
Bilingualism
  bilingual education promoted by Collier, 28
  Office of Bilingual Education and Minority Languages Affairs, 147
  professional organizations, 150
  and school success, 101
  and science/math education, 125, 129
  See also English language; Language; Tribal languages
Blackfeet Community College, 150
Blackfeet people, 5, 87, 151
Board of Indian Commissioners, 24, 44
Boarding schools, 21–27
  benefits, 23–24
  deculturization and assimilation as goal, 14, 15–16, 17, 22–23, 42, 44
  harmful effects, 22–23
  and ISEP, 73–74
  living conditions, 23, 45
  and the Meriam Report, 25–27, 45
  Myer's support for, 64
  numbers reduced, 61
  origins, 14–15
  reforms, 27
  statistics, 15, 21, 43
  typical practices, 15, 22
  See also Indian Schools system; Missionary schools
Books. *See* Language arts; Reading; Textbooks
Boyd, Robert, 54

Brophy, William, 63
Bureau of Indian Affairs (BIA), 145–146
  autocratic nature of, 59
  contact information, 145
  headquarters damaged by AIM, 32
  increasing role in native education, 16–17, 44, 59
  and the Indian Reorganization Act, 45
  and ISEP, 73–74
  Native Americans in, 72, 73
  perceived as paternalistic, 24
  policies criticized, 24, 26–27, 45 (*See also* Meriam Report)
  and post-termination education, 68–69
  and self-determination policies, 47, 71–72
  and the Snyder Act, 60
  and termination policy, 64, 67
  See also Boarding schools; Indian Schools system; *specific legislation*
Bureau of Indian Education, 71
Buses. *See* Transportation
Bush Foundation, 148
Bush, George H. W., administration of, 72

CAE. *See* Council on Anthropology and Education
CAIP. *See* Concerned American Indian Parents
California, 66, 151
California Test of Basic Skills, 102
CALLA. *See* Cognitive Academic Language Learning Approach
CALP. *See* Cognitive academic language proficiency
Cankdeska Cikana Community College, 151
Carlisle Indian School, 15–16, 44, 95
Carter, Jimmy, administration of, 72

Catholicism
  Catholic-Protestant missionary
    conflicts, 11, 16, 45
  Spanish education and
    conversion efforts, 7, 41
Cavazos, Lauro F., 33, 47
CERT. *See* Council of Energy
  Resources Tribes
Certification of teachers, 100, 101.
  See also Teacher training
Cheessehateaumuck, Caleb, 79
Cherokee Nation v.Georgia, 53
Cherokee National Historical
  Society (CNHS), 142
Cherokee people
  assimilation/acculturation, 2–3
  education among, 3, 10, 43
  historical society, 142
  learning styles studies, 87, 88
  relocation, 2, 4, 43
  sovereignty, 53
Cheyenne people, 5
Chickasaw people, 4
Child welfare. *See* Indian Child
  Welfare Act
Choctaw Heritage Press, 143
Choctaw people, 3, 4
Christianity
  education and conversion, 1–2,
    7–8, 18, 41–42, 54, 56–57 (*See
    also* Missionaries; Missionary
    schools)
  intermingling of education and,
    6–7, 8–9, 16
CIA. *See* Coalition for Indian
  Education
CIE. *See* Council for Indian
  Education
Civilization Fund Act (1819), 44, 56
Class size, 96
Classroom participation, 87–88. *See
  also* Learning styles
Clinton, William, 73
CNAIP. *See* Council for Native
  American Indians

CNHS. *See* Cherokee National
  Historical Society
Coalition for Indian Education
  (CIA), 143
Coalition of Indian Controlled
  School Boards, 35
Cognitive Academic Language
  Learning Approach (CALLA),
  105, 120–121
Cognitive academic language
  proficiency (CALP), 103, 118,
  120, 122–123
Cohen, Felix S., 67
College of Menominee Nation, 151
College of William and Mary, 42, 54
Colleges
  industrial model, 80–81
  Native American education
    before 1900, 41–42, 54
  tribal colleges, 36, 46, 150–153
  See also Higher education
Collier, John, 27, 28, 61
Colonists, European
  education among, 6–7
  education and conversion of
    Native Americans, 1–2, 7–8, 18,
    41–42
  See also Christianity
Comanche people, 5
Committee of One Hundred
  Citizens, 24, 45
Common school movement, 12–14
Community colleges, tribal, 36,
  150–153
Community schools in early
  America, 6–7
Community-controlled schools
  and the Economic Opportunity
    Act, 68
  and the Indian Education Act,
    70–71
  tribes' abandonment of federal
    system in favor of, 74
  See also Tribal control of
    education

Competitive learning environments, 86–87

Concerned American Indian Parents (CAIP), 143

Congress. *See* Federal government

Connecticut, tribal contacts and recognized tribes, 154

Content schemata, 119

Conversion and education, 1–2, 7–8, 18, 41–42, 54, 56–57. *See also* Missionary schools

Cooperative learning environments, 86–87, 90

Cornplanter, 54

Corporal punishment, 22–23

Council for Indian Education (CIE), 143

Council for Native American Indians (CNAIP), 143

Council of Energy Resources Tribes (CERT), 143

Council on Anthropology and Education (CAE), 149

Crawford, T. Hartley, 14, 43, 57

Creativity, 95

Creek people, 59

Crook, George, 57–58

Crossover effect, 104–105

Crow people, 91

Crownpoint Institute of Technology, 151

Cultural orientation, 90. *See also* Learning styles

Cultural sensitivity, 83
   and curricula, 33, 83–84, 101 (*See also* Curricula)
   of teachers, 97–99, 108, 129–130
   See also Multiculturalism

Culture, Native American
   Collier's encouragement of, 28, 61
   cultural preservation, 107, 123–124
   culturally relevant curricula, 47, 70, 90–92, 101–102, 107, 126–127, 129–130, 131 (*See also* Curricula)
   Dawes Act and, 16
   individuality not stressed, 87, 90 (*See also* Cooperative learning environments)
   interrelational worldview, 128–129
   land seizures' impact on, 63
   language's role in preserving, 123–124
   maintained by students, 17, 23
   Pan-Indian movement, 24
   religious ceremonies/customs banned, 14
   sacred lands restored, 70
   teacher sensitivity to, 97–99, 108, 129–130
   and termination policy, 64
   traditional tribal education, 1, 81, 85, 86
   and the Tribally Controlled Schools Act, 74–75 (*See also* Tribally Controlled Schools Act)
   See also Assimilation; Tribal education, traditional model; Tribal languages

Curricula
   academic failure and, 101–102
   conflicts over content, 13
   cultural balance and accuracy needed, 83–84
   cultural insensitivity, 33, 101
   culturally relevant curricula, 47, 70, 90–92, 101–102, 107, 126–127, 129–130, 131
   50/50 curriculum, 10, 15
   high- vs. low-track curricula, 104
   of Indian Schools, 15, 22, 26, 106
   indigenously developed curricula needed, 91
   materials, 90–92 (*See also* Textbooks)
   of missionary schools, 10–11

Curricula, *continued*
   rigorous curriculum needed, 105
   social justice movements and
      curriculum reforms, 31–32
   supplemental native curricula
      insufficient, 101–102, 105–106
   teaching to standardized tests,
      103
   See also specific subject areas

D'Arcy McNicke Center for the
      History of the American
      Indian, 149
Dartmouth College, 42, 54
Dawes Act, 16, 44–45, 59–60
Day schools
   vs. boarding schools, 27, 60, 61,
      64
   See also Johnson–O'Malley Act;
      Schools
Daybreak Star Press, 144
Deculturalization. *See* Assimilation
Deer, Ada, 73
Delaware tribe people, 54–55, 56
Demonstrations of learning, 87–88
Desegregation, 84
Determination of Rights and Unity
      for Menominee Shareholders
      (DRUMS), 66
Diné College, 151
Disabled students. *See* Students
      with disabilities
Discipline. *See* Corporal
      punishment
Disease
   impact of European diseases on
      native populations, 5, 23, 79
   Indian Schools system and, 23,
      26
   termination policy and, 66
Distance education programs,
      146–147
Diversity. *See* Multiculturalism
Doctrine of Conquest, 51–52
Doctrine of Discovery, 49–50

Doctrine of the Law of Nations, 52–53
Dole, William P., 17
D-Q University, 151
Dropping out
   academic performance and, 100
   causes and prevention, 95–97,
      98–99, 100, 105–106
   need to track dropouts, 106–107
   rates, 95–96
   retention and re-entry, 107
DRUMS. *See* Determination of
      Rights and Unity for
      Menominee Shareholders
Dull Knife Memorial College, 151

Economic Opportunity Act (1965),
      68
*Educating Americans for the 21st
      Century* (National Science
      Board Commission on Pre-
      College), 124
Education Amendments Act (1978),
      Title XI, 47, 73–74
Education loans, 61. *See also*
      Funding for Native American
      education: federal grants,
      fellowships, and programs
Education reforms
   Collier's policies, 28
   Committee of One Hundred
      Citizens recommendations, 45
   disciplinary focus of, 99
   Indian Nations at Risk task force,
      33–34, 47
   Meriam Report
      recommendations, 26, 27
   and paradigm shifts, 81–82
   parental involvement
      encouraged, 67–68
   principles, 25
   self-determination, 33, 47
   social justice movements and,
      29–30
   uniform education standards,
      73–74

Education, role and purpose of, 79
Educational Testing Service, 104. *See also* Standardized testing
Elders, educational role of, 1, 85, 86
Elementary and Secondary Education Act (ESEA; 1965), 62, 68–69
Eliot, John, 41
Emmons, Glenn, 64–65
English language
    cognitive academic language proficiency (CALP), 103, 118, 120, 122–123
    as common language, 6, 11, 24
    English-language instruction required, 11, 22, 26, 44
    impact of English-only instruction on students, 68
    limited English proficiency (LEP) students, 120–121
    as second language, 68, 95, 105, 121–123, 150
ERIC Clearinghouse on Rural Education and Small Schools (ERIC/CRESS), 149
Escalante, Jaime, 104
ESEA. *See* Elementary and Secondary Education Act, 1965
Eskimo people, 130–131
"Eskimos Solve the Future" (Guthridge), 130–131
ESL. *See* English language, as second language
An Even Chance (Kickingbird and Charleston), 69
Everybody Counts—A Report to the Nation on the Future of Mathematics Education (National Research Council), 124
Experiential learning
    instructional strategies/materials, 125, 130–131
    vs. intellectual learning, 86, 101

traditional tribal education, 85–86
Explorer classroom, 101
Extracurricular activities, 96

Family structure, 90. *See also* Parents
Federal government
    agencies, 145–148 (*See also specific bureaus, departments, and agencies*)
    assimilation as goal (*see* Assimilation)
    chronology of government–Native American relations, 42–47
    Collier's reforms, 27–28
    commissioner of Indian affairs established, 57
    education spending, 9 (*See also* Funding for Native American education)
    Indian Schools system (*see* Indian Schools system)
    legislation (*see specific acts and laws*)
    self-determination policies, 32, 69–75 (*See also* Self-determination)
    Supreme Court, 72, 84
    termination policy, 46, 62–68
    treaties with Native Americans (*see* Treaties)
    and tribal sovereignty, 52–53, 72 (*See also* Sovereignty of tribal governments)
Federally Impacted Areas Act (1951), 62, 65, 67
Field trips, 130
First Nations Development Institute (FNDI), 144
Florida, missionary school established, 41
FNDI. *See* First Nations Development Institute

Fond du Lac Tribal and Community College, 151
Ford Foundation, 140
Ford, Gerald, 72
Formalized education, slow growth of, 9–10, 13
Fort Belknap College, 151
Fort Berthold Community College, 151
Fort Peck Community College, 151
Foster care. *See* Indian Child Welfare Act
Franciscans, 7
Funding for Native American education
BIA funding, 17, 44, 47, 145–146
under Clinton administration, 73
Economic Opportunity Act, 68
Education Amendments Act, Title XI, 73–74
education loans, 61
federal grants, fellowships, and programs, 145–148
Federally Impacted Areas Act, 65
Indian Education Act, 46, 70–71
Johnson–O'Malley Act, 62, 65
missionary school funding, 10, 16, 17, 21, 43, 45
misuse of monies, 69
in the 19th century, 16, 17, 43, 44, 45, 59
private sources, 148–149
under Reagan and Bush administrations, 73
self-determination in use of funds, 70
for students with disabilities, 145
vocational education funds/programs, 147–148
See also Indian Education Assistance Act; Indian Self-Determination and Education Assistance Act; Native Americans Educational Assistance Act; Tribally Controlled Schools Act

Gathering of Nations, 144
GED. *See* General educational development exam
General Allotment Act (Dawes Act; 1887), 16, 44–45, 59–60
General educational development (GED) exam, 97–98
Georgia, tribal contacts and recognized tribes, 154
Gerard, Forrest J., 72
Gifted and talented programs, 92–95
Gipp, David, 91, 107
Government agencies, 145–148. *See also specific bureaus, departments, and agencies*
Grant, Ulysses S., 5, 44
Great Britain, 50–51. *See also* James I, King of England

Hampton Normal and Agricultural Institute, 14
Handbook of Federal Indian Law (Cohen), 67
Harjo v. Kleppe, 59
Harney, William S., 6
Harvard University, 41–42
Haskell Indian Nations University, 151
Haulapai Bilingual Academic Excellence Program, 150
Health
effects of termination policy on, 66
health care, 23, 26, 146
See also Disease
Higher education
federal grants, fellowships and programs, 146–147, 148
industrial model, 80–81
Native American education before 1900, 41–42, 54
Native American studies

programs, 33, 35–36, 46
and native-language courses, 124
preparation for, in boarding
    schools, 23–24
research and information flow
    controlled by, 82
self-confidence as aid to, 98
teacher education/training (*see*
    Teacher training)
tribal colleges, 36, 46, 150–153
History
    need for balance and accuracy in
        teaching, 83–84
    test scores, 95, 104
Holistic worldview, 127–129
Home learning environment, Native
    American
    characteristics, 86
    discontinuity with school
        environment, 89–90
    and intelligence test scores, 94
    and math/science, 125, 126, 130
    native language used in, 120
    perceived as "disadvantaged" or
        "deprived," 105
    and positive identity
        development, 99
Hopi people, 28
House Concurrent Resolution 108
    (1953), 64–65, 70. *See also*
    Termination policy
Hunting skills, learning, 128–129
Huron University, Si Tanka College,
    153

IACA. *See* Indian Arts and Crafts
    Association
Ickes, Harold, 27
Identity development, 99
Ideologies of education
    assimilation as goal, 10–11,
        13–16, 17, 18, 22–23, 41, 44,
        82–83, 85–86
    conflicts over role of education,
        11, 12, 13

deficit model, 103–104
industrial model, 80–81, 96
intellectual vs. experiential
    learning, 85–86, 100–101 (*See
    also* Experiential learning)
multiculturalism, 82–84 (*See also*
    Multiculturalism)
Native American ideology, 79–80
paradigm shifts, 81–82
role and purpose of education,
    79
tracking, 103–104
white ideologies, 13
See also Learning styles
Impacted Aid Act. *See* Federally
    Impacted Areas Act
Incarceration, 99
Indian Affairs, Bureau of (BIA). *See*
    Bureau of Indian Affairs
Indian Arts and Crafts Association
    (IACA), 144
Indian Child Welfare Act (1978), 47,
    72
    text of, 191–204
Indian Citizenship Act (1924), 24, 45
Indian Civilization Fund Act (1802),
    10
Indian Claims Commission Act
    (1946), 63
Indian Country Press, 144
*Indian Education: A National
    Tragedy, a National Challenge*
    (U.S. Senate Special
    Subcommittee on Indian
    Education 1969; Kennedy
    Report), 33, 46, 69, 95
Indian Education Act (1972), 33,
    46–47, 70–71, 75
Indian Education Assistance Act of
    1975 (text), 204–216
Indian Education, Bureau of, 71
Indian Financing Act (1975), 70
*Indian Givers: How the Indians of
    the Americas Transformed the
    World* (Weatherford), 102

Indian Health Service Scholarship Program, 146

Indian Nations at Risk (National Commission on Excellence in Education), 124. *See also* Indian Nations at Risk task force

Indian Nations at Risk task force, 33–34, 47, 98, 101, 124

Indian Reorganization Act (Wheeler–Howard Act; 1934), 27, 45, 60–62

Indian School Equalization Program (ISEP), 73–74, 145

Indian Schools system, 14–17, 21–27
  benefits, 23–24
  curricula, 15, 22, 26, 106 (*See also* Curricula)
  deculturization and assimilation as goal, 14, 15–16, 17, 22–23, 43–44
  harmful effects, 22–23
  and ISEP, 73–74, 145
  living conditions, 23, 45
  and the Meriam Report, 25–27, 45
  Myer and, 64
  numbers reduced, 61
  origins, 14–15
  reforms, 27
  statistics, 15, 21, 43
  teacher turnover rate, 101
  typical practices, 15, 15–16, 22

Indian Self-Determination and Education Assistance Act (1975), 33, 70, 71–73
  and Native American studies programs, 35–36
  1988 amendments, 47, 74
  text of, 216–227

Indian Trust Council Authority, 70

Individuality, 87, 90. *See also* Cooperative learning environments

Industrial model of education, 80–81, 96

Institute for Government Research, 24

Institute of American Indian Arts, 152

Instructional strategies
  to achieve academic competence, 118–119
  adaptation to native learning styles, 89–90, 108 (*See also* Learning styles)
  CALLA language development model, 105, 120–121
  culturally relevant curricula, 47, 70, 90–92, 101–102, 107, 126–127, 129–130, 131
  for English as a second language (ESL), 121–122
  gifted and talented programs, 92–95
  for limited English proficiency (LEP) students, 120–123
  for mathematics, 90, 126–127
  for reading, 90–91
  for science, 90, 125–126, 127–131
  transmission vs. experiential methods, 100–101, 125, 126–127, 130–131 (*See also* Experiential learning)
  whole language methods, 90–91, 127

Intelligence and intelligence tests, 93–95. *See also* Gifted and talented programs

International Reading Association, 149

IRA. *See* Indian Reorganization Act, 1934

ISEP. *See* Indian School Equalization Program

Jackson, Andrew, 3
James I, King of England, 1, 41
Japanese Americans, 63

Jefferson, Thomas, 7
Jesuits, 7, 41
JNCL. *See* Joint Committee for
   Languages
Johnson, Lyndon B., 68
Johnson–O'Malley Act (1934), 27,
   45–46, 62, 65
Joint Committee for Languages
   (JNCL), 150

Kansas, tribal colleges in, 151
Kaskaskia people, 55–56
Kellogg Foundation, 148
Kennedy, Edward (Ted), 33
Kennedy, John F., 68
Kennedy Report *(Indian Education:
   A National Tragedy, a National
   Challenge)*, 33, 46, 69, 95
Kennedy, Robert, 33
Keweenaw Bay Ojibwa Community
   College, 152
Klamath people, 66
Knox, Henry, 51–52

Lac Courte Oreilles Ojibwa
   Community College, 152
Lakota people
   Rosebud Sioux education
      guidelines, 36
   smallpox outbreak, 5
   Sun Dance, 14, 28
   tribal college, 152
Land
   allotment system, 16, 26–27,
      44–45, 59–60
   Indian Claims Commission Act,
      63
   indigenous rights, 49–51
   relocation of tribes, 2–4, 43–44
      (*See also* Reservations)
   Taos sacred lands restored, 69
   termination policy and, 66 (*See
      also* Termination policy)
   westward expansion by whites,
      4–5

Language
   acquisition of second language,
      121–122, 123
   author's language choices as
      factor in reading experience,
      119
   CALLA language development
      model, 105, 120–121
   cognitive academic language
      proficiency (CALP), 103, 118,
      120, 122–123
   cultural preservation role,
      123–124
   lack of common language as
      cause of conflict, 6
   and learning styles, 89
   Meriam Report on Indian
      Schools' policy, 26
   Native American Languages Act,
      269–271
   professional organizations,
      150
   science as second language,
      125–126
   test scores, 95
   See also Bilingualism; English
      language; Language
      Development; Reading; Tribal
      languages
Language arts
   Association for the Study of
      American Indian Literatures
      (ASAIL), 149
   CALLA language development
      model, 105, 120–121
   cultural bias in reading books,
      91
   high- vs. low-track curricula, 104
   instructional strategies, 118–119
   test scores, 104
   whole language methods, 90–91,
      127
   See also English language;
      Language development;
      Reading

Language development, 117–118
    CALLA language development
        model, 105
    and second-language
        acquisition, 121
    and writing, 118–119
    See also Language
Leadership skills, 23–24
Learning styles, 84–90
    cooperative vs. competitive
        learning, 86–87
    and curricula materials, 90–92
    defined, 84–85
    demonstrations of learning,
        87–88
    instructional strategies, 86,
        89–90
    intellectual vs. experiential
        learning, 85–86, 100–101, 125,
        126–127, 130–131
    and math/science curricula,
        124–125, 126–127
    shaped by cultural norms, 87–88
    and traditional tribal education,
        85, 86
Leech Lake Tribal College, 152
Legislation, 49–75
    body of federal Indian law,
        67
    in the early 20th century, 60
    in the New Deal era, 60–62
    in the termination era, 62–68
    See also Federal government;
        Treaties; *specific acts and laws*
Libraries, 141, 148
Linear thinking, 81
Literacy, 3, 6, 9. *See also* Cognitive
    academic language proficiency
    (CALP); Reading
Little Big Horn College, 152
Little Priest Tribal College, 152
Loans for education, 61. *See also*
        Funding for Native American
        education: federal grants,
        fellowships and programs

Louisiana Territory Act (1804), 4
Louisiana, tribal contacts and
        recognized tribes, 154

Mandan people, 5
Manifest destiny, 4–5
Manual skills
    hunting skills, 128–129
    manual-labor schools developed,
        14, 43
    taught in Indian Schools, 15–16
    taught in missionary schools,
        10
    traditional instruction in, 1
    treaty provisions for education
        in, 54, 56
Marks v. United States, 53
Massachusetts, tribal contacts,
        154
Mathematics
    concrete teaching materials,
        126–127
    deficiencies, 124–125
    grant money, 148
    and native learning styles,
        124–125
    stressed in current educational
        model, 81
    teaching methods, 90
    test scores, 95, 104, 124
Medill, William, 57
Menominee people, 46, 66, 70,
        151
Meriam, Lewis, 24, 45. *See also*
        Meriam Report
Meriam Report *(The Problem of
        Indian Administration)*, 24–27,
        45
Michigan
    tribal colleges, 150, 152
    tribal contacts and recognized
        tribes, 155
Minnesota
    jurisdiction over tribal lands
        assumed, 66

Minneapolis Public Schools, 144
native education policies, 107
tribal colleges, 151, 152, 153
Minorities
same-group role models needed, 103–104
textbooks demeaning to, 101
tracking and teachers' expectations, 103–104
Missionaries
Catholic-Protestant conflicts, 11, 16, 45
education and conversion by, 1–2, 5, 7–8, 18 (*See also* Missionary schools)
See also Christianity; Missionary schools
Missionary schools
acculturalization as goal of, 10–11
boarding schools initiated, 42 (*See also* Boarding schools)
colleges, 41–42
curriculum, 10–11
federal funding, 10, 16, 17, 21, 43, 45
language of instruction, 11
See also Missionaries
Mohegan people, 54
Montana
native education policies, 107
tribal colleges, 150, 152, 153
tribal contacts and recognized tribes, 155
Montoya v. United States, 53
Morgan, Thomas J., 16–17
Multiculturalism, 31–32
vs. assimilation, 82–84
caring teachers, cultural sensitivity of, 97–99
dearth of programs, 83–84
educational goals, 83
growing respect for diversity, 31–32, 83

and teacher training, 89, 100
See also Cultural sensitivity
Muskogee people, 4
Myer, Dillon S., 63–64

NABE. *See* National Association for Bilingual Education
NACIE. *See* National Advisory Council on Indian Education
NALI. *See* Native American Language Issues
A Nation At Risk (National Commission on Excellence in Education), 102
National Advisory Council on Indian Education (NACIE), 34, 71, 75
National Association for Bilingual Education (NABE), 150
National Council for the Accreditation of Teacher Education (NCATE), 34
National Council of Teachers of English (NCTE), 150
National Education Longitudinal Study (1988), 102, 104
National Indian Education Association (NIEA), 32, 35
National Science Foundation, 148
The National Study of American Indian Education. See *To Live on This Earth*
National Workplace Literacy grants, 146
Native American education model, traditional, 1, 81, 85, 86
Native American Language Issues (NALI), 150
Native American Languages Act (1990) (text), 269–271
Native American Research Information Service, 150
Native American studies programs, 33, 35–36

Native Americans. *See* Culture, Native American; Self-determination; Students, Native American; Treaties; Tribal control of education; Tribal governments; *specific tribes and groups*
Native Americans Educational Assistance Act (1988) (text), 227–268
Navajo Curriculum Center Press, 145
Navajo people, 79–80, 97, 101
Navajo Students at Risk (Platero), 105, 106–107
NCATE. *See* National Council for the Accreditation of Teacher Education
NCTE. *See* National Council of Teachers of English
Nebraska
jurisdiction over tribal lands assumed, 66
Standing Bear case, 57–58
tribal colleges, 152
Nebraska Indian Community College, 152
New Deal era, education during, 27–29
New Jersey, tribal contacts and recognized tribes, 155
New Mexico
and termination policy, 64
tribal colleges, 151, 152, 153
New York, tribal contacts and recognized tribes, 155
Nez Percé people, 5
Nichols, John, 63
NIEA. *See* National Indian Education Association
Nixon, Richard, 66, 69–70
Nonlinear thinking, 81
North Carolina, tribal contacts and recognized tribes, 155
North Dakota

native curriculum, 91
tribal colleges, 151, 153
Northwest Indian College, 152

OBEMLA. *See* Office of Bilingual Education and Minority Languages Affairs
Office of Bilingual Education and Minority Languages Affairs (OBEMLA), 147
Office of Elementary and Secondary Education, 147
Office of Postsecondary Education (OPE), 147
Oglala Lakota College, 152
Oglala Sioux people, 88, 152
Ojibwa colleges, 152
Oklahoma, tribal contacts and recognized tribes, 155
Omaha people, 5, 57–58
Oneida people, 14, 42, 55
OPE. *See* Office of Postsecondary Education
Oral tradition, 1
Oregon, 66
O'Sullivan, John, 4–5
"Outing" system, 15–16

Palouse people, 28
Pan-Indian movement, 24
Parent advisory committees (PACs), 46–47, 69, 70, 71
Parents, 67–68, 106
commitment to/concerns about education, 34
See also Parent advisory committees (PACs)
Passivity, 100–101. *See also* Learning styles: intellectual vs. experiential learning
Peace commission, federal, 6
Peace Policy, 5
Pequot people, 41
A Place Called School: Prospects for the Future (Goodlad), 96

Postsecondary Education, Office of
(OPE), 147
Pratt, Richard Henry, 15, 16, 22, 44
Praying towns, 2
Principle of Discovery, 50
*The Problem of Indian
Administration* (Merriam
Report), 24–27, 45
Professional organizations, 149–150
Protestantism
Catholic-Protestant missionary
conflicts, 11, 16, 45
education among Protestant
settlers, 6–7, 8–9
missionary schools, 10–11, 43
(*See also* Missionary schools)
Public education
desegregation's effect on Native
Americans, 84
early 20th-century advances,
24–25
Federally Impacted Areas Act, 62,
65
Johnson–O'Malley Act, 27, 45–46,
62, 65
native education in the early 20th
century, 60
principles of school reform, 25
restrictions on curricula, 106
social justice movements and,
29–32
during the termination era, 65,
67–68
tribally operated schools, 36 (*See
also* Tribal control of
education)
See also Curricula; Schools
Public Law 280 (1953), 65
Public speaking, 88

Reading
cognitive academic language
proficiency (CALP), 118 (*See
also* Cognitive academic
language proficiency)

cultural bias in reading books, 91
instructional strategies, 118–119
International Reading
Association, 149
key aspects (factors), 119
remedial programs, 105
test scores, 104
whole language methods, 90–91,
127
See also English language;
Language arts
Reagan, Ronald, 73, 75
Reality, conflicting views of, 81
*Recommendations for the
Improvement of Science and
Mathematics for American
Indians* (American Association
for the Advancement of
Science), 125
Reforms. *See* Education reforms
Religion, Native American
Collier's encouragement of, 28
religious ceremonies/customs
banned, 14
religious freedom provided, 45
Taos Pueblo's sacred lands
restored, 69
See also Culture, Native American
Relocation of tribes
by the government, 2–4, 43–44
(*See also* Reservations)
to urban areas, 66–67
Remedial programs, 105–106. *See
also* Tracking
Report on BIA Education (Bureau of
Indian Affairs), 101
Reservations
exodus to cities from, 29
off-reservation boarding schools
(*see* Boarding schools; Indian
Schools system)
problems chronicled in Meriam
Report, 26–27
reentry of boarding school youth
into reservation life, 23

Reservations, *continued*
relocation to, 2–4, 43–44
reservation schools (*See also*
Tribal control of education)
See also Tribal governments
Retention programs, 107
Riggs, Alfred L., 11
Rock Point Community School, 98
Rockefeller, John D., Jr., 24
Rocky Boys Reservation, 74
Role models, 106
Roosevelt, Franklin D., 27
Rosebud Sioux people, 36

Salish Kootenai College, 152
Sanborn, Kenneth O., 6
Santa Clara Pueblo v. Martinez, 72
Santee Normal Training School,
11
Schemata, 119
Scholarships. *See* Higher education:
federal grants, fellowships and
programs
The Schooling of Native Americans
(AACTE), 33
Schools
and academic performance (*see*
Academic failure)
buildings/facilities, 59
class participation, 87–88
class size, 96
desegregation, 84
discontinuity with home
environment, 89–90 (*See also*
Home learning environment,
Native American)
dominant culture, 108 (*See also*
Assimilation
(acculturalization): as goal of
education)
extracurricular activities, 96
language used in (*see* English
language; Language)
and learning styles (*see* Learning
styles)
and native culture (*see* Cultural
sensitivity; Curricula)
native financial responsibility for,
57
in 19th-century America, 9–10,
13
organization, 95
and parental involvement, 106
principles of school reform, 25
rural vs. urban, 9, 10, 84, 96–97,
127
school choice, 12–13
size, 96–97
social justice and, 29–32
during the termination era, 65,
67–68
transportation to, 96–97
unresponsiveness to tribal
requests, 33
See also Boarding schools;
Curricula; Day schools;
Education reforms; Indian
Schools system; Missionary
schools; Public education;
Teachers; *specific academic
subject areas*
Schurz, Carl, 15, 44
Science
bicultural approach, 129–131
deficiencies, 124–125
as dominant, integrating view of
reality, 81
"ethnoscientific" approach, 125
grant money, 148
instructional strategies, 90,
124–126, 127–131, 128–129
and native learning styles,
124–125
rational vs. holistic science,
127–129, 130
as a second language, 125–126
test scores, 104, 124
Script schemata, 119
Secondary education, difficulty
transitioning to, 99

Self-confidence, 98, 99
Self-determination
    Clinton administration's policies,
        73
    in education, 32–33, 34–36, 47,
        69–72, 73–75 (*See also* Tribal
        control of education)
    Ford and Carter administrations'
        policies, 72
    Indian Child Welfare Act, 47, 72,
        191–204
    Indian Self-Determination and
        Education Assistance Act, 33,
        35–36, 47, 70, 71–73, 216–227
    Nixon administration's policies,
        32, 69–71
    Reagan and Bush
        administrations' policies,
        73
    See also Indian Self-
        Determination and Education
        Assistance Act; Tribal
        governments
Seminole people, 4
Seneca people, 54
Sequoya, 43
Sherman, William, 6
Si Tanka College/Huron University,
    153
Simpson-Tyson, Audrey, 91
Sinte Gleska University, 153
Sioux nation
    Lakota, 5, 14, 28, 36, 152
    Oglala, 88, 152
    Rosebud Sioux, 36
Sisseton Wahpeton Community
    College, 153
Sitting Bull College, 153
Snyder Act (1921), 60
Social justice movements and
    education, 29–32
Social workers, 104–105
Society of American Indians, 24
South Dakota, tribal colleges in, 152,
    153

Southwestern Indian Polytechnic
    Institute, 153
Sovereignty of tribal governments,
    52–53, 58, 72. *See also* Self-
    determination
Spain, 49
Spanish settlers, 7, 41
Special education
    impact of social justice
        movements on, 29, 30
    as principle of school reform,
        25
    programs for disadvantaged
        children, 69 (*See also*
        Elementary and Secondary
        Education Act)
Spending on education, 9, 10, 29.
    See also Funding for Native
    American education
*Spirit and Reason: The Vine Deloria,
    Jr., Reader* (Deloria), 128
St. Mary's School (Alaska), 98
Stand and Deliver (film), 104
Standardized testing
    and cognitive academic language
        proficiency, 103, 120
    cultural bias and academic
        failure, 102–103
    test scores, 95, 104
Standing Bear, 57–58
Star Schools Program, 146–147
State governments
    choice between
        Johnson–O'Malley or Impact
        Aid, 65
    education in the 19th century,
        9
    public education of native
        children required, 46, 66
    and tribal sovereignty, 52–53
Stockbridge Indians, 55
Stone Child College, 153
Storytelling, 1, 127
Structure schemata (schema),
    119

Students (generally)
    equal plane fallacy, 108
    reading affected by life
      experiences of, 119
    tracking, 103–104
Students, Native American
    attitudes toward teachers, 97–98,
      121–122
    boarding schools'
      drawbacks/benefits, 22–24 (*See*
      also Boarding schools)
    boredom of, 100, 104, 105
    and caring vs. uncaring teachers,
      97–99
    desegregation's effect on, 84, 89
    disabled students, 29, 30, 145,
      146
    disenfranchisement,
      characteristics of, 84
    dropping out, 95–100
    English proficiency (*see* English
      language; Language)
    extracurricular activities, 96
    gifted and talented students,
      92–95
    identity development, 99
    and the industrial model of
      education, 80–81
    language of thought, 120
    resistance in boarding schools,
      17, 23
    role models needed, 106
    self-confidence, 98, 99
    self-esteem, 123
    tracking, 103–104
    in the traditional tribal
      educational model, 85, 86 (*See*
      also Tribal education,
      traditional model)
    transitional difficulties, 97, 98–99
    underperformance by, 92
    See also Academic failure;
      Intelligence and intelligence
      tests; Learning styles;
      Standardized testing

Students with disabilities, 29, 30,
    145, 146
Sun Dance, 14, 28
Superintendents. *See* Administrators
Supreme Court, 72, 84

Taos Pueblo, 69
Teacher training
    certification and competency
      testing, 100, 101
    failures of training programs,
      99–100
    for gifted and talented programs,
      95
    in multiculturalism, 89, 100
    in Native American education,
      34, 89, 100, 101, 119
    for Native American teachers, 11,
      34, 61
    See also Teachers
Teachers
    in boarding schools, 15
    caring vs. uncaring teachers,
      97–99
    cultural sensitivity required, 108,
      129–130
    expectations of students, 92,
      103–104
    in the industrial model of
      education, 80
    Native American teachers, 11, 34,
      61, 99–100
    in 19th-century America, 9
    professional organizations,
      149–150
    recruitment, 100
    standards for, 25, 100–101
    teachers' union, 31
    teaching methods and styles, 89
      (*See also* Instructional
      strategies; Learning styles)
    turnover rates, 101
    See also Elders; Teacher training
Teachers of English to Speakers of
    Other Languages (TESOL), 150

Teaching materials, 90–92. *See also* Curricula; Textbooks

Teaching methods. *See* Instructional strategies

Technology and education, 81–82, 146–147

Termination policy, 46, 62–68, 70

Terry, Alfred, 6

TESOL. *See* Teachers of English to Speakers of Other Languages

Testing. *See* General educational development (GED) exam; Intelligence and intelligence tests; Standardized testing

Text (defined), 119

Textbooks
cultural bias, 90–91, 101
reliance on, 90, 98
unknown in traditional native practices, 22

To Live on This Earth (Fuchs and Havighurst), 32–33, 46

Tracking, 103–104. *See also* Remedial programs

Trade and Intercourse Act (1834), 4

Trading posts, 5

Transitions, difficulty with, 98–99

Transportation to school, 96–97

Treaties
and colonial land rights issues, 49–51
Congressional authority, 58
early federal treaties, 14, 42, 51–52, 53–57
education provisions, 14, 26, 34, 42, 54, 55–56
and government provisions/entitlements, 6
and Native American territories, 4, 51–53

Treaty of Lancaster, 54

Tribal control of education, 34–36
Cherokee, 3, 43
and the Economic Opportunity Act, 68

and ESEA Title I, 68–69

Indian School Equalization Program (ISEP), 73–74

Indian Self-Determination and Education Assistance Act, 33, 47, 74 (*See also* Indian Self-Determination and Education Assistance Act)

indigenously developed curricula needed, 91 (*See also* Curricula: culturally relevant curricula)

native organizations, 35

and parental involvement, 106

teacher training, 34

tribal colleges, 36, 46, 150–153

Tribally Controlled Schools Act, 74–75, 272–287

Tribal education, traditional model, 1, 81, 85, 86

Tribal governments, 27
authority defined, 70
and child custody, 47 (*See also* Indian Child Welfare Act)
and Collier's reforms, 28–29
and education, 35, 47, 69 (*See also* Tribal control of education)
and federal authority, 58
federal commitment to support, 74–75
performance, 35
recognized by Indian Reorganization Act, 60–61
sovereignty, 52–53, 58, 72
See also Self-determination

Tribal languages
language courses, 36, 123, 124
as language of instruction, 3, 11, 43
Native American Languages Act (text), 269–271
used at home, 120

Tribally Controlled Schools Act (1988), 74–75
text of, 272–287

Tribes of the United States (list), 156–171. *See also specific tribes*
Turtle Mountain Community College, 153
Tuscarora people, 55

United Tribes Technical College, 153
Universities. *See* Higher education; *specific universities*
University of Arkansas at Little Rock, 145
U.S. Department of Education, 69
   contact information and programs, 146–147
   Learning Technologies Division, 146–147
   Office of Education, 9, 70–71
   Office of Elementary and Secondary Education, 147
U.S. Department of Health, Education, and Welfare, 69
U.S. Department of the Interior, 60, 147–148

Victoria, Franciscus de, 49–50
Vigil, Gilbert, 80
Virginia, tribal contacts and recognized tribes, 156

Warm Springs Indian Reservation, 87–88

Washington, George, 54
Washington (state), 107, 152
Watkins, Arthur W., 64
Watt, James, 73
Weatherford, Jack, 102
West Virginia, tribal contacts and recognized tribes, 156
Wheeler, Charles E., 61. *See also* Wheeler–Howard Act
Wheeler–Howard Act (Indian Reorganization Act; 1934), 27, 45, 60–62
White Earth Tribal and Community College, 153
White House Initiative on Tribal Colleges and Universities, 148
Willoughby, W. F., 25
Wisconsin
   jurisdiction over tribal lands assumed, 66
   tribal colleges, 151, 152
Worcester v. Georgia, 53
Work, Hubert, 25
World War II, 29, 63
Wounded Knee, 32
Writing and language development, 118–119
Wyandot people, 4

Zuni Reservation, 74